Sexscapes of Pleasure

Sexscapes of Pleasure

Women, Sexuality and the Whore Stigma in Italy

Elena Zambelli

First published in 2023 by
Berghahn Books
www.berghahnbooks.com

© 2023, 2026 Elena Zambelli
First paperback edition published in 2026

All rights reserved. Except for the quotation of short passages
for the purposes of criticism and review, no part of this book
may be reproduced in any form or by any means, electronic or
mechanical, including photocopying, recording, or any information
storage and retrieval system now known or to be invented,
without written permission of the publisher.

Library of Congress Cataloging-in-Publication Data

Names: Zambelli, Elena, author.
Title: Sexscapes of pleasure : women, sexuality and the whore stigma in
  Italy / Elena Zambelli.
Description: [New York] : Berghahn Books, 2023. | Includes bibliographical
  references and index.
Identifiers: LCCN 2022028516 (print) | LCCN 2022028517 (ebook) | ISBN
  9781800736856 (hardback) | ISBN 9781800736863 (ebook)
Subjects: LCSH: Women--Sexual behavior--Italy. | Sex workers--Italy. | Pole
  dancing--Italy.
Classification: LCC HQ29 .Z358 2023 (print) | LCC HQ29 (ebook) | DDC
  306.70820945--dc23/eng/20220701
LC record available at https://lccn.loc.gov/2022028516
LC ebook record available at https://lccn.loc.gov/2022028517

British Library Cataloguing in Publication Data
A catalogue record for this book is available from the British Library

EU GPSR Authorized Representative
LOGOS EUROPE, 9 rue Nicolas Poussin, 17000, LA ROCHELLE, France
Email: Contact@logoseurope.eu

ISBN 978-1-80073-685-6 hardback
ISBN 978-1-83695-573-3 paperback
ISBN 978-1-80758-337-8 epub
ISBN 978-1-80073-686-3 web pdf

https://doi.org/10.3167/9781800736856

CONTENTS

Preface vi

Acknowledgements x

Introduction 1

Chapter 1. A Moral and Political Economy of Women's Sexuality 27

Chapter 2. Women Pole Dancing for 'Pleisure' 51

Chapter 3. Women Pole/Lap Dancing for Work 75

Chapter 4. Women Selling Sex 102

Chapter 5. Sexscapes in the Matrix of Domination 127

Conclusions 145

References 155

Index 179

Preface

It was a warm summer evening, and I was spending it at Charlie's, a popular outdoor disco on the outskirts of a provincial town in northern Italy. That night, the venue launched a collaboration with Sexy Moon – a 'night club' (Eng. original, meaning strip club) locally renowned for its ample offer of female erotic entertainment – and I went in the hope of establishing some research contacts. As the first show began, I noticed that it was a woman in charge of overseeing the rhythm and flow of the erotic shows and the audience's mood and behaviour. It was she who introduced the performers; she who accompanied the dance performances with words and gestures of emphasis; she who instructed customers to clap when the time was right; and she who reprimanded them if they failed to express their appreciation appropriately. 'Go to the stadium with your whistles! … here, we want claps only for our girls.' I approached her during the break.

Albeit readily welcoming, Nadia did not have much time to dedicate to me. I could see her body sag and her attention fade away the more I told her about my research and why I was interested in 'pole dance' and 'lap dance' (the latter being the term Italians generically use to indicate any form of female-to-male erotic entertainment). Then, suddenly, Nadia began shouting and waving at someone behind my back. 'Zezaaa! Come here. *Come*!' I turned, and saw a tall, slender and elegant woman approaching us. 'Zeza can speak to you about pole dance and lap dance for hours!' said Nadia, stretching her right arm over the woman's shoulders and her left arm over mine before pushing us both away from her and the counter. 'Now go on that sofa and talk', she said brusquely, 'bye!'

Feeling terribly clumsy and unprepared as I sat facing her, Zeza spoke first. 'Why do you research these things?' she asked me in a suspicious, almost hostile tone. It was only after a thorough explanation of my research project and some evidence of my recreational pole dance competence that she relaxed and began talking with me. As a start, she offered that 'Zeza' was her former stage name: because *now* she was a *pole* dancer, but in the *past*, she was a *lap* dancer. 'How would you explain the difference between the two?' I asked her. 'Lap dance is fun, seductive, [it is] something playful …' she said sparklingly, as if retrieving some pleasurable memories from bygone days, 'and then, there is the stripping', she whispered, leaning towards me as if sharing a coming-of-age secret. For a moment, I saw her looking above me, towards the dance floor, where possibly a former colleague was performing a dance with the pole. Then she looked back at me, pulled her dress down to her knees, straightened her spine and solemnly added that 'pole dance, instead, is a *sport*. In Italy, few people understand this difference, but maybe research such as yours will help clarify things once and for all.'

We then chit-chatted about the physical strength and skill necessary to perform the acrobatic tricks of recreational pole dancing – nodding, laughing and clapping at each other's tales of physical pain, bruises, challenges and small achievements. Zeza told me of an accident that a friend of hers had while practising it at home,[1] and I expressed my sorrow, adding that, indeed, I found the practice too physically hazardous for me, hence my decision to stop. 'I was frequently travelling for work', I explained, 'and so, every time I returned back home, and to the [pole dance] school, I always struggled to catch up with my peers. Eventually, fearing injury, I gave up.' And then it was silence. I expected Zeza to pick up the conversation from where I left it, but she did not. 'So, what is your job, *e-x-a-c-t-l-y*?' she hissed instead.

Her sudden renewed hostility froze me, and I could not understand where it was coming from. I eventually grasped that she might have become suspicious of my good faith following my reference to some 'work' of mine that she knew nothing about – a job that was frequently taking me away from home … like a journalist, perhaps? If my mind reading was correct, Zeza probably feared that she had confided her lap dancing past in the wrong person. Realizing my slip-up, I quickly briefed her about me. I explained that I had worked several years in international development and that even though I left that career I was still occasionally undertaking freelance consultancies. While sharing this with Zeza, part of my mind was busy thinking how to divert the attention away from my outgrown 'me'. The first conversation (re)starter was a reverse question. 'And what is your job?' I thus asked her as soon as I could. 'I work in service provision', she replied. 'In which area?' I continued distractedly – still intent on fathoming how to retrieve at least a bit of the spark of our initial conversation. 'I am ashamed to tell you', she said, looking at me with eyes wide open, conveying an unmistakable plea for no further questions.

Silently cursing myself for having failed to read between the lines of her vagueness, I went back to chit-chatting about the pleasure and pain of recreational pole dancing. However, it was clear that she had withdrawn from the conversation. Shortly afterwards, in fact, Zeza stood up from the sofa, adjusted her dress and excused herself. 'May I call you to continue the interview elsewhere?' I asked her tentatively. 'Yes, you can', she said, and after jotting her phone number down on my agenda, she continued, 'but I do not know when I will be able to meet you'. I messaged her twice throughout the summer to ask whether she felt like meeting me again. In her gentle replies, she never shut the door completely, but it was never the right time either. Understanding her discreet request to be left alone, I stopped any communication. Yet, it was not too long before we unexpectedly stumbled upon each other again, albeit in quite a different setting – in the daytime, at a recreational pole dance school's opening party.

'So, what is the difference between *pole* dance and *lap* dance?' a young male compère in suit and tie read from the script in his hands. 'Gosh!' exclaimed Daniela, the owner of the school, on stage next to him, 'I have answered this question a thousand times already!' Then she grumbled, crossed her arms, looked at the audience and grumbled, grumbled and grumbled again, moving restlessly the whole time. With her hands now on her hips, Daniela turned her head back to face the scoundrel. 'Why do you ask this question? Do we look like *strappone* [whores]?' she asked disdainfully.[2] Laughs, claps and whistles followed Daniela's haughty response. 'The difference is in the context', she continued, 'here, at the school, we do it to have fun and for sport; *they* do it for money, for other *scopi* [goals; (you) fuck].'[3] Then, Daniela furrowed her brow, as if to invite her public – which included performers' friends, partners and family as well as many potential female customers – to think carefully about the meaning of her words and to let this moral-laden boundary between pole and lap dancers sink in.

The roar arising from the audience appeared to have set Daniela's words in stone. Triumphant, she and the compère walked off the stage while a group of female recreational pole dance 'students' (this is what instructors call them) came in. Barefoot and wearing plain cotton tops and shorts, ten women of different ages, body sizes and shapes performed a mildly acrobatic dance choreography to the tune of a pop love song. Zeza was one of them. Watching her absorbed in twirling on the pole to the applause of a mixed (versus male-only) and young (versus mature) audience, I wondered whether she had heard Daniela's scornful remarks on lap dancers. Suddenly, I felt deeply all the violence of the patriarchal binary dividing women into 'good' or 'bad' based on their use of sexuality. The eyes of Zeza and mine crossed at the post-performance buffet, but we conspiratorially ignored each other – for in this life of hers we were strangers, and we remained so.

Notes

1. Poles for home-based practice can easily be bought in shops and online. At the time of my fieldwork, an average quality pole cost around three hundred euros.
2. The etymology of the derogatory term *strappona* (sing. fem.) descends from the verb *strappare*, meaning 'to tear (something) apart'. It is used in some parts of Italy to describe a woman intent on making men move past their virgin status, where this change coincides with the latter's loss of the fraenum connecting foreskin and penis. Traditionally, it was women prostitutes that used to help young men accomplish this transition as part of their broader role as 'bad' women. A *strappona* is thus a woman despised for having multiple male sexual partners.
3. The word *scopi* means 'goals' when pronounced with an open 'o', and it is the second-person singular declension of the verb *scopare* (to fuck), in present tense, when the 'o' is closed.

Acknowledgements

Undertaking this research has been a profoundly transformative journey that has radically altered my understanding of what it means to be a woman and my ways of being one. I wish to start by expressing my deepest gratitude to all the self-identified women I encountered, interviewed, reflected with and nurtured personal and sometimes political relations. I am profoundly grateful to Pia Covre, the co-founder, with Carla Corso, of *Comitato per i Diritti Civili delle Prostitute* and Porpora Marcasciano, the president of *Movimento Identità Trans*. I warmly thank the volunteers with whom I shared the nights on the street sex work mobile outreach unit for the trust and support we gave each other, and the feminist and queer scholars and activists, whose knowledge and practices shaped my understanding of Italy's contemporary politics of sexuality.

For the inspiring, critical and insightful conversations around my research, especially in its early stages, I am immensely grateful to Professor Ruba Salih, Dr Caroline Osella, and Professor Lynn Welchman. My deepest gratitude goes to Professor Andrea Cornwall, Dr Rutvika Andrijasevic, Dr Pauline Oosterhoff and the anonymous peer reviewers of my draft book manuscript for their rigorous, constructive and generous comments. For the mutual processes of learning and exchange on the intersections of race, migration, intimacy and the law, I want to thank Professor Betty de Hart, Professor Marlou Schrover, Dr Guno Jones, Nawal Mustafa, Rébecca Franco, Andrea Tarchi and Jordan Dez. I wish to extend my heartfelt thanks to Professor Michaela Benson, who supported me in the final stages of this journey. I am also hugely grateful to Anita Jones, who proofread my book manuscript, combining professionalism and engagement with the subject at hand.

The genealogy of this book encompasses over ten years of my life, and many friends have contributed to it in different ways – exchanging ideas and reflections; offering support; navigating life with me. I cannot do justice to all of them, but I want to express my warmest gratitude to Maria Ferrara, Elena Capelli, Sarah Alessandroni, Erica Beuzer, Simona Bruni, Susanna

La Polla De Giovanni, Rachelle Hangsleben and Giulia Guadagnoli, and a special thanks goes to Concetta Paduanello.

Several things have changed in my life since I first started the research for this book – jobs, homes, countries. What has remained the same is the depth of the ties binding me to my mother Bruna Iori, my father Fortunato Zambelli and my sister Franca Zambelli, whom I thank for their unconditional love.

I am profoundly thankful to my partner, Dr Mattia Fumanti, without whose unwavering encouragement and support I might have never found the determination to give my research a book form.

I dedicate this book to all the self-identified women for whom feminism is a continuous learning practice that is always personal and political; individual and collective; situated and aspirational.

Introduction

This book explores how women negotiate the tension between sexuality and status in contexts where their use of the first jeopardizes the latter. In Italy, the country where I undertook research for this book and where I am from, the patriarchal division of women into 'good' and 'bad' based on how they manage their sexuality is entrenched and forceful. More broadly, this binary informs the experiences of many women living in 'Western' countries (Giddens 1992, 111),[1] albeit in different ways and as mediated by their social location. This book, then, speaks of the experiences of women living in Italy, with some of the insights it offers potentially resonating beyond the country's national boundaries.

The opening vignette offered an instance of how this patriarchal binary is reproduced in everyday life. Daniela's moral-laden juxtaposition of women pole dancing professionally in strip clubs for male customers' pleasure and women who dance alike but for their own leisure and pleasure in recreational pole dance schools posited that these two categories of women were of unmistakably different *kinds*. Fear of being on the 'bad' side of the binary kept all the women in check. Zeza hid her lap dancing past from her recreational pole dance peers, while Daniela reassured prospective female customers that their respectability would not be jeopardized if they were to attend her school.

Feminist media and cultural scholars have primarily discussed the commercial success of recreational pole dance taking off in the early 2000s as an expression of the 'pornification' (McNair 2002) or 'sexualization' of mainstream Western culture (Attwood 2006; 2009). These terms point at large-scale transformations occurring in the intertwined domains of sexual cultures and economies, encompassing the proliferation of online pornography and people's do-it-yourself sexual productions; the gentrification of parts of the erotic entertainment industry; the diffusion of retail sexual commodities and the (neo)burlesque revival. These transformations reflect and reproduce the blurring of the boundaries between 'mainstream culture and the adult commercial sex industry' (Brents and Hausbeck 2010, 9), occurring at a time when neo-liberalism (D. Harvey 2005) has met 'postfeminism'. The latter has been alternatively conceived by some scholars as a new, 'third wave' feminism (Genz and Brabon 2009) and by others as a 'backlash' against the second wave (Faludi 1991). Nancy Fraser traced its roots to the 'disturbing convergence' between the contemporary demands of capitalism and second-wave Western feminism's goals (Fraser 2009, 97–98), as the mainstreaming of some of the second wave's keywords has coincided with their radical resignification. 'Empowerment' became an individual objective that women can achieve through consumerism (McRobbie 2009; Evans and Riley 2015), their 'free choice' to become the willing sexual objects of male desire (Gill 2003, 104) and the marketization of their 'erotic capital' (Hakim 2011).[2] In the background of this new cultural landscape, structural constraints and intersecting inequalities dissolved (Gill and Donaghue 2013) in a randomized matrix of individual preferences, choices and responsibilities.

From within this cultural context, the figure of the female stripper started to circulate in Hollywood celebrity movies and 'daytime television talk shows' (Frank 2002, xxi) as an icon of the 'empowered' woman who is intensely and confidently sexual. One of the precursors of this change was the movie *Striptease* (Bergman 1996), starring Demi Moore in the role of a secretary who starts working as a stripper to pay the legal expenses in her child custody trial.[3] In parallel, pole dancing became a mainstream leisure and fitness activity for women. Starting in the US and Canada, it first expanded to some other Western countries, and, gradually, to most other parts of the globe. In academia, feminist scholars have mainly engaged with the study of women's engagement with this practice to discern whether and how it may contribute to reproducing or subverting gender relations of power between men and women. Some consider recreational pole dance to promote women's sexual objectification under a new guise (Whitehead and Kurz 2009; Donaghue and Whitehead 2011; Owen 2012). Others suggest that it may be authentically empowering for women (Holland and Attwood 2009; Holland 2010). A third perspective highlights the tension between women's individual agency and the oppressive structures under which they negotiate it (Just and Muhr 2019). At the same time, scholars doing research on women working as exotic dancers – including women who pole dance for work – remind us that real-life strippers continue to be direly stigmatized (Frank 2002, xxvi; Egan, Frank and Johnson 2006a, xix; Price-Glynn 2010, 35; Colosi 2010, 168; Barton and Mabry 2018, 615).

The book starts from this cultural ambivalence towards the figure of the woman who uses her sexual desirability for her own leisure and pleasure or for work to discuss the role of the 'whore stigma' (Pheterson 1996) in women's processes of subjectivation in Italy. It looks at *recreational* pole dancing as a 'pleisure' practice – that is, an activity that women learn in their leisure time and perform free of charge on different occasions (e.g. birthday parties, pole dance schools' public events) for the pleasure they obtain by doing it in front of an audience. Recreational pole dancing holds the promise for women to feel intensely sexually desirable, as female strippers are, by offering them non-professional stages where they can enact and enjoy such pleasurable performance of selves. However, this promise is fraught with the danger of being stigmatized as 'whores', as real-life female strippers are. This book, then, shows that many women react to this looming threat by deploying respectability 'tactics' (de Certeau 1984) through which they displace the whore stigma onto 'other women' and particularly lap dancers, 'foreign' and sex working women.[4] It thus follows the journey of the whore stigma as it travels across these different categories of women who, in different ways and at different sites, put their sexuality to work.

Women and the Whore Stigma

At the centre of this book lies the experiences of subjects who identify as women and are socially classified as such based on their appearance. Therefore, the subject 'woman' includes both cis and trans women. This choice reflects the assumption that in patriarchal and heteronormative contexts, such as Italy, humans who are perceived to occupy the 'woman' position are subjected to, and thus have to negotiate, the whore stigma. The risk, intensity and experience of this gendered stigmatization is nonetheless mediated by women's position within a 'matrix of domination', where 'intersecting oppressions originate, develop, and are contained' (Collins 2000, 227–28).[5] It is from within this dense field of power, which is structural, relational and subjective, that women construct selves.

The book adopts a Foucauldian understanding of the role of discourse in processes of subjectivation (Foucault 1990; 1984). Michel Foucault argued that at any particular historical moment discourse makes available a limited repertoire of subject positions that individuals may take up by adopting specific technologies of the self. Drawing from his work, Judith Butler elaborated the notion of the 'paradox of subjection' to describe the ambivalent 'process of becoming subordinated by power as well as the process of becoming a subject' (J. Butler 1997, 2). This concept tames Foucault's otherwise deterministic view of the self as a mere product of discourse, thereby highlighting that while no subject can exist outside of the discourse in which it comes into being it is not univocally determined by it either. Since no subject can rise above the conditions in which it was and is constantly being formed, then nobody can claim to see everything 'from nowhere' (Haraway 1988, 581) nor adjudicate what may constitute a subject's 'authentic' consciousness and agency (Moore 2001; Mahmood 2001). As the author of this book, I translate this ontological condition into an epistemological and ethical commitment to pursuing 'strong objectivity' (Harding 1993). Hence, as 'the subject of knowledge', I have been placing myself throughout 'on the same critical, causal plane as the objects of knowledge' (Harding 1993, 69).

Although Foucault did not specifically address the construction of the woman subject through the discourse of sexuality,[6] his conceptual repertoire can be adapted to fit within a broader materialist feminist analysis of sexuality and power. Indeed, in Italy, women's subjection through sexuality occurs within a patriarchal moral and political economy of their virtue and dishonour. Women are either defined by forfeiture or subsumption into sexuality: they can be 'good', like the Christian icon of the chaste woman and mother (the Madonna), or 'bad', as women whose intense sexuality is a source of male desire and contempt (the 'whore').[7] In Italian language, this binary corresponds to women's classification as either *sante* (saints) or *puttane* (whores). The latter term has a plethora of synonyms, suggesting its living and generative qualities.[8] Significantly, it also has a quasi-tautological, ontological relationship with the subject 'woman' – for example, the expression *una buona donna* (a good woman) can be ambivalently used to describe either a 'good' or a 'bad' woman.[9]

While the term 'whore' literally means 'prostitute' (Pheterson 1996, 37), its definitional scope is much broader than women selling sex. It does, indeed, potentially apply to any woman transgressing chastity norms, such as by displaying sexual confidence and skill and/or having (had) sex before or outside of marriage, with multiple partners, and/or with another woman (Pheterson 1996, 45–46). In the words of Gail Pheterson, the 'whore stigma' is an 'instrument of sexist social control' (Pheterson 1996, 20) that can equally mark women who are in or out of sex work. It is, in fact, 'a *female gender stigma*' (Pheterson 1996, 65), regulating the relationship between women's sexuality and their status based on patriarchal notions of female dis/honour. A woman's labelling as a whore harbingers danger, as it may lead her to experience 'social ostracism, denial of rights, and/or sexual and physical violence' (Pheterson 1996, 66–67).

The concept of the whore stigma is widely used in scholarship on women selling erotic and/or sexual labour (see, for example, Chapkis 1997; Nagle 1997; Sanders 2005; Hallgrimsdottir, Phillips and Benoit 2006; Scambler 2007; Robillard 2010; Grant 2014; Capous-Desyllas et al. 2020). Some of these works follow in the wake of Goffman's pioneering *Stigma: Notes on the Management of Spoiled Identity* (Goffman 1963), focusing on how sex workers negotiate the whore stigma in their everyday lives by managing the relationship between their public and private selves. Beyond the study of the erotic and sex markets, the purchase of this concept has been limited (but see Zambelli 2018; Krivonos and Diatlova 2020) – although there is an extensive body of scholarship engaging with the study of practices and experiences of 'slut-shaming'.[10] Effectively, then, the 'whore stigma' has primarily been empirically studied as an *occupational* rather than a *gendered* stigma. Yet, while women undoubtedly enduringly constitute the bulk of the sex working population (Smith and Mac 2018, 4), the effects of the whore stigma stretch well beyond the boundaries of the sex market: 'while only some women may be sex workers, all [women] negotiate [the] whore stigma' (Grant 2014, 76).

I suggest that here is where materialist feminism needs a Foucauldian notion of discourse to reconceptualize the whore stigma as both an everyday instrument of social control (Pheterson 1996) and a disciplinary device of subjection (Foucault 1977) partaking in the production of the very 'woman' subject. It operates both in the form of external checks on women's behaviour and as a technology of the self. Women's compliance with the patriarchal chastity norms underpinning the whore stigma is thus a means to cultivate their social value and human status in a sexist society. By shifting the focus of analysis from the experiences and negotiating strategies that individuals may adopt to manage their stigmatization to the structures producing it, this (re)definition of the whore stigma follows in the wake of the recent body of sociological scholarship that embeds the study of stigma in a structural analysis of power and inequality (Link and Phelan 2014; Tyler and Slater 2018; Tyler 2021).

Whilst acknowledging the *longue durée* of the circulation of the whore stigma as a disciplinary device contributing to reproduce women's structural subordination to men, its specific form (i.e. the looks and behaviours deemed 'improper' and the punishment that a transgression may trigger, etc.) changes in time and place. Hence, some of the stigmatized and stigmatizing behaviours that Pheterson identified in Western countries over twenty-five years ago may no longer be as intensely or frequently so, depending on women's different social locations. Nonetheless, the book will show that in Italy the whore stigma remains a powerful and ubiquitous device of discipline and social control of women.

Intersections of Gender, Race and Class

Women's experience of the whore stigma as an instrument of social control is not evenly shared across race, class and gender. For example, recent research has shown that in the US 'a large number of trans Latina sex workers were arrested by anti-prostitution law enforcement as they were assumed to be sex workers for being out in the street: simply for "walking while trans"' (Mai et al. 2021, 24). Intersectionality (Combahee River Collective 1977; Davis 1982; Lorde 1984; Crenshaw 1989; Collins 1998; Collins and Bilge 2016) is thus central for a nuanced and situated analysis of the forms and effects of the whore stigma. Incorporating this paradigm thus requires looking at the role of sexuality in the creation and reproduction of class-based, gendered and racialized hierarchies of power and rule both in Western European countries (Mosse 1996) and their former colonies (Stoler 1995).

In eighteenth-century North-Western Europe, the rise of the bourgeoisie was accompanied by the formation of its attendant ideology of respectability. Sexuality became a social class marker, and the middle classes adopted the exercise of moderation in the pleasures of sex as their self-ascribed distinctive trait (Foucault 1984; Mosse 1996). Nevertheless, compliance with this austere behavioural code was unequally demanded of men and women. The sexual double standard granted middle-class white European men leeway to enjoy some premarital and extramarital heterosexual sex without jeopardizing their status in society. However, this latitude was inadmissible for middle-class white European women, whose chastity was constitutive of their value on the marriage market and in society. Women's very expression of sexual desire was problematized as a sign of their purportedly incomplete evolution and/or natural-born deviance (Lombroso and Ferrero 1903). As chastity became a distinctive property of 'respectable' white middle-class women, promiscuity, sexual excess and impropriety became the defining markers of their female others – that is, working-class women and female prostitutes. Women's use of space crucially signalled and reproduced this gendered and class-based boundary: since respectable women ought to remain secluded within the walls of the home, '"women of the streets" [became] a euphemism for prostitution' (Skeggs 1997, 46–47).

In colonial contexts, sexuality was deployed to mark a people's purported stage of modernity based on a racialized temporality culminating in Western civilization. Nineteenth-century evolutionary social theory theorized humankind's teleological progression from 'primitive promiscuity, marriage by capture, and exotic forms of sexual abuse' to the perfection of Victorian sexual morality (Lyons and Lyons 2011, 68). 'Inferior races' were imagined as sexually degenerated (Mosse 1996, 39–40) and at the mercy of their sexuality (Mosse 1996, 153–54), and these racist and sexist stereotypes fed into white Europeans' self-condoning 'white men's burden' narratives. It was a Khoikhoi woman, Saartjie Baartman, who was made to signify this racist and sexist hierarchy of rule between the white colonialists and the racialized people under their domination.[11] Back in the European metropolises, these racist depictions of 'primitive' sexuality contributed to shoring up further the edifice of the sexual double standard. '[C]onfronted with lecherous savage ancestors, [white European men] might excuse their visits to [female] prostitutes as inevitable expressions of male nature' (Lyons and Lyons 2011, 70). Conversely, white European middle-class women were warned that their 'elevation above the primitive was tenuous at best and depended upon strict adherence to domestic norms' (Lyons and Lyons 2011, 70). The distinction between unchaste white European women and the racialized people living under European colonial domination was deemed to be so tenuous that by the end of the nineteenth century 'the perception of the prostitute … merged with the perception of the black' (Gilman 1985, 229). White European female prostitutes became 'the metropolitan analogue of African promiscuity', and they came to be represented as 'white Negroes' (McClintock 1995, 56).

The book will show that today these intersecting gendered, class-based and racialized stereotypes continue to shape the tension between women's sexuality and their status in Italy. For example, they contribute to making some places and practices unevenly accessible to women across race, and they influence the different exchange values attributed to women's erotic and sexual labour (Chapter 5). They are also refracted in (women's) 'exotic value' – a novel concept that I coined to capture the ambivalent attraction and contempt underpinning the changing relationship between race, place and a woman's heterosexual desirability. In her ethnography of women working in the exotic dance industry in New York and San Francisco, Siobhan Brooks defined 'racialized erotic capital' as a property of (women) matching normative beauty standards, which, in the US, generally correspond to 'someone who is White, young, and/or has a lean body' (Brooks 2010, 7). Differently, as I will show, my concept of exotic value is ambivalent, situational and fluid (Chapter 5). It encapsulates both the erotic power of the 'pornotropics' (McClintock 1995, 22) and contempt for people coming from an 'anachronistic space' (McClintock 1995, 30). It may vary based on the 'racial grammar' (Bonilla-Silva 2012) of the (male) beholder of the gaze and (women's) race manipulation skills and possibilities.

Crossing Boundaries and Binaries

The book's preface highlighted how some women negotiate the tension between their use of sexuality and their status by reproducing moral-laden hierarchies of power among them. In Western countries, these relational processes of subjectivation and othering have rarely been the object of ethnographic enquiries. Feminist scholarship on women's engagement with practices of sexualized consumption, erotic and/or sex work primarily follows in the wake of the sex wars' debate on women's oppression or liberation (Chapter 4). Ethnographic studies of contemporary pleasure practices, such as recreational pole dancing (Holland 2010; Griffiths 2016) and (neo) burlesque (Cervellon and Brown 2014; Blanchette 2014), prevalently discuss their significance for the reproduction or challenge of the unequal gender relations of power between men and women.[12] Likewise, ethnographies of women exotic dancers mainly focus on the gender relations of power at play with their regulars (Frank 2002; Egan 2006) or the club's management (Colosi 2010; Price-Glynn 2010) (but see Brooks 2010 for an intersectional analysis). Ethnographies of women selling sex mostly discuss the labour dimension of their activity, including studies focusing on one (Sanders 2005; Day 2007; Agustín 2007) or multiple sex market segments in one or more countries (Chapkis 1997; Bernstein 2007; Mai 2018).

The blurring of the boundaries between practices of sexualized consumption (including pleasure) and erotic and/or sex work constitutes the backdrop to some of these studies. However, at the empirical level, they generally follow rather than cut across the leisure/work and consumer/worker binaries. This categorical approach best illuminates the peculiar conditions shaping women's experiences in a specific site and/or occupation. However, one of the unintended effects of this epistemological structure is that it isolates women who are in sex work from women who do not engage in sex work, thereby contributing to reproducing this morally laden binary. It also obstructs a relational (i.e. intra- and trans-categorical) understanding of women's subjectivation processes and the othering process and power hierarchies these rest upon and reproduce. Hence, while a few scholars have highlighted that some sex workers managed the whore stigma by displacing it onto another category of women (Brennan 2004; Andrijasevic 2010; Robillard 2010; Rivers-Moore 2013), this discussion has rarely been pursued relationally (but see Parreira 2021), let alone across the non-/sex working women binary and/or intersectionally.

This book seeks to contribute to these bodies of ethnographic work by exploring how women negotiate the whore stigma across a continuum of sites of pleisure, erotic and sex work. This field design offers two main advantages. First, it contributes to the empirical study of the 'sexualization of culture' by allowing the surfacing of imaginary and material points of contact between them. Second, and most importantly, it enables travel across, rather than reproduction of, the non-/sex working women binary. By bringing together the narratives of women pole dancing for pleasure, women who pole/lap dance for work, women selling sex and the author's subjectivity – as reflected in this writing – the book will explore the workings of the whore stigma as a disciplinary device of the subjection of women. It will identify recurrences in the gendered, racialized and class-based othering processes underpinning women's negotiation of the tension between their use of sexuality and their status. By tracing commonalities across the non-/sex working women binary, the book will foreground the intersecting structures of oppression under which Italian and migrant women in Italy negotiate selves. In doing so, it aims to contribute to a materialist feminist politics of liberation.

Sexscapes of Pleasure

Each of the sites where I undertook this research have women's commodification of their sexuality at their core, albeit in different ways. Recreational pole dancers paid to learn enacting a peculiar practice of (hetero)sexiness for their pleisure, while lap dancers performed erotic and emotional labour, and sex workers performed sex work, for male customers' pleasure.[13] The book will show that these practices of consumption and work did not strictly belong to any discreet site of either leisure (pleasure) or work but cut across them, engendering the perception of a continuum. Some women moved between these sites at different times of their lives, and the practices moved themselves, blurring the boundaries between mainstream leisure and the erotic and sex markets. For example, recreational pole dance instructors were often invited to perform commercial shows in a wide range of non-sex establishments (Chapter 2). Accepting to do so implied venturing out of the protective 'recreational' label, losing the pivot of their 'distinction' (Bourdieu 1984) from their ambivalently admired and despised female other – that is, the 'lap dancer'. Lap dancers, for their part, recurrently faced male customers' requests to perform 'extras' – that is, to sell them sex acts, thereby being effectively treated as 'prostitutes' (Chapter 3).[14] These sites were also intertextually intertwined in women's respectability tactics. Indeed, many recreational pole dancers and lap dancers' claims of dignity and value largely rested upon the absent presence of the women inhabiting the next site along this continuum, who occupied the metonymical position of the 'whore'. All across these sites, women's gendered stigmatization was visually signified by their physical proximity to a vertical pole: that which they danced with in recreational pole dance schools and 'night clubs', or that which they waited underneath (the streetlight) to be picked up for work.

In this book, I use the notion of 'sexscape' (Brennan 2004) to refer to the cultural landscape and the sites of pleisure and work wherein I undertook fieldwork. Drawing from Arjun Appadurai's work on the new landscapes engendered by contemporary global cultural flows at the end of the last century (Appadurai 1996), Denise Brennan defined 'sexscape' as 'both a new kind of global sexual landscape and the sites within it' (Brennan 2004, 15). In her ethnography of Dominican women's engagement in sex work, she posited that Sosúa – the site where she did fieldwork – was so radically altered following its inclusion in international sex tourism circuits that it had become 'a "sexscape" of sorts' (Brennan 2004, 14). In later years, Brennan returned to this concept to anchor its scope to the scale of transformations that the sex trade may trigger in the social relations constitutive of a site. In particular, she objected to its use as a synonym for commercial sex venues in the 'developed world', as their presence, she argued, 'by no means defines social and economic life outside of these [red light] districts. Neither do the female citizens of these places necessarily become associated with sexual availability' (Brennan 2010, 312). Some scholars have used Brennan's notion of sexscape to study the racialized sexual economies developing in international tourism sites in the shadow of the structural inequalities between economically wealthier and poorer countries (Lamen 2014; Jaiteh 2018). Other scholars have moved away from its strict definitional boundaries, albeit without explicitly discussing their theoretical underpinnings.[15]

In this book, I expand Brennan's concept of sexscape in two directions. First, I return to Appadurai's original work to put the cultural dimension of globalization back to centre stage. I shall thus widen the scope of this notion beyond the sphere of commercial sex practices and sex work sites to encompass the effects of the global circulation of sexual images, artefacts and commodities on imaginaries and practices of self-making. Unfolding in the wake of the cultural glamorization of the figure of the female stripper, the globalization of recreational pole dance thus offers a site to explore the role of the imagination in the production of modern subjectivities (Appadurai 1996, 31), akin to Jonathan Skinner's work on the transnational consumption of the salsa dance (Skinner 2007; 2016). The book will show that appeals to 'modernity' and its (newly) coterminous 'sexual freedom' were central in female recreational pole dancers' negotiation of this practice in what many described as a 'backward' country.

Second, I shall redefine the link between sex work and the 'forces of a globalized economy' (Brennan 2004, 16) to consider the impact of international migration on the structure and composition of the erotic and sex markets in Western European countries. Over the past thirty years, in fact, large numbers of cis and trans women have been migrating to Western Europe from countries economically impoverished by predatory neoliberal policies and the enduring legacies of the transatlantic slave trade and European colonialism in order to sell sex (Agustín 2007; Chimienti 2010; Mai 2013; Oso 2016). In Italy, the impact of these migratory flows on the sex market is visibly reflected in a prevailingly migrant street sex working population (Chapter 1; 4; 5). Similar processes have transformed the labour market for female-to-male erotic entertainment (Chapter 3; 5).

Therefore, my notion of a 'sexscape' includes but is not limited to erotic and sex work sites – as it inter alia encompasses sites of leisure (pleasure) – and it is not spatially confined to economically poorer countries, because both people and cultural imaginaries travel across national borders. In this book I focus on what I have defined as *sexscapes of pleasure* – sites, that is, at the core of which similarly lies the commodification of (women's) sexuality, albeit in different ways. Women may themselves consume it (i.e. in the form of pleasure practices) or perform it to produce someone else's pleasure (i.e. erotic and sex work practices).

A Multi-scaped Ethnography

The object of a multi-sited ethnography is the study of a 'cultural formation, produced in several different locales', rather than the study of 'the conditions of a particular set of subjects' (Marcus 1995, 99). Whereas I pursued my research in one country only, I did not study the specificities of women's experiences in one discreet location. Instead, I explored how Italian and migrant women negotiated the whore stigma – that is, a cultural formation regulating the relationship between women's sexuality and their status – across multiple sites. My research thus unfolded through juxtaposition and comparison of different but interconnected sexscapes in a culturally similar site. In this sense, it could be said to consist of a multi-scaped, more than a multi-sited ethnography.

'Bringing people of widely divergent classes and cultures into a common framework allows us to render visible aspects of social life that rely on, or even consist of, invisibility in their individual contexts' (Herzfeld 2015, 18). Indeed, the contrast between sites of pleisure and erotic and sex work allowed me to identify some of the effects of the matrix of domination producing women's uneven distribution across them (Chapter 5). Thus, the book will show that race, nationality, class and gender heavily affected women's presence, visibility and position in these sexscapes. For example, some sites were exclusively inhabited by 'white' Italian cis women (the inverted commas underlining the ambiguity and instability of this racial descriptor when applied to this nationality (Chapter 2; 5)); in other sites there were none. Trans women were either absent from or invisible in pleisure and erotic work sites, but they were the highest paid on the street for their sexual services.

This book is based on ethnographic fieldwork I conducted in some cities in northern Italy, mainly throughout August 2012 to October 2013, and less intensely until September 2015. This generic spatial qualification reflects an ethical concern for ensuring respondents' anonymity – something that I discuss in-depth later in this Introduction – whilst preserving the veracity and meaningfulness of the analysis that follows. As an Italian (cis) woman, I did research at 'home' (Jackson 1987), in the sense that I studied my 'own society, where "others" are both ourselves and those relatively different from us, whom we see as part of the same collectivity' (Peirano 1998, 123). However, before I started it, I had spent almost a decade away from Italy, having made a home in different countries, particularly in the occupied Palestinian territories and Lebanon, where I lived for years while working in international 'development' projects. Home, to me, back then as much as now, was both 'peripatetic and multisited' (Amit 2000, 8). Hence, when I travelled to Italy for fieldwork, I had already defamiliarized enough from the society in which I was born to be able to feel and work with and through 'the duality of belonging and alienation, familiarity and investigation' characterizing the traditional distinction between 'home' and 'field' in ethnographic fieldwork (Knowles 2000, 54).

I undertook participant observation in three sexscapes (which I describe next); I interviewed Italian and migrant women inhabiting them or who had in the past and I participated in local activities (workshops, debates, marches) concerning the politics of sexuality in Italy from feminist and queer standpoints. Interviews were open-ended and revolved around the relationship between women, their work,[16] and the society in which they performed it – including questions on when and how they first started doing their work, what they liked and disliked about it, and how they felt they were socially perceived for being in it. Interviews with sex workers rights' activists also addressed the history of their organizing in Italy and the transformation of the sex market following the closure of female brothels in 1958 (Chapter 1; 5). Interviews were reciprocal (Chapkis 1997, 7), as women could and sometimes did turn some of the questions back on me or posed new ones, contributing to a joint reflection on the issues at stake. The power relations between us were nonetheless structurally uneven. Moreover, the intense politicization of women's sexuality characterizing the Italian context at the time of my fieldwork (Chapter 1) may have impacted on what some women felt like sharing or omitting during the interview with me. Therefore, in my analytical and interpretive work, I have never stopped asking myself 'why a story is told in this way, how the location of the speaker shapes the tale, how the position of the audience affects what is heard, and … what is at stake politically, personally, and strategically in invoking this particular version at this moment in this context' (Chapkis 1997, 212).

I now turn to the description of the three sexscapes where I undertook my research. For each, I provide the rationale underpinning their inclusion in my field and a description of the research activities undertaken. Subsequently, I briefly describe the profile of the women inhabiting them that I encountered and/or interviewed.

Recreational Pole Dance Schools

When in September 2011 I started developing my research, I purposefully moved to London from Beirut, where I previously lived and worked for years as a consultant in international gender and development projects. Newly arrived, I was quite disoriented by the abrupt shifts in the rhythms and scale of my social world. One day, while at a hula-hoop class in my newly 'local' gym, I overheard two white British women discussing the remarkable body toning effects of 'pole dance'. Flabbergasted, I turned and asked them to tell me more about it. A long-time fitness regular, I had never stumbled upon this activity before. The only dance with a pole that I could think of was that which women performed in strip clubs for *work* – that is, neither for leisure nor exercise. The women were themselves astounded at my surprise and encouraged me to go and try it myself at one of the many gym clubs offering it in town. As I reached for my computer that night to do some research online, I realized that pole dance classes were indeed taught everywhere in England, including in mainstream fitness club chains. By contrast, there were very few venues offering them in Italy, and these were only ad hoc 'pole dance schools'. The choice to include the latter in my field thus emerged from this contrast in scale and a two-fold assumption: first, that in a few years, the market for this pleasure practice in Italy would have similarly boomed (as it indeed has) and second, that, accordingly, in that precise historical moment, its identity formation was at a liminal stage (Turner 1979). What I mean is that, in Italy, pole dancing was still largely associated to its strip club genealogy and so the few women navigating its transition to a pleasure activity were seeking ways to practice it without incurring in its stigmatized and stigmatizing association with real-life female strippers. There and then, therefore, women could be seen actively negotiating the tension between the 'pleasure and danger' (Vance 1984a) of their sexuality and their status as 'good' or 'bad' women.

At the start of my fieldwork, I thus enrolled in a beginner's class to gain competence on the kind of workout involved in the activity. I disclosed my researcher identity to the school's owner, instructors and peer pole dance 'students' (this being many instructors' term of choice to describe the women attending their classes), but I did not subsequently interview any of them. Gradually, I began establishing contacts with other instructors, in other schools, which I later interviewed; I participated in schools' open days, celebrations, and local and national contests, and I familiarized myself with the practice's emerging identity by reading pole dance blogs and watching online pole dance performances. I then undertook fourteen in-depth interviews with women recreational pole dance entrepreneurs and/or instructors, many of whom also performed commercial pole dance shows outside of the strictly recreational pleisure context.

I furthered my understanding of women's negotiation of their practice of recreational pole dancing in two ways. First, I realized in-depth interviews with students of an atypical class, gender and/or age profile. I thus interviewed a young woman in a precarious job who became so fond of it that she started attending daily classes despite the high costs involved; an opposite-sex couple who learned it the DIY way due to economic constraints; and the mother of a prodigious teenager, who spoke of her daughter's ambivalent experiences of admiration and stigmatization in relation to her practice. Second, I contrasted recreational pole dancing with other leisure activities that appeared to me to be similarly infused with a promise for women to feel sexy and desirable, thereby falling under the pleasure category. While on the field, many pole dance schools introduced classes of (neo)burlesque and a triad of circus disciplines (aerial silk, trapeze and circle) combining grace and strength – that is, two attributes characterizing physical activities stereotypically classified as 'female' (I.M. Young 2005). In order to understand these ongoing transformations, I thus interviewed four burlesque instructors; a burlesque 'student' who also sold sex toys at home through ad hoc meetings and 'parties' (McCaughey and French 2001; Curtis 2004); one instructor of aerialism and one instructor of 'Oriental' dance.

'Night Clubs'

As earlier relayed, the mainstreaming of recreational pole dancing as a pleasure activity is historically embedded in the glamourization of the figure of the female stripper, who professionally pole dances for male customers' pleasure, in strip clubs. Most recreational pole dancers were ambivalently seduced and disturbed by this material and imaginary proximity, and, indeed, their respectability narratives were largely set against the women working at these sites (Chapter 2) – hence my decision to include women working as lap dancers in my field.

Entrepreneurs and managers of female-to-male erotic entertainment venues in Italy use a broad range of exclusively English terms to present their businesses ('sexy bar', 'sexy disco', 'lap dance', etc.). However, the 'vernacular' expression in use is 'night clubs' or simply 'nights'.[17] Likewise, the women working in these places are generically defined with the English term 'lap dancers', corresponding to 'exotic dancers', which encompasses women 'stripping, lap dancing [and] table dancing' (Frank 2007, 502).

Ethnographies of women working as exotic dancers have been authored by scholars who had insiders' access to these venues (Frank 2002; Egan 2006; Price-Glynn 2010; Brooks 2010; Colosi 2010; Law 2012). Aesthetic considerations made me refrain from pursuing a similar path. As an outsider, however, gaining access to these venues was not straightforward. While in many Western countries such as the US and the UK the market for erotic entertainment underwent a process of gentrification and diversification, in Italy, this transformation has not taken place (yet?), and 'night clubs' largely cater to male customers only. Except for some rare women-only or 'women welcome' events, women can only enter if they accompany a man who is considered responsible for them, like a guardian (Chapter 3). In the face of these tight, practical constraints, I considered the possibility of asking a male friend to come with me and pretend that it was the other way around and build my access route from within. Yet, the thought of taking up this subordinate position in my own research was uncomfortable. Eventually, I opted for attending mixed, 'women welcome' events and nights (Preface; Chapter 3), to which I often went in the company of some female friends. Once inside, I was able to approach some female staff members, who later mediated my access to women working there as lap dancers. Scholars who did not have a direct, work-based entry route into these venues have likewise relied on gatekeepers (Bott 2006, 25–26; Dahinden 2010, 331). I subsequently interviewed two women who worked as human resource managers and nine lap dancers. Thanks to contacts in the recreational pole dance space rolling in, I was also able to interview two former 'acrobatic strippers' – that is, women performing acrobatic-intense erotic shows and who toured night clubs as special guests. Once off stage, acrobatic strippers perform the same emotional and erotic work as their colleagues, so that in common parlance their peculiar job profile is similarly subsumed under the generic 'lap dancer' category.

I furthered my understanding of women's work in this sexscape by comparing it with proximate occupations in which women provide some form of emotional and/or erotic labour, albeit from without the boundaries of the female-to-male erotic entertainment market. I thus interviewed a go-go dancer working in LGBTQ+ clubs and four *ragazze immagine* (image girls). The latter work in discos (but also commercial settings such as trade fairs), where they are paid to beautify the venue by virtue of their physical presence and provide bespoke companionship to male customers, thereby contributing to increasing their alcohol consumption (Zambelli 2018).[18]

Street Sex Work Areas

In many recreational pole dancers and lap dancers' eyes, women selling sex constituted their utmost female other, which they dreaded being identified with, hence my choice to include the sex market – specifically, the street, which is both its most stigmatized segment and the most accessible one for an outsider due to its visibility in public spaces. Some of the women selling sex explicitly identified as 'sex workers', which is a political and foremost class identity that 'de-eroticizes the public perception of the sex worker' and 'force[s the] recognition of sex workers outside of a sexual transaction' (Grant 2014, 125). For the migrant cis and trans women whom I met while they were selling sex on the street, however, their work appeared to be more a 'temporary activity rather than an identity' (Chapkis 1997, 185). In this book, I thus refer to the latter as 'sex working' women because although there and then sex work was their main occupation and source of livelihood, addressing the identity question would have required using other research methods than those that I describe below. This term is also better at capturing the multifaceted temporalities underpinning the women's engagement in the sex trade. Whilst for some it constituted and may long remain their primary occupation, others engage in it flexibly, such as in response to an acute economic need, as a buffer between other jobs, cyclically, seasonally, or in other ways still.

Akin to scholars who have researched street sex work ethnographically (Agustín 2007; Bernstein 2007), I entered the field by collaborating with associations offering outreach sexual and reproductive health information and safer sex items to cis and trans women selling sex on the street.[19] I shared my research project with the associations, and after completing a technical training course for volunteers, for a year I regularly went out with one of them on their night-time outreach service. Over time, I developed a degree of familiarity with some women, with whom miscellaneous conversations emerged from our nonetheless mainly health-focused exchanges. However, right from the start, I decided not to approach sex *working* women for interviews. The power imbalance between us was dire, partly because of the self-ascribed 'helper' position I occupied and partly because many of them were probably undocumented migrants. In those circumstances, any unusual personal questions coming from anyone sitting inside the outreach van may have been cause for suspicion, and I did not want to risk jeopardizing in any way the association's street credibility or the effectiveness of their interventions.

Instead, I interviewed women sex *workers* who were open about their current or past engagement in the sale of sex, either because they were public figures and/or because they had publicly shared their experiences. Most had street sex work experience, with some having worked on the street only and others having instead worked mainly indoors. I thus interviewed three Italian women sex workers and two pioneering sex workers' rights activists (who consented to my use of their names): Pia Covre, who co-founded with Carla Corso the *Comitato per i Diritti Civili delle Prostitute* (Committee for Prostitutes' Civil Rights; from now on: *Comitato*) and Porpora Marcasciano, who is the president of *Movimento Identità Trans* (Trans Identity Movement, MIT).

The Women

Women's presence across this continuum of sexscapes of pleasure reflected marked patterns of racialized, class-based and gendered segmentation (Chapter 5). Recreational pole dance entrepreneurs and instructors were overwhelmingly Italian cis women. Although some Italian cis women worked as lap dancers, the latter were prevalently Eastern European cis women. On the street, except for a few Italian trans women, people selling sex were mostly migrant cis and trans women from Eastern European and Latin American countries, respectively. Women were predominantly white, but their whiteness was internally stratified (Garner 2007) based on their nationality and also carried, as I will show, some exotic value.

Women's ages prevalently ranged from late twenties to mid-thirties, other than Italian women who were or had been in sex work, most of whom were older than forty. Except for Porpora Marcasciano, all the women I interviewed were cisgender. This outcome was neither by design nor coincidence but reflects the workings of intersecting structures of oppression, including homo- and transphobia (Chapter 5). Likewise, I did not encounter in these sexscapes women whom society could have labelled as 'disabled' based on their appearance.

Except for a handful of women who relayed being of middle-class origins and who were working (or had worked) as either lap dancers or sex workers, most of the women were part of the working class – in the sense that it was work rather than inherited wealth that was the source of their relative economic security. Most Italian women pole and lap dancers had completed or were in higher education, while most migrant lap dancers relayed having entered this job right after high school. I do not have this information for the migrant street sex working cis and trans women because it did not emerge during the conversations we had while on outreach service.

Ethics

The research that this book is based on received ethical clearance by the School of Oriental and African Studies (SOAS, University of London). It is premised on the respect of human dignity and integrity and its thrust arises out of a commitment to social justice, of which the elimination of any form of discrimination is a milestone.

All the women that I encountered and/or interviewed were subjected, as women, to the whore stigma, though some more intensely than others due to their engagement in erotic or sex work. Street sex working cis and trans women's migrant status exacerbated their social vulnerability further – hence my choice (earlier explained) not to interview them. I always sent the women I wished to interview – all of whom were adults – detailed written information about the research objectives, the interview's main topics, their rights as participants and the confidentiality procedures. I did so to ensure that they had sufficient time and information to decide whether they wished to proceed. Before the interviews started, women were reminded that they could refuse to respond to any question, stop the interview at any time, and/or withdraw their consent to its use even after completion, without the need to provide any explanation.

Interviews were all audio-recorded with the women's permission. I transcribed each audio file verbatim and anonymized interviewees to prevent their identification: I changed names and ages as well as cities of birth, residence and work, and omitted references to peculiar events or circumstances. I then sent the women the transcript for their verification, inviting them to let me know if they wished for me to cut or alter any further information.

An Intimate (Auto)Ethnography

I designed my research project in the aftermath of a wave of sex 'scandals' revolving around the (then) Prime Minister Silvio Berlusconi (Chapter 1). In an interview of that time that went viral, one of the female escorts involved argued that '[i]f you are a beautiful woman, and you want to sell yourself, you have to be able to do it because beauty is a *valore* [value; asset] that not everyone has or is paid for. ... *Se sei una racchia* [if you are a skag], *se fai schifo* [if you are minging], you must stay at home.'[20] Her words elicited widespread condemnation, and admittedly – and shamefully (Probyn 2010) – it was my sense of disorientation in the face of this blunt social Darwinist statement of the survival of the most beautiful that puzzled me into researching the relationship between women, sexuality and the market. What I had not anticipated was that in its course I would have learnt to trace the roots of this otherness within myself.

A cis Italian woman born and raised in a working-class family and neighbourhood, the risk of being labelled a *puttana* (whore) was an immanent and polymorphous threat, for which no haven was ever safe enough. Since my adolescence, I have seen the 'whore' label applied only apparently incoherently to girls discovering their sexuality with male peers from within and without a long-term relationship; girls and women in a relationship with a man after breaking up with another; girls and women for some reasons considered to be 'misbehaving'; and women who did not themselves 'misbehave' but whose offspring did – in fact, the Italian translation of the expression 'son of a bitch' can be equally rendered as *figlio di puttana* (son of a whore) and *figlio di buona donna* (son of a good woman). The space separating the subject 'woman' from the subject 'whore' was so narrow and unstable that, in hindsight, it appears as if it was a lingering tautology in the process of its making.

Well into my late adolescence, these were the only connotations of *puttana* I knew, meaning that I did not know it similarly applied to women selling sex. To be honest, for a long time, I just did not know that there was such a trade. Some sex working women were regularly stationed on the main street close to where I lived with my parents, but I do not remember the latter every saying a word about their presence. Nor did I ever ask my parents who the women standing still in the dark of the night were. It was as if their existence was being denied despite their incontrovertible presence in front of me. As a result of this suppression, I must have become accustomed to the women's illegibility, leaving me with no lingering questions to raise. Still, growing up, I had frequently heard some young men using the circumlocution *vattene sui viali* (go on the boulevards) to mean that, for whatever reason, they considered the girl or the woman to whom they addressed it to be a *puttana*. When one night I eventually ended up there, on those boulevards, I realized the literal sense of that expression.

A female friend and I were out with some male friends a few years older than us (they already had a driving licence and a car). Suddenly, they decided to drive towards the city centre out of 'boredom'. Once we hit the boulevards encircling it, instead of going into town, they started driving all around it, in fits and starts. Each time they spotted a sex working woman, they slowed the car down – almost stopped it in front of her – and then started honking, shouting and gesturing insults, just to speed away immediately afterwards, before the women could lash back at them. As I learnt then, that was the so-called *puttan tour* (whore tour). A typically male youth 'leisure' practice and homosocial bonding ritual, this activity does not necessarily entail such violence against sex working women; in fact, some male youth do 'approach them to strike up a conversation' only (Crowhurst and Eldridge 2020, 171). Still, for the two female adolescents in the back of the car, the experience of this violent spectacle instilled in us the terror of ever being on its receiving end.

Now a cisgender heterosexual woman in her mid-forties, I was single for most of my life. I have always thought of myself as an independent woman striving to go for what felt good to her and refuse what was not, rather than feeling bound to fulfil a straight life at all costs. This research, however, shook some earth beneath my feet. I began to wonder how my ex-partners viewed my independence and sexual 'freedom', and the more I delved into it, the more I sensed the forcefulness of the patriarchal binary splitting women into either *sante* or *puttane*. Starting from myself, I eventually learned that a woman's classification as a 'whore' does not depend on her receipt of money for sex but on her being a woman in the first place (Pheterson 1996, 65).

Therefore, the journey that I narrate in this book is simultaneously an autoethnography (Ellis and Bochner 2000; Ellis, Adams and Bochner 2011) and an 'intimate ethnography' (Waterston and Rylko-Bauer 2006). It is written from the perspective of a cultural 'insider', who, whilst researching her own society, becomes aware of the violence underpinning her own subjectivation – violence that is simultaneously personal and political, visceral and structural, epistemic and material, embodied and disavowed. To date, the 'intimate Other' at the centre of the 'intimate ethnography' field has primarily been an ethnographer's family member.[21] Differently, the intimate Other in my research is not primarily a physical person with whom I stand in an intersubjective relationship but a figure that is both archetypical and mundane and that is constitutive of my own subjectivity – the whore. Therefore, while making features of my 'culture' accessible to 'outsiders', this book also reflects the outcome of the process through which I have come to know the woman I was *terrorized* not to be(come) – the woman who confidently displays and uses her sexuality on her own terms, whether for pleasure and/or for work. Writing this book, then, is not just an end in itself. In sharing this journey, I seek to elicit epiphanies of liberation from the constitutive violence of the whore stigma that non- and sex working women are subjected to – albeit in different ways, and as mediated by their social locations.

I distinctively identify the early seeds of this intimate (auto)ethnographic plunge in a conversation I once had with an Italian male researcher. At the end of a conference, I shared my early puzzle for the recurrent stigma displacement and othering processes that I was observing among the women in my research. As soon as I finished my tentative illustration, he burst into laughter. 'What a class solidarity!' he exclaimed sarcastically. Flabbergasted at his unempathetic reaction, I could not put my gut feelings into words, as back then I did not discern the flaws in his reasoning yet. Now I know that mine was an outburst of 'feminist rage' (Ahmed 2017) against his male privilege, as he added insult to the injury of the structural gendered violence under which women negotiate their subjectivities. I have also learned that there is more than one reason why the struggle for sex workers' rights matters to me.

Book Outline

Chapter 1 sets the historical and conjunctural context for understanding the moral and political economy of sexuality in Italy, particularly the forcefulness of the binary juxtaposition of 'good' and 'bad' women. Starting from a puzzling and widespread contemporary nostalgia for *case chiuse* (closed, i.e. tolerance houses), it traces the special place that female prostitution occupies in the sexual politics of the Italian nation state and the Catholic Church. It subsequently offers an overview of the key transformations in the country's social and legal discipline of sexuality following its rapid post Second World War modernization, including the formation of the contemporary ethnonationalist discourse in which the figure of the migrant and the prostitute have come to overlap. In conclusion, it sketches the specific historical context in the aftermath of which I undertook fieldwork, consisting of the era of sexual-economic austerity following the sex 'scandals' involving the media tycoon and former Prime Minister Silvio Berlusconi.

Chapter 2 discusses how women recreational pole dance entrepreneurs and/or instructors managed the tension between sexuality and status, which this pleasure practice touches upon. It foregrounds how, behind an official desexualizing script, many women were attracted to this activity for its promise to make them feel sexier whilst remaining respectable. The chapter illustrates how women used metaphors of healing and modernity to affirm the pleasure involved in their own and their students' practice. Nevertheless, it also shows that many of them negotiated the whore stigma arising from the practice's strip club association by displacing it onto a category of 'other women', whom they depicted using intersecting gendered, class-based, and racialized stereotypes. In conclusion, the chapter traces recreational pole dance's journey to respectability, showing how it seemingly relied on the discursive erasure of the very same women that first introduced this practice in Italy while working in 'night clubs'.

Chapter 3 illustrates how the real-life women embodying recreational pole dancers' ambivalently admired and despised female other – that is, 'lap dancers' – negotiated the whore stigma from within their workplaces. It shows how women inhabited contexts where their skills were simultaneously valued and feared and where the lingering possibility that they may be available to provide male customers with commodified sex on demand exacerbated their gendered stigmatization. Subsequently, the chapter discusses the most recurrent discursive repertoires – narratives of self-entrepreneurship, familial sacrifice and love – that women mobilized to dignify themselves at work. It will also show that, akin to most recreational pole dancers, many lap dancers managed the whore stigma by displacing it onto another category of female others, who in their case mainly consisted of women selling sex from within and without the night club.

Chapter 4 shifts the focus onto the women embodying recreational pole dancers and lap dancers' ultimate female other – that is, women selling sex. Against the background of the feminist sex wars on the nature and regulation of prostitution, and particularly the debate on boundaries in sex work, the chapter highlights how women claimed value through or despite their work. It argues that some sex working women claimed it in their endurance in a challenging, sometimes hazardous, always precarious and harshly stigmatized job, which sustained their own and their family members' livelihood needs and social mobility aspirations. It also shows that some sex workers claimed value in their capacity to negotiate the structurally unequal relationship between capital and labour a bit more in their favour. Together, I will contend that Italian and migrant sex working women and sex workers' narratives offered ways to conceptualize the relationship between women's sexuality and status beyond patriarchal-defined notions of female virtue and dis/honour.

Chapter 5 analyses the effects of the matrix of domination on the presence, visibility and position of different categories of women in the three sexscapes previously discussed. It particularly describes sexscapes' racialized and gendered segmentation at the crossroads between racist and sexist constructions of sexuality of colonial roots, a political economy of migrant labour exploitation and restrictive prostitution and migration laws.

The Conclusions outline the book's theoretical and empirical contributions. These mainly sit within the ethnographic study of women's subjectivation in contemporary Western countries, the sociological study of (the whore) stigma and scholarship on migration, intimacy and work. They finally offer reflections on future lines of investigation.

Notes

1. Giddens also included the qualifier 'Christian', but I wanted to highlight here the caveats of this specification when unaccompanied by the acknowledgement of the intertwinement of race and religion in Europe's colonial conquest (Wynter 2003); the endurance of native and enslaved people's cultures (Mintz and Price 1992) despite the horrors of colonization, slavery and racial segregation; and the super-diversity (Vertovec 2007) characterizing contemporary life in these countries' 'global cities' (Sassen 1991).

2. Hakim described 'erotic capital' as 'a nebulous but crucial combination of beauty, sex appeal, skills of self-presentation and social skills [making] some men and women agreeable company and colleagues, attractive to all members of their society and especially to the opposite sex' (Hakim 2011, 1). Developed in a heteronormative framework, this concept is premised on the so-called 'male sex deficit' – that is, the assumption that men are naturally endowed with 'greater sexual desire [than women]', leaving them 'frustrated from an early age' (Hakim 2011, 3). Women's heterosexual desirability thus becomes an asset to potentially take advantage of (Hakim 2011, 57).
3. More recently, the movie *Hustlers* (Scafaria 2019), starring Jennifer Lopez, portrays the adventures of a crew of female strippers financing their glamorous lifestyles by tricking wealthy male strip club patrons.
4. In his pioneering *The Practice of Everyday Life*, Michel de Certeau theorized the difference between strategies and tactics based on the *'types of operations* and the role of spaces: strategies are able to produce, tabulate, and impose these spaces, when those operations take place, whereas tactics can only use, manipulate, and divert these spaces' (de Certeau 1984, 29–30).
5. Patricia Hill Collins posited the existence of a relationship of scale between the concept of the matrix of domination and the intersectionality paradigm. The latter, she said, 'refers to particular forms of intersecting oppressions, for example, intersections of race and gender, or of sexuality and nation. … In contrast, the matrix of domination refers to how these intersecting oppressions are actually organized' (Collins 2000, 18).
6. He did only marginally in his discussion of the problematization of the 'hysterical woman' (Foucault 1990, 103).
7. In feminist psychoanalytic accounts of the formation of the subject, the women's division in this binary is seen as a reflection of male split sexuality. Sigmund Freud posited that in the Oedipal phase the male infant experiences the mother as 'both virginal, pure, noble, sexless (as a consequence of his repression of his own sexual wishes about her), and a whore, the result of his realization that, long before his birth, the mother has already been unfaithful to him (with the father)' (Grosz 1990, 129). In adult life, men manage this ambivalence by 'embodying its elements in separate "types" of women, either virgin or whore, subject or object, asexual or only sexual', reserving 'asexual admiration' to the first, while feeling 'sexually attracted to, yet morally or socially contemptuous of, the second' (Grosz 1990, 129).
8. The dictionary of synonyms and antonyms by the 'Treccani' Italian Encyclopaedia of Science, Letters, and Arts lists the following equivalent terms: *bagascia, baiadera, baldracca, battona, bella di notte, buona donna, cagna, cocotte, cortigiana, donnaccia, donna da marciapiede (o di malaffare o di strada o di vita o, di facili costumi), donnina allegra, etera, falena, gigolette, lucciola, lupa, malafemmina, marchettara, mercenaria, meretrice, mignotta, mondana, passeggiatrice, peripatetica, prostituta, putta, (ragazza) squillo, sgualdrina, taccheggiatrice, troia, vacca, zoccola*, call girl (Treccani 2003). Note that *strappona* (Preface) is not included in this list. There are in fact many more synonyms to be retrieved from the wide range of dialects and languages spoken across Italy.
9. This equivalence can be found among the *accezioni particolari* (particular meanings; under point 'e') of the term 'woman' listed by the 'Treccani' Italian Encyclopedia of Science, Letters, and Arts, next to 'streetwalker' and 'prostitute' (Treccani n.d.).
10. The practice of 'slut-shaming' consists of 'deliberate efforts to discredit people by associating them with sexual deviancy, especially sexual immodesty and promiscuity' (Sweeney 2017, 1579). This notion partly resonates and partly diverges from the whore stigma. Melissa Gira Grant argued that what is lost in the shift from 'whore

11. Saartjie Baartman, an indentured servant, was brought from the British Cape Colony to Europe to display her purportedly 'abnormal' sexual organs under the 'stage name' of 'Hottentot Venus' (Gilman 1985; Magubane 2011). For a contemporary reading of her 'illegible will', see Hershini Bhana Young (2017).
12. As discussed for recreational pole dancing, feminist media and cultural studies scholars who have researched women's engagement with (neo)burlesque have primarily discussed it along the sexual objectification/empowerment binary. Some scholars consider women's enjoyment of this activity as a manifestation of their internalized oppression (Siebler 2014), while others offer more nuanced interpretations (Regehr 2012); for example, acknowledging its body-inclusivity and positivity (Ferreday 2008) and/or its queering possibilities (Dodds 2013).
13. The term 'sex work' was coined in 1978 by sex worker and activist Carol Leigh, member of the new-born organization COYOTE (Call Off Your Old Tired Ethics), as part of the struggle to recognize prostitution as a legitimate service work (Chapkis 1997, 70).
14. Here and in the rest of the book I use the term 'prostitute' either to underline its deployment in a stigmatizing discourse – as in this specific case – or for reasons of historical congruity, to describe specifically *women* who used to sell sex before the term 'sex worker' was coined. I discuss the gendering of the 'prostitute' subject later in the book (Chapter 1). In all other circumstances, I use the term 'sex worker' or 'sex working (person)' whenever referring to adults who consensually perform sex acts in exchange for money.
15. Elina Ihamäki (2013) used the concept of sexscape to study a Russian countryside border town where Finnish male tourists travel for sex tourism purposes, driven by their racialized desire for Russian-speaking women. Eileen Yuk-Ha Tsang (2019) used it in her ethnography of a class-based section of commercial sex venues in Dongguan, China. The edited volume by Paul Maginn and Christine Steinmetz (2014) consists of a series of case studies set mainly in Western countries; however, it does not explicitly engage with Brennan's objection to using 'sexscape' for commercial sex venues in economically 'developed' countries.
16. While I look at recreational pole dance as a leisure (pleisure) practice, I interviewed mostly women working in this sexscape as instructors and/or entrepreneurs.
17. Note that Italians use the generic term 'disco(teca)' (from discotheque) to refer to the venues that in English usage correspond to 'night club'.
18. There is a male equivalent for this occupation, i.e. *ragazzi immagine*, but the latter typically work in LGBTQI+ venues mainly to attend to male customers' entertainment.
19. In fact, the outreach unit did not go to the areas of male prostitution. The overwhelming majority of the volunteers were women, and as Porpora Marcasciano – president of *Movimento Identità Trans* (Trans Identity Movement, MIT), with street sex work experience – explained to me during her interview, 'You cannot send a woman operator to contact a male street sex worker because the relationship gets completely warped … Handing him a condom is like a statement that you are seeing him there, that he is prostituting himself, that he is selling sex to other men. … So, men do offer sexual services, but they feel guilty about it, and so the relationship [with their customers] frequently turns violent. As Pier Paolo Pasolini said, in our cultural system, a man selling homosexual services feels the need to stress that it is not true [that he is doing it/that he is gay].' On the tension between male sex work

and masculinity formations, see also Victor Minichiello, John Scott and Denton Callander (2013, 264).
20. 'Intervista shock di Terry De Nicolò, escort ospite di Berlusconi' (Shocking interview with Terry de Nicolo', escort [who was a] guest of Berlusconi), 16 September 2011. The original interview is no longer available on YouTube. It can be found on some private web pages and social media accounts by searching for this title. However, all those that I have checked for the purpose of providing a link for the reader's easy reference contain highly stigmatizing language – hence my choice not to provide any.
21. The works of Alisse Waterston (2014) and Barbara Rylko-Bauer (2014) engage with their father and mother's biographies, respectively, narrating how their lives were profoundly disrupted by antisemitism, racism, Nazism and the Holocaust in Europe and transformed through migration and exile on the other side of the Atlantic. Christine Walley's ethnographic account of deindustrialization, unemployment and class inequality in the United States (2015) revolves around her father – a steel factory worker who lost his job to this epochal economic transformation. Susan Slyomovics' anthropological and legal discussion on the relationship between violence, economic reparations and the law (2015) starts from the diverging views of her mother and grandmother, who survived Nazi concentration camps and extermination centres.

Chapter 1

A MORAL AND POLITICAL ECONOMY OF WOMEN'S SEXUALITY

Midday on a Sunday in autumn, and I am driving towards the trattoria recently opened by Gina, an old friend of mine. Her venue lies in the hills across which ran the *linea gotica* (gothic line) – the natural and political border splitting Italy in two throughout the last stages of the Second World War.[1] It was from here that the Italian volunteer combatants known as *partigiani* (partisans) fought against the Nazi Fascists, and where the latter accomplished bloody civilian massacres. Today, these events continue to be actively remembered through official commemorations, student educational activities, political tourism tours and a wide range of cultural productions. The intensity of this memorialization marks the foundational place of the country's *Resistenza* (resistance) against Nazi-Fascism in Italy's national identity.

Gina and I first met approximately twenty years ago, at a local *Festa dell'Unità* (Unity Festival), where we both volunteered in one of the many pop-up restaurants raising funds for the former Italian Communist Party.[2] Since then, many things had changed in our lives. I had been away from Italy for almost ten years, working in relief and 'development' projects in the occupied Palestinian territories and Lebanon. Meanwhile, she divorced and started her life anew by opening a business. Her trattoria had a typically rustic feel – furniture made from thick oak wood, a big fireplace and peasants' work tools hung on the walls. As I moved across the room to take my seat at the table, I was struck by something looking out of place in the otherwise well-matched interior design. Curious, I went closer to look at it and saw that it was a tin placard reproducing the price list of a female brothel – the *Casa delle Sorelle Fraschini* (Fraschini Sisters' House) – offering customers '*signorine dall'Italia e dall'Etiopia*' (Misses from Italy and Ethiopia). It was dated 'XIV EF' – that is, the fourteenth year of the 'Fascist Era': 1936.[3] That was when, after repeated military assaults and wars against the Ethiopian people, including the use of chemical weapons against combatants and civilians (Del Boca 1969; Sbacchi 2005), Italy claimed control over their country and, with it, the birth of the Italian Empire.[4]

This was an interesting piece for my research and definitely an unexpected place to find it. 'Where did you get that?' I asked Gina when she came to greet me. She turned to look at the placard. 'That one?' she said, shrugging her shoulders nonchalantly, 'Oh, well! I bought it at a local flea market.' Then Gina picked up a cigarette (smoking in public venues was banned, but there were no customers around, so she did as she pleased), and when she looked at me again, I saw a naughty twinkle in her eyes, as if the presence of this object ought to tell me something intimate, perhaps cheeky about her. She then steered the conversation elsewhere, leaving me mumbling about when, how and why ephemera from imperial brothels had become vintage decor.

****

A middle-aged and lefty woman's fascination with female brothels that were shut down by law before she was born indexed the peculiar nostalgia circulating in Italy at the time of my fieldwork. While in many Western European countries consensus for the so-called 'Swedish' prostitution model criminalizing the purchase of sex was gaining momentum,[5] in Italy, some major political parties were veering in the opposite direction (Crowhurst 2019), demanding the reopening of *case chiuse* (closed houses, meaning tolerance houses) instead. The term *casa chiusa* (sing.) aptly conveys the country's ambivalent attitude towards female prostitution. Although until 1958 the state authorized their existence, it also mandated that their doors and windows remain shut and prohibited their establishment in the proximity of schools, public buildings and churches (M. Gibson 1999, 32). This spatial containment thus suggests that female brothels were considered objects of shame and danger for the 'health' of the social body.

This chapter offers a historical and conjunctural contextualization of the relationship between women's sexuality and their status in Italy, thereby providing the backdrop for the sociocultural dynamics discussed in the rest of the book. It traces the political and moral economy underpinning the entrenched patriarchal division of women into 'good' and 'bad', focusing on the role of the state and the Catholic Church, whose political and spiritual seat lies at the heart of Rome.[6] The chapter illuminates the special place that state-regulated female prostitution occupies in the history of 'modern' Italy (this adjective qualifying the newness of the nation state born in 1861 against its preceding political formations), spanning its birth, its colonial and imperial history, until the present time. Next, it provides an overview of the key post Second World War transformations in the country's social and legal discipline of sexuality, encompassing the dismantlement of the system of state-regulated female prostitution (1958); laws disconnecting sex from marriage and reproduction (throughout the 1970s) and the establishment of Italy's first sex workers' organization (1982). The 1990s saw the increasing globalization of the sex market following the arrival of cis and trans women from countries in Latin America, Eastern Europe and Africa. Against this background, the chapter discusses Italy's nostalgia for the female brothel as an expression of a broader ethnonationalist 'affective economy' (Ahmed 2004) with colonial roots. In conclusion, it describes the wave of national(ist) indignation arising in the context of the sex 'scandals' involving the (then) Prime Minister and media tycoon Silvio Berlusconi, the aftermath in which my fieldwork unfolded.

A Pillar of the Nation

Since as far back as Aristotle, the prostitution of women was considered a 'vaccine' against male soldiers' homosexuality (Rossiaud 2013, 12). Indeed, the early seeds of the European system of state-regulated female prostitution arose in military contexts, where men were compelled to live in exclusive contact with one another for long periods of time. It was Napoleon I who, at the dawn of the nineteenth century, while pursuing his imperial project, set up the first medically supervised female prostitution camps in order to preserve the health of his troops (M. Gibson 1999, 24). Analogous concerns for male soldiers' sexuality and sexual health underpinned the issuance of the Contagious Diseases Acts in some districts in England, in 1864–66 (Walkowitz 1980, 4).

Likewise, the government of the political formation that steered Italy's nation-building process in the second half of the nineteenth century first introduced female prostitution in a military context. The Kingdom of Piedmont-Sardinia, then in a war against the Austrians, authorized by decree the opening of state-controlled brothels in Lombardy to support the allied French army fighting on their side in the Second Italian War of Independence. The following year (1860), the decree was turned into law, which became known as the *Regolamento Cavour* (Cavour Regulation).[7] The jurisdiction of *Regolamento* grew organically with the country's expanding frontiers, replacing a 'patchwork of law and custom with a homogeneous statute applicable to all communes, urban or rural, that harboured prostitutes' (M. Gibson 1999, 15).

It could well be said, therefore, that the prostitution of women played a part in the very making of modern Italy. This role, nonetheless, did not come with any positive recognition. Rather, women prostitutes were made to occupy the position of the 'abjects' of the nation (McClintock 1995).[8] They were, in fact, 'simultaneously rejected but necessary to its functioning' – akin to other social categories that were central in the making of 'modern industrial imperialism', including enslaved people, people living under colonial domination and domestic workers (McClintock 1995, 72). It is, in fact, quite significant, I contend, that *Regolamento* was never published in the country's *Gazzetta Ufficiale* (Official Gazette).[9] Technically, its absence may be justified by the fact that the law was issued a year before the Kingdom of Italy was born (1861). It nonetheless hints at *Regolamento*'s exceptionally extrinsic status and the country's profoundly entrenched ambivalence towards women selling sex. Tellingly, during a Parliamentary debate, an Italian MP said that this law 'never appeared in the Official Gazette, nor in the collection of laws and decrees; [because] some things should be known by those who are interested in them, but it is better not to publicize them undeservedly' (quoted in Turno 2003, 105).

The system of state-regulated female prostitution, first elaborated by Alexandre Parent Duchâtelet for the city of Paris (Parent Duchâtelet 1840), organized its containment within a chain of state-surveilled spaces: the brothel, the hospital for venereal diseases, the prison and the corrections house (Corbin 1985, 16–20). It thus ensured men a regularly accessible and safe outlet for heterosexual sex in ways that would have served the 'healthy' – that is, functional – reproduction of the family and the nation. Female prostitutes' organized availability was also key to protect the virtue and value of middle-class women on the marriage market – of which their virgin status was a keystone – and the cultivation of men's heterosexual dispositions.

Different from other European countries that managed brothels at the municipal level, in Italy, the central state was directly and actively involved in the enforcement of the division of women into 'good' and 'bad' in the city (M. Gibson 1999, 36).[10] Any woman selling sex had to register with the public authorities, and she could work either in a brothel or independently, as a *meretrice isolata* (isolated prostitute). From then onwards, women registered to work as prostitutes had to undergo compulsory, bimonthly vaginal checks at the hands of public health officers. Results were recorded in a *libretto* (book) that had always to be kept readily available for police inspection in the brothel (where it was in the owner/manager's hands) or on the prostitute, if she worked on her own (M. Gibson 1999, 88). Since the performance of female respectability required seclusion within domesticity, the morality of any woman moving on her own in public spaces was questionable. Indeed, the vice squad could arrest her, enforce a vaginal test and, if found ill with a venereal disease, enforce her hospitalization and registration as a prostitute (M. Gibson 1999, 132).

Once undertaken, registration was substantially indelible. The police considered applications for cancellation only based on 'marriage, sickness, entrance into a reformatory, starting an "honest" job, or the guarantee of support by a respectable citizen', but even on these terms many applications were unsuccessful (M. Gibson 1999, 143). Class nonetheless mediated the likelihood of a woman's enforced registration. This bureaucratic act was indeed more frequently imposed on 'migrant, unemployed and homeless women' than 'mistresses, courtesans, and other categories of higher class prostitutes' (M. Gibson 1999, 148). Married women were also often spared registration (M. Gibson 1999, 95) – as if the overlap between the figure of the wife and the prostitute was inconceivable, leaving law enforcers in doubt over which patriarchal authority (i.e. the state or the husband) should prevail in the determination of women's legal and moral status.

The system of state-regulated prostitution was extended to Italy's colonies. Upon landing at Massawa (Eritrea), in 1885, Italians immediately separated women selling sex from the rest of the population, making them 'live instead in a segregated area' (Barrera 1996, 25). It was likewise implemented in Tripolitania and Cirenaica (Schettini 2019) – that is, territories formerly under the Ottoman Empire that Italy colonized and unified in 1934 under the flag of 'Italian Libya'. The Italian colonialists initially prohibited the employment of Italian women in the colonial brothels out of concern for the country's national and racial 'prestige'. Nevertheless, male soldiers and settlers' demand for sex was so high that this rule was soon lifted (on Tripolitania and Cirenaica see Schettini 2019, 58; on the Horn of Africa see Pankhurst 1974, 177).

After declaring the birth of the Italian Empire (1936), the fascist regime outlawed some types of intimacies between Italian male settlers and native women.[11] Regarding female prostitution, new regulations by the then Italian Ministry of Colonies Alessandro Lessona to the vice-king Graziani (reproduced in Rochat 1973, 189–90) recommended the opening of tolerance houses, 'even mobile, with women of the white race [sic]', and the prohibition of local men's access to them. In November 1936, Vittorio Gorresi, an Italian journalist, reported that the regime established 'a special Office P. under the Ministry of Colonies' and launched a tender among the 'best tolerance houses' to branch out in the Italian East Africa (quoted in Stefani

2007, 132). The objective was to spare 'at least the high ranks' from having sexual contact 'with the coloured [sic] *sciarmutte* [whores]' (Vittorio Gorresi quoted in Stefani 2007, 132).[12] These racist prostitution policies nonetheless failed, as the number of white women working as prostitutes in Italy's colonial brothels remained incommensurably low compared to the demand for commodified sex.[13]

Italy's defeat in the Second World War coincided with the end of the fascist regime, the Kingdom and the Empire.[14] The system of state-regulated female prostitution, though, survived intact this epochal earthquake. Overall, its exceptional durability is testimony to its pivotal role in the country's moral and political economy of sexuality. Between *Regolamento Cavour* (1860) and the so-called 'Merlin Law', which, nearly a century later (1958), shut the brothels down, it underwent only minor changes, which substantially revolved around the degree of intensity of state surveillance over women.[15]

A Lesser Evil

The organized availability of female prostitutes was similarly functional in the scaffolding and tenability of the sexual politics of the Catholic Church. The latter's position on the prostitution of women can be traced back to a major theological shift occurring between the second half of the eleventh century and the beginning of the twelfth. The reforms proposed by Thomas Aquinas inaugurated a relatively more relaxed approach towards sex (Hirshman and Larson 1998, 45–47; Rossiaud 2013, 31–32), which was disconnected from original sin and conceived as both natural and necessary for the reproduction of the godly-ordained natural order – humankind included. Sex, however, ought to be enacted with moderation and within the boundaries of reproductive heterosexuality and monogamous marriage. Acts detached from reproduction were considered to be *against* nature, and the Church condemned sodomy, masturbation, onanism and bestiality (Rossiaud 2013, 28–31). In parallel emerged the figure of the *meretrix publica*, indicating women visibly asking for money in exchange for sex (Rossiaud 2013, 7). By the end of the thirteenth century, the official position of the Church was that female prostitution was 'the lesser of two evils' – the worse evils being homosexuality, adultery and incest (Rossiaud 2013, 12). Such a principle was enshrined in the *De Regimine Principum*, authored by Thomas Aquinas and completed by Bartholomew of Lucca around 1280. In it, the latter quoted 'an interlinear gloss' that appeared in a manuscript of the *City of God* a few decades earlier, stating that '[t]he public woman is, in society, what is a bilge on boats and a sewer in a building. Take the sewer away, and all the building will be infected' (Rossiaud 2013, 12).

Throughout the thirteenth to the end of the fifteenth century, however, there was in Western Europe a degree of osmosis between prostitution and marriage, and women selling sex enjoyed social, economic and religious rights (Rossiaud 2013, 254–55). Female prostitutes frequently attended marriages and received gifts 'in exchange for the freedom conceded to an old customer' (Rossiaud 2013, 255). Not just a symbolic ransom, as Rossiaud suggests, the meaning of these gifts may also be interpreted as an expression of appreciation for the women's work of cultivating the groom's heterosexual dispositions until marriage. From this perspective, one could conceive the existence of a 'traffic' (in Levi Strauss' terms) in men, as their exchange between a 'bad' and a 'good' woman marked the passage from a propaedeutic in heterosexuality to its investment within legitimate forms of reproduction and generationality.

The schism in Christianity provoked by the rise of Protestantism led to the Catholic Church's implementation of strict boundaries separating legitimate and illegitimate sex. While Luther and Calvin desacralized marriage and allowed divorce, the Catholic Church reaffirmed this contract's sacred (Hirshman and Larson 1998, 49–51) and indissoluble status.[16] The Council of Trent (1545–1563) condemned any form of sex taking place before or outside marriage, including fornication, adultery, concubinage and prostitution. Nevertheless, the latter was not prohibited, suggesting that it maintained its status as a 'necessary evil'. This activity was, in fact, regulated in the *Stato Pontificio* (Papal States) (McCarthy and Terpstra 2019), which remained under the temporal rule of the pope until its annexation to the Kingdom of Italy. In late sixteenth – early seventeenth-century Bologna, for example, women could legitimately sell sex if they paid a fee to the *Ufficio delle Bollette* (Office of Receipts) (Ferrante 1987, 989–90; McCarthy and Terpstra 2019); the latter also functioned as an arbitration court to settle women prostitutes' disputes with their clients (Ferrante 1987, 990–92) – suggesting that the women were subjects of law and had (workers') rights.

Since the birth of the modern Italian nation state, the influence of the Catholic Church on its moral and legal discipline of sexuality has always been forceful *and* has coexisted with Italy's century-long system of state-regulated female prostitution. The politics of sexuality of both institutions, in fact, largely aligned with each other. Italy's new Civil and Penal Code reaffirmed the normativity of heterosexual marriage and the sexual double standard (Balestracci 2020, 14). In parallel, 'sodomy' became a crime under the Kingdom of Italy, thereby breaking with the established pattern of 'tolerance' for male homosexuality that characterized most of the preceding political formations (Ponzio 2019, 108).[17] Female homosexuality was never criminalized (Balestracci 2020, 15) – an apparent latitude that arguably rather indexed its status as inconceivable in the minds of the legislators.

Male prostitution was similarly unthinkable: Italian prostitution laws have always assumed that the 'prostitute' subject is a woman, and this remains the case today: Article 3.5 of the current Merlin Law (more on this later) criminalizes any person who 'induces into prostitution an adult *woman*' (my emphasis), and Article 4.3 doubles the punishment if the person found guilty of aiding and abetting prostitution is a relative, including the *husband* (but not the wife). This gendering of the prostitution subject is not only factually incorrect – as men and LGBTQI+ people sell sex too (see e.g. Browne, Cull, and Hubbard 2010; Rinaldi 2019; Scott, Grov, and Minichiello 2021) – but it is also harmful, because it reinforces the quasi-tautology between the subject 'woman' and the subject 'whore' (Introduction).

Nonetheless, there were a few issues on which the Italian state and the Catholic Church held diametrically opposing views, particularly where marriage was concerned; the state considering it a rescindable civil contract and the Church an indissoluble sacrament. Between the birth of Italy and the rise of Fascism, the Italian government tried multiple times to introduce divorce – nine, to be exact – but '[e]ach one was a failure largely because of Catholic opposition' (Pollard 2008, 36).[18] However, a similarly vocal divergence in matters of female prostitution was not as apparent, suggesting that the two institutions might have had little disagreement on its 'necessity' – although an in-depth investigation into the Church's archives is needed to shine more light on this.

Eventually, the efforts of the state and the Church to fully control women's sexuality were only partially successful. Clandestine, occasional and part-time prostitutes always outnumbered registered ones (see M. Gibson 1999, 95 on the period under state-regulated prostitution, and Bellassai 2006, 30 after the Merlin Law). In the countryside, the demanding nature of agricultural work required women's help too – hence, the impracticability of their spatial seclusion in the home. In contexts where today's children are tomorrow's helpers in the fields, people living off the land considered women's fertility more valuable than their virginity at marriage. Indeed, at the beginning of the twentieth century, premarital sex among engaged partners was customary, as the marriage proposal overrode the importance of the wedding ceremony (P. Willson 2011, 15). Many couples would wait for pregnancy confirmation before getting married (Parca 1965, 84; Sorcinelli 1993, 306).

This scenario changed rapidly following Italy's defeat in the Second World War, which was to be followed by a sweeping wave of economic, social and cultural modernization.

The Rise of Sexual-Economic Modernity

Akin to what many feminist scholars have observed in several countries across the globe (see e.g. Yuval-Davis 1997; Abu-Lughod 1998; Moghadam 2013), in post-Second World War Italy, 'modernity' had a woman's face. Already before the end of the war, women were identified as a special target of the Allied troops' media propaganda, who wished them to know that 'from now on, they too will count' (Edoardo Anton, quoted in Garofalo 1956, 2).[19] In 1946, Italians were called to cast their ballot for the referendum on the country's form of government, determining its transmutation into a Republic and the election of a Constituent Assembly. This was the first time that Italian women were granted suffrage to vote in national elections, except *meretrici isolate* – that is, women lawfully selling sex but autonomously. This proscription was abolished the following year (P. Willson 2011, 235). Nonetheless, its enforcement at such a critical nation-(re)building moment reveals the structural contempt for women using their sexuality independently from the patriarchal-capitalist institution of the female brothel of the time. The year that Italy became a Republic also saw the launching of the *Miss Italia* (Miss Italy) beauty pageant – the first competition requiring women to walk the catwalk in revealing attire[20] – foreboding the overlap between women, modernity and commodities that was to intensify in the following years.

A beneficiary of the US-sponsored Marshall Plan – the programme that promoted the post-Second World War economic recovery of Western European countries – Italy underwent a very rapid process of transformation, which took over a century to unfold in other countries (P. Willson 2011, 199). The so-called *miracolo economico* (economic miracle) transformed the country into an industrial power, and '[m]illions of Italians were catapulted out of poverty and rural isolation through migration to the cities and greater access everywhere to mass culture and commercial leisure' (Cullen 2013, 38). Italy's modernization unfolded along the intertwined axis of mass consumerism and women's emancipation (Gundle 2007, 114) – both epitomized by female figures: the housewife endowed with the latest electrical appliances and the 'sexy' woman wearing make-up and revealing attire (P. Willson 2011, 203–4).

These transformations alarmed the Catholic Church, which feared their impact on Italians' sexual mores. At that time, Italy was one of few Western European countries where divorce was prohibited and female prostitution was legal (Tambor 2006, 134)[21] – a legal tandem similarly characterizing two countries with a prevalently Catholic identity and population: Portugal and Spain. The Catholic Church reacted to the US influence by condemning 'cosmetics, beauty contests, "immoral dress" and modern dances' (Pollard 2008, 135). It also strove to uphold the value of women's chastity; for example, by proclaiming the canonization of Maria Goretti (1950), a young woman who died at the turn of the twentieth century while resisting rape (P. Willson 2011, 231). Nonetheless, the pressure to disconnect sex from marriage and reproduction was growing.

It was in this context that, in the summer of 1948, Lina Merlin – the only woman senator in the Republic of Italy's first Parliament and a socialist – proposed a bill to abolish the state-regulated prostitution of women. Her initiative was perceived to be so disruptive that it was metaphorically portrayed as a terrorist attack at the heart of the state: journalist Anna Garofalo described it as 'the first bomb exploding in Parliament' (Garofalo 1956, 91). While, in 1949, the United Nations General Assembly approved the Convention for the Suppression of the Traffic in Persons and the Exploitation of the Prostitution of Others, it took Italy ten years of parliamentary debates to approve the so-called *Legge Merlin* (Merlin Law), and only with a secret ballot (Bellassai 2006, 18).[22] The text of the law, however, was very different from senator Merlin's original bill, mainly due to the compromise struck with the party holding a nearly absolute majority in Parliament – Democrazia Cristiana (Christian Democracy) – and whose support was necessary if the law was ever to pass. This required a shift of emphasis in the justification of the law from women's rights to containment of social pollution (Tambor 2006, 138–40; P. Willson 2011, 259–60). Throughout this decade, the Catholic Church abstained from any direct commentary on the bill's parliamentary debate (Tatafiore 2012, 176) – a striking silence when compared to its vocal battles against any law that, in subsequent years, aimed at disconnecting sex from marriage and reproduction (more on this later).

The Merlin Law abolished brothels and shut down existing ones. Women were allowed to sell sex autonomously, although under quite constraining circumstances. The exchange of sex for money between two consenting adults was allowed, but pretty much anything else was criminalized. The law prohibited solicitation both in private and public spaces, and the definition of the crime of aiding and abetting prostitution was so broad that prostitution became 'simultaneously allowed and prohibited everywhere' (Tatafiore 2012, 154). This paradoxical condition pushed the women out into the street, which became the default place where sex could be sold without breaking the law. The state, in fact, could not tax them for their use of public soil or else it would have become itself a third party illicitly profiting from their work – this being also the rationale underpinning women's law-mandated income tax exemption.

The new prostitution law was nevertheless quite unpopular among men and women alike. Interestingly, the latter were said to be its 'fiercest enemies'

(Anna Garofalo, quoted in Azara 2017, 64), seeing the brothel as a convenient outlet to cultivate their sons' heterosexual orientation, funnel their premarital sex and satisfy their husbands' sexual 'needs' without affecting their marriage, as a lover might have. Brothels became mythological objects, celebrated in 'descriptions, narrations, nostalgic memories, emotional testimonies' (Serughetti 2019, 56), and as this chapter's initial vignette suggests, so they remain today.

While men mourned the loss of the institution affording them heterosexual sex on demand, they kept negatively judging women having sex outside of marriage. A few years after the Merlin Law was enforced, a study on men aged between 20 and 50 years of different social classes found that 81% regretted the closure of the brothels (Parca 1965, 215–16) and 75% – that is, approximately the same proportion – held in contempt women engaging in premarital sex (Parca 1965, 12–13). The latter were nonetheless increasing in number. A collection of women's letters to female weekly magazines revealed that their boyfriends increasingly put pressure on them to give them the 'love proof' (Parca 1959, 6) – that is, to have full vaginal intercourse – implying the women's loss of their virgin status and, with it, their patriarchal-defined female honour. A study carried out in 1964–65 with female adolescents (13–19 years old) living in major cities across the North/South divide[23] found that most did not consider premarital sex to be 'immoral' (L. Harrison 1966, 104); a fifth had already had 'full sexual intercourse' (L. Harrison 1966, 116) and many doubted their boyfriends' masculinity if they did not demand more than a kiss (L. Harrison 1966, 58–59).

The late 1960s were the years when the seeds of Italy's sexual revolution were planted. Akin to what happened in the US and many other Western countries, Italian second wave feminists put the discipline of sexuality at the centre of their battles to retrieve control of their body from the state, the medical profession and the Church. During the next decade, most of their demands were codified in law: the state legalized divorce (1970),[24] contraception (1971)[25] and abortion (1978),[26] and it equalized gender roles and rights within the family (1975).[27] The Catholic Church fought everywhere against these norms – in the street, in the parishes, in the press and Parliament – but unsuccessfully, and referendums to abolish the divorce and abortion laws failed.

At the same time as these battles were being fought and won, soft porn and erotica exploded in the mass media (Missero 2019, 86–87; Balestracci 2020, 104). Private, commercial TV channels thrived 'on the nexus between desire, image, and the female body' (Gribaldo and Zapperi 2012, 24), and so did the booming advertisement industry (Balestracci 2020, 133). The level of sexism, 'voyeurism and fetishization of women's bodies' reached such levels that some feminist scholars interpreted it as a backlash against the freedoms that feminists had won for all women (Gribaldo and Zapperi 2012, 15; 17). Amid this cultural economy, the media empire of Mr. Silvio Berlusconi – the man who was to be one of Italy's most long-running Prime Ministers – thrived.

Sex Workers Take the Floor

Although the state abolished brothels, it did nothing to eliminate the stigmatization of women selling sex and failed to acknowledge their rights as women, workers and citizens. In its founding manifesto, Italy's first sex workers' rights organization – *Comitato* – denounced that the state 'tolerated' women prostitutes 'only as long as [they] are whores, informants, victims of a pimp' and that they instead harshly 'persecuted and blackmailed' prostitutes whenever claiming their citizens' rights (Comitato per i diritti civili delle prostitute 1983). The birth of *Comitato*, in 1982, followed in the wake of the emerging sex workers' movement in the US and Europe, which had the demand 'for freedom from police violence' at its core (Grant 2014, 22). In fact, it was the women's subjection to institutional violence that first triggered their protest. Carla Corso – one of two co-founders of *Comitato* – recounted in her memoir that the organization was born 'after the umpteenth episode of violence' that occurred while working in the proximity of the Aviano NATO Air Base. 'We were fed up with what was going on in Pordenone [a city close to the base], with all the abuses against prostitutes, especially by the Americans' (Corso 1991, 173). In that position, the women were exposed to intersecting structural vulnerabilities – as women, prostitutes and Italian citizens.

At that time, in fact, despite the feminist victories in the domains of sexuality, marriage and reproduction, the Italian state did not recognize women's full ownership of their bodies nor protect them from male sexual violence – in the home or in the streets. Mitigating circumstances for 'honour crimes' and the 'redemption' of rape through shotgun weddings were abolished only in 1981 (P. Willson 2011),[28] and until 1996,[29] rape was considered an offence against 'public morality' rather than a crime against the person subjected to it. Against this backdrop, the purported perpetrators' privileged position as American citizens exacerbated the women's structural vulnerability. From an international relations perspective, in fact, Italy's position towards the US was that of a satellite country in the face of a mighty economic and military superpower that had, to some extent, remade the country anew. The Anglo-American troops first occupied Italy militarily, then liberated it from fascism, and the US-funded Marshall Plan powered the country's post-war reconstruction. Italy occupied a geopolitically strategic position during the Cold War,[30] and it hosted a considerable number of US military, based on agreements that have long remained secret.[31] Reports documenting the occurrence of incidents of sexual violence involving US soldiers stationed abroad corroborate Carla's account.[32] Taken together, these elements suggest that the women inhabited a challenging position, one where their experiences of violence were doomed to be institutionally dismissed.

In those years, the sex market was undergoing a rapid and radical transformation. After the closure of the brothels, the sudden visibility of women selling sex on the street engendered the public perception of their quantitative increase (Angioletti 1979, 40), and complaints arose 'from the most diverse sectors of civil society, both secular and Catholic. Fathers and mothers wrote [to the Ministry of Interior] to preserve the integrity and modesty of their daughters and sons. Parishes rose up, starting petitions and collecting thousands of signatures at the exit from Sunday Mass' (Azara 2022, 275). These perceptions were exacerbated in the 1990s, following the arrival of sex working cis and trans women from Latin America, Africa and the former Soviet bloc. In her interview with me, Pia Covre, the other co-founder of *Comitato*, recounted that

> the arrival of these big migratory waves changed the relationship between supply and demand; the condition of the offering subject changed. Suddenly, we had a vast supply [of sexual services] on the market and very fluctuating prices because [migrant] women did not know how much we [Italian street sex working women] asked. They asked what to them was a lot, but they did not realize that for us and the market back then they should and could have asked for much more!

By the end of the 1990s, street sex working women were mainly from Nigeria and Albania (P. Willson 2011, 325). A similar transformation had already taken place in the market for trans women's sexual services, following the arrival of large numbers of migrant trans women from Brazil (Tatafiore 2012, 90). In those years, Italy was to '[Brazilian] travestis what El Dorado was to the Spanish conquistadores of the New World. It [was] the land of fabled riches to which one travels in order to make one's fortune and return with enough money to realize one's dreams' (Kulick 1998, 166). Competition pressure pushed Italian cis and trans women to shift indoors to stem the race to the bottom (Corso 1991, 227–28; Tatafiore 2012, 140). The street sex market thus became, by and large, dominated by migrant cis and trans women – and so remains today (Chapter 5).

Making the Streets Respectable

Against the backdrop of Italy's increasing migration anxieties (King 1993, 289–90; Zincone 1998, 77; Mingione and Quassoli 2000, 41; Merrill 2006, 79), an ethnonationalist affective economy arose in which the figure of the prostitute and the migrant came to overlap (Peano 2012, 423). Cleaning the streets of prostitution became coterminous with containing migration, with the aim of making the nation look 'respectable' (Stoler 1997) again. Italian women and men organized petitions and local demonstrations against urban blight, while the state launched a wide-scale operation of repression and regulation of the street sex market (Tatafiore 2012, 139). In parallel, the request to change the Merlin Law and reopen *case chiuse* became the object of public debate (Tatafiore 2012, 149).

These – the early 1990s – were also the years when Italy's political class was largely swept away by the judicial investigation into political and economic corruption known as *Mani Pulite* (Clean Hands). Many key figures of the ruling parties were found guilty (Ginsborg 2007, 501–5). From the ashes of this political earthquake arose a new political formation, Forza Italia (Forward Italy), whose leader – Mr Silvio Berlusconi – ruled the country for almost fifteen years, in coalition with two strange bedfellows. While the Lega Nord (Northern League) campaigned for the secession of Italy's northern regions, Alleanza Nazionale (National Alliance), the heir of the Fascist Party (Tarchi 2003, 142), had instead a strongly nationalist and unitary agenda. However, there were some priorities that they all shared: halting migration,[33] protecting the 'natural' family[34] and removing prostitutes from the streets.[35] These were all supposed to be met via the December 2002 government bill to criminalize prostitution in 'a public place or in places open to the public' and to decriminalize it in rental flats. However, the bill did not go through, so some local mayors moved into direct action, imposing administrative measures on street sex working women and their customers in the name of 'urban safety' and 'decorum' (Garofalo Geymonat 2014, 91).

The demand to reopen (female) brothels, which some Italian political parties have been explicitly campaigning for (Crowhurst 2019; Abbatecola 2019), needs to be understood within a broader racist and sexist cultural and political economy of sexuality, with colonial roots. In his analysis of contemporary race relations in Britain, Paul Gilroy coined the term 'postcolonial melancholia' to describe the country's longing to restore its lost imperial power and prestige – both inextricably linked to whiteness – while disavowing its structural violence (Gilroy 2010, 82). Likewise, I suggest that the nostalgia for the specifically fascist-era brothel, which this chapter's opening vignette reflected, contributes to the disavowal of the racist and colonial violence that reached its apex in this historical period, culminating in the promulgation of Italy's *Leggi Razziali* (Racial Laws).

After I first stumbled upon the imperial brothel price list hanging on the wall of Gina's trattoria, I did some research online, and I found a whole marketplace for such objects as part of a broader circuit of vintage commodities and cultural initiatives celebrating *case chiuse*. There were placards, keyrings, room dividers and briefcases, all dated sometime between the 1920s and 1930s – that is, during the period broadly corresponding to the 'Fascist Era'. Like Gina's, some of these price lists appealed to male customers' racialized desire, as they referenced the presence of different categories of female prostitutes, including women living under Italy's colonial domination. For example, in 1939 (Year XVII of the Fascist Era), the tolerance house *'Madama Elvì'* offered *'signorine francesi, bellezze nere abissine, giovanotte emiliane'* (French Misses, black Abyssinian beauties, young Emilian bachelorettes).[36] In 1930 (Year VIII of the Fascist Era), *'Dalla Tripolina'* (At the Tripolina's) advertised the presence of *'signorine delle colonie italiane'* (Misses from the Italian colonies).[37] Nevertheless, the allure of the racialized women coming from Italy's colonies was ambivalently evoked and concealed – for none of the images printed on these brothel price lists portrayed women other than white or white-passing. Then, there was a newly established *Museo delle Case di Tolleranza* (Museum of Tolerance Houses) that a private citizen set up after the opportune retrieval of a brothel hidden behind a building's walls.[38] Its opening came with a calendar of social events evoking those bygone times. Interestingly, however, the women featuring in their glossy advertisements resembled more the fashionable flappers of the 1920s and 1930s than female prostitutes mundanely working in the Italian *case chiuse*. The use of this aesthetic, then, contributed to dignifying the nostalgia for the pre-Merlin Law female brothel whilst concealing its fundamentally patriarchal and extractive character.

Today, I contend, this romanticized yearning for the female brothels of those bygone days contributes to concealing the intersecting racist and sexist agendas underpinning some parties' demand to reinstitute them. In a contemporary context where the street sex working population overwhelmingly consists of migrant cis and trans women, the demand to reopen (female) brothels partakes in an affective and political economy of ethnonationalism, in which the despised figure of the prostitute and the migrant have come to overlap. In fact, when contextualized against the backdrop of Italy's increasingly restrictive migration laws and xenophobic political rhetoric, the (neo)brothel could be seen to serve multiple purposes. Whilst reinstituting men's comfortable access to commercial (hetero)sex on demand, it would also remove prostitution from public sight and contribute to containing migration further by funnelling the migrant sex working population into an additional space of semi-detention. All of this whilst generating new tax revenues for the nation.

Nevertheless, notwithstanding these pressures, the Merlin Law persists unchanged. Between 1979 and 2018, one hundred and sixty-four prostitution bills were presented in Parliament to modify it (Serughetti 2019, 61). Of these, twenty were presented in the XVIII legislature (2013–18), and none was ever examined in Parliament.[39] Eventually, it seems that the status quo is preferred to the risk of setting in motion a reform pathway that could end up curtailing further or altogether erasing men's capacity to purchase sex legally. At the same time, as the next section shows, their counterparts in this exchange – that is, the women selling them sex and more broadly using their sexuality as an economic resource – continue to be harshly stigmatized for doing so.

From *Bunga-Bunga* to Sexual-Economic Austerity

> I observe the girls who, these days, go in and out of the police headquarters: they carry designer bags as big as suitcases, 'Manolo Blahnik' shoes, gigantic sunglasses costing as much as renting a flat. It is to own these [objects] that they spend nights dressed up as nurses giving and receiving fake injections from an old billionaire [the then Prime Minister Silvio Berlusconi] obsessed with his virility. They think that this is what it means to be lucky ... because this is what they have seen and heard, [and] what the ruling power offers – his TV and his [female] leaders, the women politicians elected for their mistress skills, TV starlets turned into ministers. ... This is the damage produced by the *quindicennio* [fifteen years] that we have traversed,[40] this is the political crime that has been accomplished: the vacuum, the free fall towards the cathodic Middle Ages, and at last, Italy reduced to a brothel. (De Gregorio 2011)[41]

The extract above is from the blog post significantly entitled *Le altre donne* (The other women). It was authored by Concita De Gregorio – then director of the left-wing newspaper *l'Unità* (Unity)[42] – in the heat of the sex 'scandals' involving the then Prime Minister Berlusconi. At the end of May 2010, Karima El Mahrough – a young Moroccan woman, which the press called by the professed stage name *Ruby Rubacuori* (Ruby the Heart Stealer) – was arrested in Milan on charges of theft. Berlusconi himself called the police station to have her released as an act of diplomatic courtesy, suggesting that she was the niece of the then President of Egypt, Hosni Mubarak. He was subsequently put under investigation for abuse of office and the alleged unlawful purchase of sex from a minor.

This incident was the peak of a wave of sex 'scandals' involving the then Prime Minister at the crossroads between political conduct and private life

(Dominijanni 2014), including the organization of kinky '*bunga-bunga*' parties at his private residence.[43] Female prostitution reappeared at the core of the country's national identity, taking on a markedly racialized character. In the blog post above, in fact, the 'other women' are effectively equated to prostitutes and juxtaposed with 'the majority of *Italian* women' (my emphasis), thereby hinting at the existence of a national(ist) 'female respectability line'. Race further fragmented the 'bad' women category from within, so that contempt and blame disproportionately fell on migrant women (Giuliani and Lombardi-Diop 2013, 135; Gribaldo 2018).

A few days after the publication of the blog, a group of women professionals and politicians – the founders of what will become known as the *Se Non Ora Quando* (If Not Now, When, SNOQ) movement – launched a mass demonstration in the name of 'the dignity of women and the [national] institutions' (SNOQ 2011). Drawing from language reminiscent of nineteenth- and early twentieth-century social purity movements (Walkowitz 1980; Wanrooij 1990; Dyhouse 2013), their appeal warned against young women's Faustian bargain of beauty for power, which risked polluting 'social life and the models of civil, ethical and religious awareness'. In so doing, they reproduced the patriarchal division of women into 'good' and 'bad', and it was only after they were called out on this that the organizers invited sex workers to participate in the demonstration (Redazione XXD 2011).

A few months afterwards, at the beginning of November 2011, the then President of the Italian Republic appointed as lifetime senator Mario Monti, a former European Union (EU) commissioner in matters of finance and trade. A few days later, Berlusconi resigned, and Monti took his place, leading a technocratic government that included numerous figures from the private sector. Together, they unleashed an era of economic and sexual austerity. Neoliberal reforms increasing precarity and eroding the entitlements of the many were compounded by interventions to chastise the public sphere. Workers' protection from illegitimate, unfair and discriminatory layoffs were modified to their detriment, and a new pension law increased the age of retirement.[44] Concomitantly, the state rose to the role of the benevolent patriarch. A new law increased the penalties for perpetrators of *femminicidi* (femicides) and introduced the mandatory arrest in flagrante delicto of domestic violence perpetrators,[45] while suddenly, campaigns on violence against women became ubiquitous (Eretica 2013). I grasped the full scale of this discursive shift when, in the changing room of a popular gym I used to patronize, I overheard a woman quoting her eleven-year-old daughter on the subject of choosing her boyfriend carefully: 'he should be someone I know ... because nowadays there are many feminicides.'

Attitudes towards women using their sexuality as an economic resource nevertheless remained ambivalent. On the one hand, and as part of the country's newly moralizing atmosphere, the stigma attached to sex working (women) acquired a peculiarly national(ist) connotation. The Merlin Law-mandated income tax exemption (based on the fact that selling sex is not considered 'work') was resignified as tax evasion, fuelling new forms of repression and state surveillance.[46] Today, welfare chauvinism explicitly underpins the Northern League's campaigns to reopen *case chiuse* (Crowhurst 2019, 375). On the other hand, the media continued fuelling a voyeuristic obsession with the women involved in Berlusconi's sex 'scandals'. In this gendered economy of desire and contempt, the figure of the fallen woman – that is, the *santa* who turns into a *puttana* – came to occupy a central place. Local news recurrently reported that some Italian housewives were starting to sell sex to cope with the consequences of the economic crisis and that higher education female students were doing the same, albeit out of lifestyle aspirations (see, for example, Redazione 2014a; 2014b). It was in this ambivalent affective landscape that, as I show in the rest of the book, the women I met and interviewed negotiated the tension between their sexuality and their status.

Conclusions

This chapter has foregrounded the central role that women's sexuality has consistently played in modern Italy's sexual politics. State-organized female prostitution was a key pillar in the scaffolding of the country's 'national heterosexuality' (Berlant and Warner 1998, 553); it lay at the heart of the national and imperial project, and it lasted for almost a century, surviving intact major political upheavals – including two World Wars, fascism, its collapse, the end of the Kingdom and the birth of the Republic. Following the country's political demise and the material destruction left by the Second World War, Italy's rapid modernization was simultaneously economic and sexual. The year marking the take-off of the country's *miracolo economico* (economic miracle) which historians conventionally identify in 1958, was also when female brothels were shut down. In the following two decades, Italy underwent a full-scale (hetero)sexual revolution, encompassing a set of legal reforms disconnecting sex from marriage and reproduction. In parallel, the media and advertisement industries thrived on the increasing visual overlap between women and/as commodities.

The centrality of the prostitution of women in Italy's politics of sexuality further emerges when considering the powerful influence of the Catholic Church on the country's social and legal discipline of sexuality. The magnitude of its power manifested clearly in the battles against the legalization of divorce and abortion and, more recently, against any norm that would disconnect sexuality from reproduction and 'nature'.[47] The summer of 2013 saw the outburst of a full-scale war on the so-called 'ideology of gender'.[48] In subsequent years, it has contributed to blocking 'the implementation in schools of a strategy against homophobia and transphobia'; abandoning the 'discussion of the bill on hate crimes related to sexual orientation and gender identity', and watering down Italy's law on same-sex civil unions (Garbagnoli 2016, 198; 200).[49] Against this background, this chapter has suggested that the coexistence between Italy's century-long system of state-regulated female prostitution and the mighty influence of the Catholic Church was not a paradox but a demonstration of the centrality of this group of abject women in the political and moral economy of heteronormativity of the state and the Church.

The chapter has further foregrounded the ethnonationalist dimension of this politics of sexuality in a context where the figure of the prostitute and the migrant have come to overlap. I have suggested that Italians' longing for the female brothel finds expression through the registers of nostalgia and contempt. It can manifest itself in the form of a postcolonial melancholia for the 'good old 1920s–30s' – that is, the years when Italy was 'manfully' fascist and had an Empire (at least for part of that period). Moreover, at a time when the street sex working population overwhelmingly consists of migrant cis and trans women, the (neo)brothel could be seen to function as a space of containment and tax revenues generation. In parallel, respectability was discursively resignified as a racialized national property – one that only Italian women may embody.

The next chapter will show that these notions of female respectability and dishonour underpinned the narratives of some of the women I encountered in my fieldwork. The book now moves on to discuss them, starting from the women who walked a thin 'female respectability line': recreational pole dancers.

Notes

1. The Kingdom of Italy entered the Second World War in 1940 as an ally to Nazi Germany. On 3 September 1943, it signed the Armistice of Cassibile with Anglo-American Allies. The agreement was made public a few days later (8 September), after which Germany attacked the Italian forces. Quickly, Germany occupied most of the Italian territory that was not under the control of the Allied troops, establishing a puppet state led by Benito Mussolini – the Repubblica Sociale Italiana (Italian Social Republic). The gothic line marked these two opposite fronts, running for over 300 km, from Massa-Carrara (Tuscany region) on the west coast to Rimini (Emilia Romagna

region) on the east coast. The war continued on Italian soil for more than a year and a half until the German forces surrendered by signing the *Resa di Caserta* (Surrender of Caserta), which became effective on 2 May 1945.
2. On 3 February 1991, little more than a year after the fall of the Berlin Wall (on 9 November 1989), the Italian Communist Party was dissolved and renamed Partito Democratico della Sinistra (Left Democratic Party, PDS). Later that year, some dissidents established the Partito della Rifondazione Comunista (Communist Refoundation Party). Whereas the latter still exists, the former was dissolved again in 1998, giving way first to the Democratici di Sinistra (Democrats of the Left) and eventually to the present-day Partito Democratico (Democratic Party).
3. The fascist regime introduced the Fascist Era calendar year in 1927. Its beginning was retroactively made to coincide with the National Fascist Party's armed March on Rome (28 October 1922), after which the King of Italy, Victor Emmanuel III, appointed Benito Mussolini as Prime Minister. It remained in use in the Repubblica Sociale Italiana until Italy's liberation in 1945.
4. Italy first attempted to colonize Ethiopia in December 1895, but the Ethiopian army overpowered its troops. In October 1935, Italy launched a new military campaign. Benito Mussolini announced victory on 9 May 1936, and the King of Italy was proclaimed the Emperor of Ethiopia. The Italian colonies in the Horn of Africa – Eritrea, Somalia, Ethiopia – were unified under the flag of the Africa Orientale Italiana (Italian East Africa). The Italian Empire also included the territories of present-day Libya.
5. Sweden's prostitution model (also known as the 'Nordic' or 'Equality' model) became law in 1999 as part of the Violence Against Women Act. Under it, the sale of sex is allowed, but its purchase constitutes a crime. In 2014, the EU Parliament approved with a non-binding resolution the 'Report on sexual exploitation and prostitution and its impact on gender equality' (Honeyball 2014) which recommended its adoption. Within the EU/EEA, the Swedish model has since been adopted by Norway (2009), Iceland (2009), France (2016) and Ireland (2017).
6. The Vatican City State is an enclave within Rome. It became an independent state under the *Patti Lateranensi* (Lateran Treaty) signed between the Kingdom of Italy and the Holy See in 1929. The Treaty, which regulates State-Church relations, was subsequently incorporated in Art. 7 of Italy's republican Constitution.
7. *Regolamento del servizio di sorveglianza sulla prostituzione* (Regulation of the service of surveillance of prostitution), ministerial decree, 15 February 1860. Italy's Prime Minister at the time was Camillo Benso, Count of Cavour – hence, the naming of the law after him.
8. McClintock drew this concept from the work of Julia Kristeva, who described the 'abject' as a liminal category of undesirable elements emerging in the process of individuation and separation between the subject and the object, the self and the other, evoking 'judgment and affect … condemnation and yearning' (Kristeva 1982, 9–10).
9. Cursory research of *Regolamento* in the year-by-year collection of the laws of the Kingdom of Piedmont-Sardinia held at the University of Turin – which are part of the online Archive of Law and Constitutional History (http://www.dircost.unito.it/root_subalp/1860.shtml) – did not return any results either. Nevertheless, further in-depth archival investigation is needed to confirm or refute this initial impression.
10. Data contained in a 1949 report of the then Minister of the Interior Mario Scelba in Parliament reported licensed brothels in two hundred and seventy-six municipalities (out of eight thousand) and highlighted the uneven distribution between urban and

11. rural areas (Bellassai 2006, 29). In the countryside, in fact, the registered brothels were only a few.
11. In 1937, concubinage was prohibited by decree, and two years later it was criminalized. See Royal Decree n. 880/1937, *Sanzioni per i rapporti d'indole coniugale fra cittadini e sudditi* (Sanctions for relationships of a conjugal nature between citizens and subjects); Law n. 1004/1939, *Sanzioni penali per la difesa del prestigio di razza di fronte ai nativi dell'Africa Italiana* (Penal sanctions in defence of racial prestige in front of the natives of Italian Africa).
12. The term *'sciarmutte'* is an Italianized version of the Arabic term *'sharmuta'*, meaning 'whore'.
13. In 1937, in Addis Ababa, there were forty-seven white female prostitutes selling sex to white men only; in 1938, in Asmara, there was only one licensed brothel to serve an Italian settler population of almost sixty thousand people (most of whom were unmarried men) and unknown numbers of transit workers and soldiers (Stefani 2007, 134).
14. In spring 1941, the British troops occupied Italian East Africa, and in February 1943, the Axis troops were pushed out of Libya. Following the signature of the Paris Peace Treaties (10 February 1947), the newborn Italian Republic formally lost all its overseas territories. The United Nations nonetheless handed Italy the *amministrazione fiduciaria* (Trust Territory) over Somaliland until 1960, after which the country became independent.
15. In 1888, *Regolamento Crispi* (Crispi Regulation) abolished compulsory registration for individual prostitutes and the *sifilicomi* (hospital for venereal diseases) (Greco 1987, 57). However, three years later, *Regolamento Nicotera* (Nicotera Regulation) reintroduced and tightened compulsory registration (Greco 1987, 57). Laws promulgated during the fascist regime exacerbated the medical and police checks on brothels and on independent prostitutes; expanded the definition of soliciting and increased police repressing powers (Bellassai 2006, 25).
16. While marriage was indissoluble, it could be annulled based on the determination that the union never existed due to lack of valid consent.
17. Most of the political formations later subsumed under the Kingdom of Italy did not criminalize sodomy (Ponzio 2019, 108), reflecting the influence of the 1810 Napoleonic Code and the French Revolution's erasure of religious-inspired crimes. However, male homosexuality was criminalized in the Kingdom of Piedmont-Sardinia, and as its Penal Code was extended to the newly established Kingdom of Italy, sodomy automatically became a crime everywhere – except the former *Regno delle due Sicilie* (Kingdom of the Two Sicilies) (Ponzio 2019, 108). Decriminalized in 1889 by the new Penal Code (Ponzio 2019, 108), male homosexuality was still punishable on grounds of public order and morality (P. Willson 2011, 7). It was explicitly criminalized again during fascism and defined as a political crime against the Italian 'race' – along with the practise of abortion and being an antifascist – to be punished with confinement (P. Willson 2011, 116–18).
18. On the debates over divorce in the history of modern Italy, see also Mark Seymour (2016).
19. Edoardo Anton directed the *Ufficio Conversazioni* (Office Conversations) of the Radio controlled by the Allied troops' Psychological Warfare Branch (PWB). Anton spoke these words while presenting to journalist Anna Garofalo the purpose of the radio program *Parole di una donna* (A woman's words) – running three times a week, at the peak hour (2 PM) – which she was appointed to run.

20. *Miss Italia* was the heir of the yearly competition *5000 lire per un sorriso* (Five thousand Liras for a smile), which was launched in 1939 to promote a toothpaste brand. Women wishing to participate were required to send only a close-up picture of their (smiling) faces to a magazine.
21. Austria also had a system of state-regulated female prostitution, but divorce had already been legalized (1938).
22. Law n. 75/1958, *Abolizione della regolamentazione della prostituzione e lotta contro lo sfruttamento della prostituzione altrui* (Abolition of the regulation of prostitution and fight against the prostitution of others).
23. The North/South divide has been at the heart of Italy's national identity since its very establishment as a unified modern nation state. For a foundational materialist critique of the roots of the *questione meridionale* (southern question), see Antonio Gramsci (1966). Vito Teti (1993) and Antonino De Francesco (2012) provide a thorough overview of how discourse and material inequalities partake in its reproduction throughout the history of Italy.
24. Law n. 898/1970 *Disciplina dei casi di scioglimento del matrimonio* (Regulation of the cases of dissolution of marriage).
25. The Constitutional Court declared illegitimate Art. 553 of the Penal Code that criminalized incitement to anti-reproductive practices, which was part of Titolo X (Chapter Ten) on crimes against 'the integrity and health of the *stirpe* [race]' (Balestracci 2020, 79).
26. Law n. 194/1978 *Norme per la tutela sociale della maternità e sull'interruzione volontaria della gravidanza* (Norms on the social protection of motherhood and the voluntary termination of pregnancy).
27. Law n. 151/1975, *Riforma del diritto di famiglia* (Reform of family law), abolished the role of the breadwinner and gave women and men equal rights and duties within the family.
28. Law n. 442/1981 *Abrogazione della rilevanza penale della causa d'onore* (Repeal of the criminal relevance of the honour clause).
29. Law n. 66/1996, *Norme contro la violenza sessuale* (Norms against sexual violence).
30. Italy hosted the second-largest Communist Party in Western Europe and bordered the Communist bloc to the east – factors that increased its geopolitical importance. Its position at the centre of the Mediterranean was strategic for US military interventions in conflicts unfolding in the Middle East, particularly after the so-called 'Suez crisis' (1956).
31. The text of the agreement was eventually made public following the tragic *Strage del Cermis* (Cermis massacre) in February 1998. Twenty people died when a US aircraft flying too low cut a cable supporting an aerial lift cable car. For a recent account of what happened and where the investigation is currently at, see Godfrey Holmes (2019). On the presence of US and NATO military bases in Italy and their legal status, see e.g. Alfonso Desiderio (2008) and Davide Testa (2020).
32. A report analysing reported incidents of violence against women in East Asia (Philippines, South Korea, Japan) stated that

> Although the [US] military has a policy of "zero tolerance" for sexual violence and harassment, and most military personnel do not violate women, this [violence against women] is an officially recognized problem in U.S. military families, for women in the military, and in communities near bases in this country and overseas. Military leaders often attribute it to a few "bad apples", but these incidents happen far too often to be accepted as aberrations. Women

organizers see them as systemic – an integral part of a system of military violence. (Institute for Policy Studies 1999)

On the specific case of Okinawa (Japan), see Takazato Suzuyo and Kutsuzawa Kiyomi (1999).

33. Law n. 189/2002 *Modifica alla normativa in materia di immigrazione e di asilo* (Changes in Regulations on the Matter of Immigration and Asylum) is known by the name of its first two signatories, Umberto Bossi, then leader of the Northern League and Minister of Institutional Reforms and Devolution, and Gianfranco Fini, then leader of National Alliance and deputy Prime Minister. It criminalized irregular migration, tied migrants' residence in the country to their possession of a work contract and introduced a set of other restrictive measures in the domain of family reunification and asylum.

34. National Alliance propelled 'love of family, church and nation' (Fella and Ruzza 2013, 44) and condemned 'informal marriage, divorce, abortion and sterilization' (Tarchi 2003, 151). The Northern League also was a firmly Catholic party (Pollard 2008, 65). Initially, this allegiance did not feature strongly in the party's political rhetoric. However, it became increasingly evident in the early 2000s, in the context of the EU debate on the inclusion of a statement on its 'Christian roots' in its Charter of Fundamental Rights. For example, the League's official history (*Cronistoria della Lega Nord – Dalle origini ad oggi*, in thirteen volumes) includes no direct or coded mention of homosexuality up until 1999. It does from 2000 onwards, as the party took a position in defence of the 'natural' family. Afterwards, 'prostitution, pornography and paedophilia' – the latter circulating as a code word for homosexuality – became more prominent in the party's political rhetoric (Lega Nord 2002, 28).

35. In National Alliance's 1995 political programme, prostitution was seen as an 'alarming' phenomenon, next to drugs and immigration, and the party demanded a new law to punish its exercise in public spaces (Alleanza Nazionale 1995, 34). The then leader of the Northern League, Umberto Bossi, vehemently demanded that brothels be reopened (Crowhurst 2019, 378–79). For example, in a speech reported in the *Cronistoria*, he argued that '[p]rostitutes have to stay in ad hoc [i.e. closed] houses', because street prostitution 'provoked the crisis of love weddings by constituting a readily available sexual alternative to the wife, just outside the door' (Lega Nord 2002, 28)

36. Retrieved May 2021 from https://www.classicarte.it/www_classicarte_it/files/cdn/targa-tabella-insegna-in-metallo-riproduzione-tariffario-bordello-anni-2086_250.jpg. Note that in popular culture women from the Emilia Romagna region (i.e. *emiliane*) are exoticized for their purported exceptional sexual skills – hence their special mention in this brothel pricelist.

37. Retrieved May 2021 from https://www.arterameferro.com/targa-in-latta-riproduzione-tabella-dalla-tripolina-bordello-casino.html.

38. The tale of the origins of the Museum is the following:

In 2010, [some] colleagues intent on demolishing a building in Carsara, in the province of Pordenone, called Davide Scarpa. He is fond of history, and they found a pile of cloth that appears to be old. Davide Scarpa buys it for a thousand euros from the owner and then spends years on its restoration. The objects found are the remnants of a fascist era brothel: probably somebody hid them to save them from oblivion. Thus, the treasure exposed in the 'Museum of Tolerance Houses' was born. (FuoriPorta n.d.)

39. This was evincible through a search for the prostitution bills on the *Fondazione Openpolis* website. Retrieved May 2021 from https://parlamento17.openpolis.it/argomento_leggi/PROSTITUZIONE/filter_act_leggi_type/DDL/filter_act_ramo/0. The website was reworked so this page is no longer available.
40. The use of the term *quindicennio* intentionally evokes a parallel with the fascist *ventennio* (twenty years), thereby equating Silvio Berlusconi to Benito Mussolini.
41. Originally, this blog post appeared on its author's own blog, at this page: http://concita.blog.unita.it/le-altre-donne-1.266857. Today, however, it no longer exists.
42. The newspaper was founded in 1924 by Antonio Gramsci to be the voice of the Italian Communist Party. After the latter was dissolved (1991), the newspaper aligned itself with the voice of its majority heir (the Democratic Party of the Left) and subsequent transformations (see endnote 2, this Chapter). Today, it no longer exists.
43. The etymology of the term '*bunga-bunga*' is uncertain. However, at that time, it was associated with Silvio Berlusconi's friendship with the Libyan President Muammar Al-Gaddafi.
44. Law n. 92/2012, *Disposizioni in materia di riforma del mercato del lavoro in una prospettiva di crescita* (Norms on the reform of the labour market in a prospect of growth), modified Article 18 of the *Statuto dei lavoratori* (Workers' statute), which protected employees from illegitimate, unfair and discriminatory lay off. Art. 24 of the Decree-Law 201/2011, *Disposizioni in materia di trattamenti pensionistici* (Norms on public retirement schemes) increased retirement age.
45. Law n. 119/2013, *Conversione in legge, con modificazioni, del decreto-legge 14 agosto 2013, n. 93, recante disposizioni urgenti in materia di sicurezza e per il contrasto della violenza di genere, nonché in tema di protezione civile e di commissariamento delle province* (Conversion in law, with modifications, of the decree law 14 August 2013, n. 93, introducing urgent norms in the domain of security and against gender-based violence, and in the domain of civil protection and receivership of the provinces).
46. For example, in Bologna, *carabinieri* (gendarmerie) conducted a 'census' to estimate the volume of street sex workers' earnings and their potential income tax revenues (Redazione 2012).
47. For example, Law n. 40/2004, *Norme in materia di procreazione medicalmente assistita* (Norms on medically assisted reproduction), limits access to medically assisted reproduction to heterosexual couples, and bans '[g]amete donation and surrogate motherhood' (Riezzo et al. 2016). The influence of the Catholic Church on its formulation is inter alia acknowledged by Giovanni Bianco (2011).
48. In 2016, 'during a closed session with Polish bishops, Pope Francis stated, 'In Europe, America, Latin America, Africa, and in some countries of Asia, there are genuine forms of ideological colonization taking place. And one of these – I will call it clearly by its name – is "gender"' (quoted in Corredor 2019, 613). However, the roots of this discourse lie in the late 1980s–mid-1990s, when the Church prepared to defend the 'natural order' against the rising international influence of the feminist and LGBT movements (Garbagnoli 2016).
49. Law n. 76/2016 *Regolamentazione delle unioni civili tra persone dello stesso sesso e disciplina delle convivenze* (Norms on the civil unions between people of the same-sex and discipline of cohabitations). The law does not recognize the right of same-sex couples to enter into a marriage contract but only a civil union. For a feminist and queer critique, see Marina Franchi and Giulia Selmi (2020).

Chapter 2

WOMEN POLE DANCING FOR 'PLEISURE'

On a late Saturday morning, towards the end of the summer, I drove to an open day weekend organized by a new pole dance school that was presenting its courses to prospective customers. The venue lay in an industrial area, which I found puzzling, as I had expected the school to be in a more central one, easier to reach without private motor vehicles. All along the road, I did not see any board or sign advertising the school's presence, and at its street number, all I could see was a big warehouse. Doubting whether I was in the right place at all, I pulled the car over and took out my phone to double-check.

'Hi! I am looking for a dance school … do you know where it is?' asked a female voice coming from the distance. As I lifted my head, I saw a young woman smiling and walking towards me. I could not imagine there being more than a 'dance' school in such a desolate place and so I wondered whether it was fear of my judgement that made her omit the word 'pole'. 'I am going to the same place', I replied conspiratorially, 'let us walk together'. Monica and I then started walking down the side of the warehouse to see if there was an entrance to the school.

'Excuse me!! Excuse me!! Are you going to … ?' Monica and I turned in the direction of the voice to see a woman, more my age than Monica's (who must have been in her mid-twenties), gesturing to us and gasping as if she had run miles. When she reached us, she remained silent – her unfinished question still lingering in her eyes. Guessing the reason for her hesitation, I reassured her that, yes, we were also going 'there'. 'Finally!', Giulia exclaimed, visibly relieved, 'It took me an hour to drive here, but this is the nearest school to my hometown ... .' We continued our exploratory walk together, and, eventually, we found a door at the back of the warehouse. No boards, no placards, no name on the bell – just a taped piece of white paper with the handwritten word *Ingresso* (Entrance). We pulled the door open, and there the pole dance school was, at last.

The first thing I saw was a long queue of women waiting to give their name and contact details to a woman in a tracksuit sitting behind an office desk. I joined them, signed up to try all the classes, and then roamed around, waiting for my turn. The pole dance room was ample, with a high ceiling. Its interior design mixed elements of a gym or dance studio (the parquet floor; a full-wall mirror) and night entertainment venues (disco lights) with some cosy decor (purple tulle curtains). And then there were the poles – plenty of them, organized in three rows. In stainless steel, each stretched approximately three meters from floor to ceiling and could operate in either stationary or spinning mode – the latter function boosting performers' twirling speed. Next to each pole, two women were alternating exercise under the guidance of a young female instructor, and to the sound of some catchy electro-pop-rock music. Everyone was barefoot and wore shorts and a T-shirt – the school's recommended outfit for the day. Next door, there was a smaller multipurpose room for non-pole dance courses. There were hooks on the ceiling to hang aerial silks, circles and trapezes, and some 'sexy chair' dance props in a corner – foldable plastic chairs and wedge-heel shoes of different shapes and sizes. Over time, I observed that this set-up was common in the schools that I visited throughout my fieldwork, many of which lay in similarly industrial areas, where rental costs were cheaper.

When my turn came, I felt unfit and clumsy like never before in my life. Lifting my body up the pole was incredibly hard – and in fact, I could not, learning first-hand that pole dancing was, on the whole, quite physically challenging (Griffiths 2016). My sexy chair try-out session was no less of a disaster. Wedge-heel shoes were a first for me, and while trying to strut around the chair, I was quite worried about twisting my ankles. I was in good company, though: few of the perhaps one hundred women I saw that day moving in and out of the school looked either sporty or confident walking in high heels. Driving back home that evening, I felt as if I had set foot on an incipient, booming female business.

****

The image of three women converging on a place that none dared to name conveys the ambivalent attraction and fear, pleasure and danger

(Vance 1984a) projected on a new leisure practice that touched upon the tension between women's sexuality and their status. 'Pole dance' is an activity blending dance moves and acrobatic tricks that is performed on, around and with a vertical pole. The first recorded performance is said to have occurred in a strip club in Oregon, US, in 1968 (Holland 2010, 38). However, some alternative tales trace its origin elsewhere, to more 'respectable' practices – including the Mallakhamb, the Maypole dance and the Chinese pole (Holland 2010, 38). Whilst acknowledging that these different genealogies are not necessarily incompatible, the historical conjuncture matters. The current mainstreaming of pole dancing as a female pleasure activity, in fact, unfolds within a cultural landscape in which the glamorized figure of the female stripper circulates as the epitome of the confident and sexually liberated (white) woman (Introduction). Its success, therefore, is entangled with the formation of this new Western sexscape.

In September 2012, when I began fieldwork, the recreational pole dance market in Italy was in its early stages, but it lay on the threshold of a significant scale shift. At that time, the practice was taught only in a few main cities, prevalently in the economically wealthier northern regions. Two years later, Giulia's hometown had two pole dance schools, and today, there are hundreds of venues offering classes across the country, including mainstream gym clubs.[1] Generally, the women attending them – referred to as 'students' by their instructors – were overwhelmingly Italian, 'white' (a racial descriptor of which I will say more later) and in their late twenties/early thirties. Most of the pole dance school's owners that I interviewed were in their thirties, and they usually worked as instructors themselves, generally helped by other young women they employed.

This chapter explores recreational pole dance entrepreneurs and/or instructors' narratives of when and how they first approached this practice and the main reasons they saw as constitutive of its burgeoning commercial success. It starts by showing the centrality of women's desire to feel sexy and desirable in their engagement with this pleasure practice and their fear of being stigmatized as 'whores' for doing so. It will show that the imagined and material contiguities between recreational pole dance and 'lap dance' – which in Italian usage functions as a broad, generic synonym of female-to-male erotic entertainment (Introduction) – primarily featured in their narratives as a source of aggravation. Against this background, the chapter will thus illustrate the respectability tactics that women used to negotiate their access to a stigmatized and stigmatizing activity without jeopardizing their status. These, as I show, largely relied on their disidentification from the figure of their despised female other – the 'lap dancer' – whom they described using intersecting gendered, class-based and racialized stereotypes.

Feeling 'Sluttier' and Desirable

'What made you start practising pole dancing?' I asked Francesca, sitting at her kitchen table – my question marking the beginning of the interview, after some informal chatting over breakfast. The moment I switched on the audio recorder, Francesca's expression and posture changed radically – she suddenly became serious, crossed her arms on her chest, laid back on the chair and with deadpan eyes on mine, she said, 'Okay, I started …' Then she paused to give me a long, frank look. She reprised. 'Okay, I will give you the two versions', she said, 'the official and the real one'. The official script revolved around her fondness for any type of *sport* – pole dance merely being her latest craze in an endlessly expanding list. Her private script, however, had nothing to do with sports or fitness but had the power of the erotic at its core: 'The truth is that, basically, I was in a night club [Eng. original, meaning strip club] with my boyfriend, and we saw this girl dancing with the pole, and she danced, well, in a more athletic way than the others, and I was shocked. From there, I did some research.' Francesca spoke these words swiftly as if wishing to throw them out all at once just to get back to safety as soon as possible. Then she fell silent again, waiting for my reaction.

Francesca's concealment of the context in which she came to know and develop her interest in pole dancing, I suggest, indexes the gendered anxieties emerging from and projected on a practice touching upon female chastity norms. Indeed, she likely refrained from publicly admitting to having been in a night club in fear of the whore stigma – for a 'good' woman should have never been there in the first place. At that particular moment, these anxieties were possibly more intense than usual following the recent wave of sex 'scandals' involving the former Prime Minister Berlusconi (Chapter 1). Although the latter had exited the political stage for over a year, the media kept fuelling the voyeuristic blend of curiosity and contempt for the 'other women' who used to entertain him (in exchange for money, gifts and/or positions) purportedly by, among other things, staging pole dance and burlesque shows at his private residence (see e.g. BBC News 2012; McKenna 2012). In front of an Italian female researcher who may have been a feminist (a political identity that most women in these pleisure spaces looked on as oppressive and chastising), Francesca might have also anticipated being negatively judged for her yearning to emulate a 'sexually objectified' woman – to be seen, that is, as suffering from false consciousness and 'internalized oppression' (Bartky 1990).[2] Hearing my attentive silence, Francesca eventually reprised her tale: 'Obviously, I do not tell this to anyone. If someone asks me, "How did you discover pole dance?" [I do not say] "Ah well, I was in a night club with my boyfriend." I mean … I just do not! I always say: "I discovered it on YouTube".'

The two versions of Francesca's story aptly convey the ambivalent fascination and fear that she projected onto the body of the female pole/lap dancer who left such an impression on her. It was the power of the woman's sexuality that had earned her a place on stage in a venue where men paid for the pleasure to watch her dancing – that power, however, was inseparable from the whore stigma. Hence, when I shared that some female friends of mine looked forward to coming along with me to try pole dancing, she nodded in recognition of their drive:

> Women's curiosity stems from the fact that you hang on to a pole, and eventually, every woman wants to be like that – I mean, to be charming and seductive. A woman really likes to have this role, because in normal society, we cannot be like that. We … I mean, [taking this reasoning] to its extreme [limits]: we would all like to be, let's say, sluttier, wouldn't we? But we cannot dress in a certain way; we cannot wear certain shoes; we cannot make certain types of movements. We have taboos … We are compelled … not in terms of *coercion*, but we are compelled *to be* [my emphasis] in a certain way. So, we all need a relief valve to feel like hot chicks; to feel like hotties; to feel a bit slutty. It is bad to think it this way, but, actually, it is a bit like that, which pushes many people [towards recreational pole dancing].

Underneath Francesca's explanation of the factors driving the commercial success of this practice lies the tension between women's sexual oppression and liberation. Against the background of the constraining norms disciplining women's comportment in 'normal society', this pleasure practice thus appears to offer them an opportunity to safely perform the woman who is intensely sexy and desirable – that is, without jeopardizing their 'respectable' status. However, this possibility is strictly space-bound, as it can only exist within the pole dance school and cognate spaces and occasions (e.g. celebrations, contests). It is also premised on the absence of money flows circulating between the performers and their audience. As I show later in this chapter, when women performed *commercial* pole dance shows, they relayed feeling that their audiences perceived them in ways that they did not necessarily enjoy. In that moment, in fact, they were no longer protected by the dignifying 'recreational' label, and they were thus seen as lap dancers – that is, 'bad' women – pole dancing for money.

Women's desire for sexiness is ambivalently and inextricably entangled with the pleasure and danger arising from the intense sexuality of the figure of the 'whore' (Introduction). It is a longing to feel 'sluttier' and *hence*, more *hetero*sexually desirable. My assumption of the women being prevalently heterosexual arises from two factors – one cultural, one conjunctural. First, the glamorized figure of the female stripper underpinning and fuelling the globalization of this practice (Introduction) dances for the pleasure of strip clubs' male customers – hence, in an ultimate heterosexual space. Second, all the women that I encountered and interviewed during my fieldwork were or had been until recently in an intimate relationship with a man. This, however, does not mean that recreational pole dance is appealing to heterosexual women only: I have myself interviewed a man practising it, and across the country, there surely are LGBTQI+ students and instructors. However, at that time, they were probably few and/or not particularly visible.

Scholars who have discussed women's recreational pole dancing in other Western contexts, such as the UK, Australia and Denmark, have observed that, both in marketing outlets and women's narratives, this activity was explicitly associated with the themes of sexual liberation and empowerment (Whitehead and Kurz 2009; Holland 2010; Donaghue and Whitehead 2011; Griffiths 2016; Just and Muhr 2019). Conversely, Francesca's two tales of her engagement with this practice suggest that women like herself – and her students, as she relayed – did not feel in the position to claim these goals openly. Indeed, akin to her public script situating recreational pole dance within the austere and respectable family of sports, the official discourse circulating at that time in the Italian pole dance online community stressed the activity's chaste and even domestic orientation. For example, a blog post published on *Pole Dance Italy* listed nine 'good reasons' to start a course (D'Amico 2014). The first was to become 'very strong' and being able 'to carry *buste della spesa* (grocery bags) by [oneself]'; feeling 'more sensual and self-confident' came only second to last (D'Amico 2014). As I show next, for some recreational pole dancers this discursive difference marked Italy's 'backwardness'.

Walk Like a Modern Woman

Recreational pole dancers' management of the tension between their sexuality and their status did not only unfold in the domain of language and discourse, but it was also material, in more than one way. At the time of my fieldwork, the field was traversed by a growing rift between schools that placed the performance of sexiness at their core (from now on 'sexy' schools) and schools that rejected it, rather affirming its sports status (after this, 'sporty' schools).[3] Globally, pole dancers' dress code was a key site where the activity's identity was being formed and contested. For example, at the 2014 Pole World Cup, in Brazil, 'a costume committee' checked all entrants' outfits and disqualified any competitor wearing 'heels, bikinis, thongs, leather, rubber or latex' or performing '[a]ny movement relating to sex' (Speed 2014). Footwear was a similarly tense terrain. In sporty schools, performing barefoot was a must, whereas sexy schools did not prohibit nor prescribe any specific aesthetic but encouraged women to try pole dancing at least once using wedge-heel shoes. In her ethnography of recreational pole dancing in England, Samantha Holland suggested that some women straightforwardly expressed the pleasure that they felt in learning how to wear 'stripper heels' (Holland 2010, 2) – a term unambiguously evoking the strip club imaginary (Holland and Attwood 2009, 174). In my research in Italy, however, I observed that the feelings women anticipated by wearing this prop were more complex and ambivalent, indexing the tension between pleasure and danger that characterized their engagement with this practice.

Magda, another recreational pole dance instructor, relayed having first discovered this activity in Los Angeles, where she lived for some years as a temporary migrant worker. I asked her whether she found significant differences in how it was taught there compared to Italy. 'Gosh!' she exclaimed, bursting into loud laughter. For a moment, she looked at me with incredulous eyes, perhaps wondering whether my question was for real. As I did neither reformulate nor withdraw it, she then explained that:

> The style is *totally* different. It is *many, many* light years away. *There*, you play a lot with sensuality, and they do not mind if you have a strip club background. *There*, the heel is essential; they make you wear it right from the first class. … And it is not a short heel: [they make you wear] *wedge heels*! Movements are much more sensual – the choreographies I have learnt [there], and I am teaching to girls [here] are much more … I mean, there is sensuality. They are not vulgar but … anyway, there is 'floorwork' [Eng. original] … .[4] However, if you perform these movements here [in Italy], they burn you on the stake! Here, we just do them behind closed doors!

Magda's words suggest that a woman's un/freedom to perform pole dance the sexy way (i.e. in wedge heels), outside of the strictly recreational pleasure spaces, indexes a country's stage of modernity. Interestingly, her juxtaposition of the US and Italian contexts foregrounds a reversal of the relationship between sexuality and modernity underpinning white Western Europeans' early colonialism (Introduction). In their analysis of the discursive shift in anthropological representations of 'primitives' between 1885 and the First World War, Andrew and Harriet Lyons observed 'a tendency to replace fictive images of lascivious savages with representations of primitives as either less highly sexed than civilized men and women, less imaginative in their exercise of the sexual function, or blocked by taboo or environmental restraints from the full exercise of their libidos' (Lyons and Lyons 2011, 69). Consistent with this shift, today a (white) woman's membership of Western modernity is no longer signalled by her chastity and modesty but by her uninhibited display of sexiness in public. For example, within the contemporary secular/multicultural debate in Europe, a particular way to perform sexuality has become the hallmark of Western modernity, and feminist, postcolonial and queer scholars have amply discussed this trope both in relation to the rights of women (see, for example, Duits and Zoonen 2006; Werbner 2007; J.W. Scott 2009; Fassin 2010; Bracke and Fadil 2012) and LGBTQI+ subjects (see, for example, Puar 2007; El-Tayeb 2011; Bracke 2012). This discursive shift has been partly driven and exacerbated by the consumerism fuelling late capitalism, as 'the ephemerality of goods' is inextricably linked 'with the pleasures of the senses' (Appadurai 1996, 85). In Italy, this pleasure has been particularly conveyed through the strong visual overlap between women and/as commodities (Chapter 1). In the contemporary Western sexscape, therefore, recreational pole dancing puts women in the paradoxical position of being modern consumers of their own commodified sexuality.

Albeit not explicitly mentioned, the mighty presence of the Catholic Church filters through Magda's description of Italy as an oppressive and 'backward' country. To be *bruciata* (burnt, fem. past principle) on the stake was the defining capital punishment that the Inquisition tribunal dispensed to people accused of heresy and witchcraft, and in the eyes of the religious authorities, women were the witches par excellence (Tavuzzi 2007, 229; Mazzone and Pancino 2008; Federici 2018). Significantly, in Italy, this term has also long been used to derogatorily mark the women who lost their virgin status before marriage (L. Harrison 1966, 160). Magda's deployment of this fire metaphor, therefore, effectively conveys the intersecting religious and secular roots of the whore stigma in Italy. It also relays the intensity of the risks awaiting women outside of the school's overwhelmingly homosocial perimeter and community. Choice of footwear, she recounted, is a particularly delicate issue:

> I am about to do a [paid] night show in town wearing [high heel] boots … but it is a risk! I keep wondering, 'shall I wear them, shall I not?' The bar knows me already, and I aim to perform some beautiful choreographies. I have done it already with boots … but the boot is aggressive. However, in the US they use it for performances. After all, it is just a boot, right? The first times I performed in Italy, I kept thinking, 'shall I wear it, shall I not?' until the very last moment. … Then, eventually, I would not.

It is important to underline that the bar where Magda planned to perform her pole dance show was not an erotic entertainment venue but an ordinary bar seeking to offer its male and female customers 'something different'. Yet, when pole dancers agree to perform these commercial gigs, they no longer dance for pleisure; they receive money to dance for someone else's pleasure. As the dignifying 'recreational' qualifier dissolves, the women lose the thrust of their defence against the whore stigma and experience being perceived as *lap* dancers instead. Ulrich, for example, another pole dance instructor, recounted her latest pole dance performance 'for *animazione* (entertainment)', in a disco, with evident annoyance:

> I do it [only] for the money because it does not give me [any] satisfaction. People do not look at you, they do not pay attention, and as soon as they see the pole, they think you are about to do something obscene and undress. In fact, sometimes they get it *wrong* because this is *not* lap dancing. You cannot touch me or try to give me money or whatever. Absolutely not!

Be(coming) Woman

Experiencing oneself as 'liberated' from everyday sexual oppression was not the only pleasure women associated with recreational pole dancing. For some, the practice offered a healing potential. 'What gives me more satisfaction in working here [in the pole dance school] is that girls are all a bit like this' said Tiziana, hunching over to portray an insecure woman shying away from her body,

> or they are chubby, and they tell each other 'No, I will never be able to do that thing; no I will not do it', or they hide when you ask them to show you what they have learnt. [But] in a few weeks, they really learn to take out what they have inside: whether it is femininity – maybe they just lack expressiveness – or elegance, or confidence … .

'And you see that they change', she continued, referring in particular to the women who do not match the 'slender ideal' (Bordo 1993, xxi), 'but they really change *here*', she said vehemently, tapping on her forehead. 'I see how they first come dressed in whatever. Then slowly, slowly, they start to take care of themselves. So, it really is also a homoeopathic medicine. It helps a lot'. As other scholars have observed (Just and Muhr 2019, 2), Tiziana found pride in being in the position to help other women feel good in their bodies, whatever their shapes and sizes (Holland 2010). However, in her words, this healing effect is explicitly linked to women's charm potential – as their capacity to display 'femininity' and look 'elegant' and 'confident' is intrinsically relational, and more specifically produced through the eyes of the (male) beholders of the gaze.

Tiziana's juxtaposition of a woman's inner and outward-oriented self suggests that she considered this charm potential to be constitutive of the 'woman' subject: it is just a matter of learning how best to express it (Donaghue and Whitehead 2011, 451). The description of recreational pole dancing as a 'homoeopathic' medicine indicates that its learning curve is imagined as a *natural* healing process that does not threaten the gendered order of things. The cloak of nature thus disguises the performativity of gender (J. Butler 1990) and the functionality of women's cultivation of their heterosexual desirability within the broader economy of heteronormativity (Meyers 2002). By learning the 'technologies of sexiness' (Radner 1993; Evans and Riley 2015) required to occupy the position of the woman who is intensely heterosexually desirable (i.e. the stripper, as a metonym of the whore), women may pursue the promise to resolve the gendered anxieties projected on the loss of their place as the object of male desire (Berlant 2012, 57). Nevertheless, doing so also exposes them to the risk of being stigmatized as 'whores'.

One of the respectability tactics that recreational pole dancers in Italy used to manage this tension between pleasure and danger was the deployment of desexualizing language. For example, some would call the pole a 'perch' instead. More eminently, the followers of both the sporty and the sexy schools classified this practice as a *disciplina* (discipline). A term evoking austerity, rigour and sacrifice, it circulates as a synonym of 'sport' in the Italian and English language alike. Indeed, 'granting an activity the status of "sport" – as well as denying it this status – is laden with cultural and political assumptions' (Besnier, Brownell and Carter 2018, 4). Its use to qualify recreational pole dance seems to represent an attempt to detach this practice from the strip club genealogy, either because it is explicitly rejected (read: the sporty school followers) or ambivalently desired and feared (read: the sexy school followers). Yet, the use of this term also readily evokes a very Foucauldian notion of discipline, as that through which subjects come into being within discourse. The convergence of these two acceptations of discipline struck me one day while at a pole dance school end-of-year party, as an instructor presented the 'sexy chair' dance as 'a discipline enhancing [a woman's] plasticity and sensuality'.

The nature of the pleasure that women experience practising recreational pole dance lies at the core of feminist scholarly debates on whether this activity may 'empower' them. One of the cornerstones of this discussion is the presence and role of the 'male gaze' (Mulvey 1975).[5] Some scholars have suggested that the substantially female homosocial space in which pole dance is practised affords women the possibility to explore what sexiness means to them (Holland and Attwood 2009, 180) away from the male gaze (Holland 2010, 2–3). Others have argued that as the male gaze operates through discourse its productivity does not depend on men's actual physical presence (Donaghue and Whitehead 2011, 452–53; Owen 2012, 89). In my research, I consistently observed the excitement with which women approached their performances in front of their (always male) partners and (always mixed) friends. Indeed, in addition to their schools' public events (end-of-year performances, showcases, etc.), many women actively looked for and created stages to pole dance in front of them. Some would pay to do so, by, for example, renting pole dance platforms to perform at their birthday parties. This pleasure, I argue, was an important part of what they were paying and working out hard for.

Recreational pole dancing was thus learnt as a social practice – that is, for the self-with-others, and its orientation always exceeded the boundaries of the pole dance schools. From this perspective, the latter's homosocial character resembled a female changing room, where women got ready and exchanged tips with one another on how to look good on stage. And yet, why should women's cultivation of their heterosexual desirability be judged as an expression of their 'false consciousness' and 'internalized oppression'? Surely, women were learning to perform sexiness in some arguably narrow ways. Nonetheless, the pursuit of the promise to feel sexier and desirable was potentially available to each woman.

But was it? Let me delve a bit deeper.

Embodying Hard Work

In the narratives of most recreational pole dancers, the difficult disentanglement of their practice from lap dance recurred as a source of concern and aggravation, one that, however, they could resolve neither on the aesthetic nor kinetic level. Whether in sexy or sporty outfits, women are recommended to wear as little fabric on their bodies as possible to better grip the pole with their flesh. Meanwhile, the image of a woman dancing with and on a vertical steel pole readily evokes women working in strip clubs. Against this blurred backdrop, recreational pole dancers used a range of respectability tactics to 'disidentify' (Skeggs 1997) from their despised female other – that is, the 'lap dancer', circulating as a metonym of the whore. To this end, as I show, they would deploy intersecting gendered, class-based and racialized stereotypes.

'When I started pole dancing professionally, for my family to understand, it was ... I am still struggling', said Tiziana shaking her head, disheartened. Her eyes were looking above me, at the woman sitting behind my back: her mother. When I saw the latter coming in during the interview, I wondered whether her arrival had been by chance or intentional – and if it was the latter, what did she come for? Did she come to protect their family's respectability, prepared to step in if need be? Did she want to impress me with her motherly pride for her entrepreneurial daughter? Did she seek to enjoy some reflected glory – for the fact a stranger had come from far away to ask her daughter for an interview? Whatever the reason, it immediately became clear to me that, from then onwards, the mother had become the daughter's primary audience. Tiziana continued:

> even for my mother, who is my biggest supporter now [it was difficult to accept] … the first time she saw me [pole dancing] on a video, she screamed '*Noooo*! What are you doing?!' But then she started following me [on social media] and coming here to the school, and then she began saying, 'Oh my God, how much work out! How many sacrifices! What bruises you have!' She saw that I have corns, and some pain here and there, up and down … so, she realized that I do not go *a Bruciata*.

The mother smiled and nodded in agreement, but, evidently, I missed some of their intertextual references. 'What does "going *a bruciata*" mean?' I asked. '*Bruciata* is a famous place, a street, actually an area, where streetwalkers stand by a bright pole, under streetlights', she explained quickly, as if eager to remove that troubling association from the minds of the three of us. As earlier observed, in Italy, the term *bruciata* has long been used to describe an unchaste woman. I do not know whether there was any causal relationship between the name of this locality and the actual physical presence of sex working women. Still, Tiziana's juxtaposition of the latter with herself further attests to the threatening, immanent presence of the whore stigma hovering above recreational pole dancers' heads.

Women selling sex on the street constitute another category of women whose proximity to a vertical pole (the streetlight) signifies their female 'dishonour'. It is thus not coincidental that the nature of the relationship between a woman and the pole constitutes another source of distinction (Bourdieu 1984) and boundary making for recreational pole dancers. As I observed during the nights out with the mobile outreach unit (Chapter 4), for the women selling sex, proximity to a streetlight is both a competitive advantage and a safety measure. From under it, women are more visible to their potential customers in the night landscape, and they can also gather a better first impression of the men approaching them. Sometimes, seeing a car approaching, I saw some women improvising pole/lap dancing moves using the streetlight as a prop. However, overall, they did not work *with* it: they simply stood under its light waiting for potential customers. Their relationship, that is, was instrumental. Differently, recreational pole dancers claimed dignity and value in their committed and respectful engagement with the pole. Francesca, for example, relayed that 'the pole is like a partner … in a *pas de deux* or in a couple-dance.' When I asked Heather – another pole dance instructor – to explain the difference between pole and lap dance, she first tried to demonstrate it to me by making a circular movement of her pelvis. In my eyes, however, that looked more like an 'Oriental' dance move rather than a pole/lap one, so I asked if lap dance was, then, 'like "belly dancing"'. *'No'*, she stated in quite a peremptory tone,

> lap dance creates a magnetic field from the dancer's belly-uterus zone towards another person, and you *use* the pole … . Then there is the stripping, though stripping is not necessary [it does not necessarily take place], whereas pole dance is dancing *with* the pole – which is no longer an object that you use but it is that which enables you to do [acrobatic tricks], understand? In fact, one could lap dance even without the pole or use it only slightly – such as holding it with your hands and rubbing against it – and then spend the rest of the time on the floor or on someone's lap. [Instead] such things are unheard of among us [recreational pole dancers]. And anyway, no lap dancer will ever have our bruises, understand?

Like Tiziana, Heather located the ultimate distinction between lap dancers and recreational pole dancers in the latter's bruised body. In my (short) attempt at learning this practice, I experienced first-hand the screaming pain of squeezing the pole with my bare inner thighs to hold my grip on it or use my bare feet to leverage the weight of my body to climb it. Bruises – their colour, position, duration – were also the object of much small talk in changing rooms and at the margins of showcases and contests. They attested to one's seriousness and determination in learning to pole dance, notwithstanding the pain of it, whilst offering a terrain of camaraderie through self-irony. I myself recurrently resorted to 'bruise talk' whenever trying to convince someone that recreational pole dance is, in fact, a physically demanding activity. Yet, in Tiziana and Heather's words, bruises circulated in a moral economy of women's honour and shame, like stigmata, ennobling the hardworking, respectable recreational pole dancer and marking her distance from the 'other women' using the pole, as Daniela said, 'for other *scopi*' (Preface). For Tiziana, then, her bruises proved to her mother – and anyone else – that she was *not* a B/*bruciata* woman.

Elegant, Not Vulgar

As is becoming evident, social class is central in recreational pole dancers' respectability tactics, as is more broadly in the social perception of cultural representations of sex and sexuality. It does in fact similarly underpin the subjective classification of cultural artefacts as either erotic or pornographic,[6] whereby the stigma on the latter reflects its association with working classness (McNair 2002, 52; Deller and Smith 2013; Philpott and Ferris 2013, 201). Analogously, in contemporary media productions, *white* women's display of sexuality signals their 'empowerment' when associated with markers of middle class-ness and their 'white trash' status if associated with working class-ness (Attwood 2006, 85; Gill 2009). Scholars who have researched women's exotic dancing and/or recreational pole dancing observed that the latter's mainstreaming is embedded in the broader process of gentrification of parts of the sex industry and specifically the rise of 'gentlemen's clubs' (Egan 2006, 10; Holland and Attwood 2009, 166; Colosi 2010, 21; Owen 2012, 84). It is therefore inseparable from the discursive resignification of the figure of the female stripper, who is no longer a 'vulgar' woman, but a 'glamorous' one instead. Speaking about the UK context, some scholars have suggested that recreational pole dancing's 'high media profile and its association with female celebrities' constitutes one of the reasons why women enjoy practising it (Holland and Attwood 2009, 173). In my research, however, I observed that women were often wary of this proximity for the polluting dangers it could unleash. Heather, for example, said:

> Take Shakira's *Rabiosa* video (de Laiguana 2011): there is an X-pole – which is the pole we use: the tough one, not the toy poles! – and all that she does is a back hook [spin], ok? However, that is an easy exercise that even a stripper can perform! Obviously, this exacerbates people's doubts about what pole dance really is. Or take Kate Moss in the White Stripes' video (Coppola 2003). Again, she does a back hook, and they call it 'pole dancing'. I mean, I do not say it is not, but if you take the stereotypical [female beauty] look, a [top] model and you have her doing a very banal exercise … well, whoever sees that will think 'well, ok, I see that [trick] also in night clubs [Eng. original, meaning strip clubs], so pole [dance] is lap [dance].

Amidst this blurred, hazy pole/lap dance continuum, appeals to glamour and modernity offered women another means to negotiate their distinction and, with it, their respectability, as Tiziana did in the following exchange with me. I had just asked her what her views were on the pole dance-with-python performance of one of the most renowned international pole dancers of the time (Judd 2012), whose intensive workshops sold out quickly all across the globe, including Italy. When I watched that video recording, I could not help but find the woman's pole dancing and snake charming skills impressive. However, I also found it undoubtedly highly erotically coded. In Western countries, in fact, the woman-and-snake imagery evokes original sin – that is, Eve's seduction by a snake – Eve representing the ultimate archetype of the unchaste woman. The performer's combination of the pole and the snake, then, could not but unmistakably evoke the figure of the woman whom men desire and despise for her sexuality – that is, the whore. 'Did you find that performance provoking?' I asked Tiziana. Visibly peeved, she replied that whether something is provoking depends on which part of the world you come from. In Europe, everyone is very modest; but overseas, in Australia and America, it is an established *sport* [my emphasis], so they [the performers] can express themselves freely. Last Saturday, I was in Milan for a workshop with one of the most famous pole dancers in the world – an Australian [woman]. She represents my idea of pole dance: whether barefoot or in high-heeled shoes, she always performs with elegance and sensuality. It [the performance] is never vulgar. There is *never, ever* any vulgarity whatsoever.

Tiziana taught recreational pole dancing the 'sexy school' way, and her mobilization of the protective 'sport' label conveys her alarm at the heightened risk of stigmatization arising from this strongly erotically charged performance. Like Magda, she deployed the modernity trope to defuse it, suggesting that the 'problem' was not the performance itself but Italy's backwardness. Next, she used social class to secure her position, reclaiming the embodiment of 'elegance and sensuality' versus 'vulgarity'. In her longitudinal ethnography on white working-class women in North West England between the end of the 1980s and early 1990s, Beverley Skeggs argued that, against their classification as 'sexual, vulgar, tarty' (Skeggs 1997, 115), the women used glamour as 'a way of holding together sexuality and respectability', thereby being able to 'negotiate being glamorous and desirable – to which they all aspire – whilst not being marked as rough and common' (Skeggs 1997, 110). Likewise, I contend, Tiziana's appeal to glamour constitutes a respectability tactic through which she disidentified from 'vulgar' women – women, that is, who are stigmatized for their use of sexuality, including in exchange for money.[7]

As anticipated in this book's preface, the distinction between the woman who pole dances for her pleasure and the woman who does it for the money that men pay for their own pleasure lies at the core of recreational pole dancers' respectability tactics. Some scholars observed that, on pole dance studios' websites, recreational pole dancers were portrayed as women 'empowered through choice and control of intent' (Whitehead and Kurz 2009, 236) and juxtaposed with 'professional pole dancer[s]', who were depicted as 'sexually objectified' (Whitehead and Kurz 2009, 233). Women who pole danced for pleasure were thus imagined as better off and 'freer' than women who pole danced for work, and their differential consumer buying power thus functioned as a discursive marker of this gendered and class-based distinction. Some scholars have indeed noted the high price of recreational pole dance classes (Holland 2010, 114; Owen 2012, 80), which, in some cases, may have been intentionally deployed as a barrier to working class women's attendance (Griffiths 2016). In my research, I similarly observed that pole dance classes were indeed quite expensive. At the beginning of my fieldwork, an hour's group class cost twenty euros, and a package of four cost seventy euros – the latter corresponding to a monthly membership at a mid-range gym club granting daily access to a wide range of courses and facilities. A year later, and despite the arrival of new competitors on the market, prices increased further. Still, at a closer look, the purported conflation between women, consumer buying power and respectability did not seem to hold up.

'Tell me something about your students', I asked Francesca, 'who are they, on average?' 'It is a *fritto misto*', she replied quickly – with this expression meaning that her students consisted of women across all age groups, body sizes and occupations (Holland 2010, 83; 99). Such inclusivity, however, did not seemingly apply across nationality. Hence, when I specifically inquired about this dimension, Francesca suddenly stiffened up. 'I have *very few* foreign students', she said,

> luckily, I have very few girls who work in night clubs [i.e. lap dancers] and come to learn pole dance because the relationship [with them] automatically breaks down as they are difficult to manage. I had several experiences, and none of them ended up well.

I asked Francesca to tell me more about these challenges, to which she replied that

> They [lap dancers] have little respect. So, for example, last minute, they will not show up. They are well off, so, for example, they immediately buy a package [of classes] because they think that money can buy pole dancing skills … . But it is not like that; it is not that if you pay me more you become better at it. But they interpret … they give this value to money, they have a view of the person slightly … consumerist, I do not know how to explain it, but they have little respect for my profession, so I have never liked teaching them … it is surely due to the work that they do.

In Francesca's words, lap dancers' high consumer buying power does not index their empowerment but their female 'dishonour', because it derives from their involvement in a stigmatized activity. Their work, she suggests, leads the women into thinking that money can buy anything, but in that recreational, pleisure context, it is not money but hard work (read: bruises) that can earn women a stage. Women working in night clubs are thus depicted as female 'bodies out of place' (Puwar 2004), and as I discuss in depth next, Francesca's 'metonymic slide' (Ahmed 2004, 119) between the figure of the foreign woman and the lap dancer conveys the racialized and gendered qualities of their discursive exclusion.

The 'Eastern European Lap Dancer'

Testimony to the expanding recreational pole dancing market for Italy, throughout my fieldwork I witnessed the opening of many pole dance schools. These events were normally accompanied by a series of open days and evenings designed to attract potential customers. One of these was so crowded that the management had to halve the duration of the try-out classes to give everyone a chance, and many of us sat squeezed against each other on the floor. From there, I looked at the restaging of my initial clumsiness when I myself first tried pole dancing.

'Wow! That was tough!' I suddenly heard from somebody sitting behind me. When I turned to look, my eyes met those of a distinguished woman, Giovanna, in her mid-forties – slender, an immaculate hairdo, gold jewellery hanging from neck and ears and a designer bag squeezed between her chest and her bent legs. 'True', I replied, 'pole dancing is tougher than most people think.' The moment I uttered these words, I saw her instinctively pulling her legs closer to her chest – as if she feared that I could aim for her bag; as if she thought that the space she was in was dodgy; unsafe. Still, she nodded and continued chatting with me. 'It has been several years since I have been horse riding and doing fitness classes, and I am fed up with that', she offered – perhaps feeling that she owed me an explanation as to why a woman like *her* was *here*. I asked whether she was planning on starting a pole dance course. 'I have been thinking about it a lot, but I have been hesitating until now', she said distractedly – her eyes scanning the room as if to scrutinize its tiniest details. 'I expected to see a *herd* [my emphasis] of foreign women hanging to a pole', she added pensively, 'but I see only normal women – Italian, and from any age bracket. I feel it is a proper environment.'

As most of us sat silent under pounding music, I wondered what made her assume that 'we' – the undifferentiated group of women around her – were Italian. Several scholars have observed that the recreational pole dance space is overwhelmingly white (Whitehead and Kurz 2009, 231; Holland 2010, 92; Whitehead and Kurz 2011, 231; Griffiths 2016). However, the translation of this observation in the Italian context is not straightforward, partly because Italians' whiteness has always been a contested and precarious property (Chapter 5). Still, any category is always relational, and whiteness has long been constructed as a residual position: 'an unmarked marker of others' differentness' (Frankenberg 1993, 198). Possibly, then, it was the absence of visibly Black, Arab, Asian and Latinx women in the room that, in Giovanna's eyes, qualified the space as Italian *and* white. At a time when respectability had become a national/ist property (Chapter 1), this may have made the space look/feel respectable to her. That assumption was nonetheless fallacious, as the overwhelming majority of lap dancers and street sex working cis women I encountered were white (Chapter 5). Nationality was thus the device through which Italian women reproduced, in this context, the gendered and racialized otherness of the 'lap dancer'.

Soon afterwards, I began to observe that the metonymical slide between 'foreign women' and 'lap dancers' was recurrent. Akin to Francesca, Floriana said that her students included 'a bit of everything – from the surgeon to the lawyer, the architect to the university student'. 'Italians and foreigners alike?' I asked.

> Mainly Italians. We do not have many foreigners. I was sure that the school would have been *flooded* [my emphasis] by Eastern European girls working in night clubs [i.e. lap dancers] and wanting to learn something more. However, the truth is that we have none, probably because they are not interested in it. I also think that the cost of the course matters: nowadays, to pay seventy euros a month is no small thing … .

The contradiction between Francesca and Floriana's explanation of why women working as lap dancers did not (apparently) attend the pole dance school foregrounds the tautological character of the latter's discursive exclusion. While Floriana attributed their absence to their relative economic poverty vis-à-vis Italian women, Francesca considered them to be unfit for recreational pole dancing because she deemed the source of their high consumer buying power to be dishonourable. Concomitantly, the circulation of the 'herd' (Giovanna) and 'flood' (Floriana) metaphors in association with 'foreign' women conjure imageries of invasion and danger that are consistent with the affective economy of ethnonationalism in which the figure of the migrant and the prostitute have come to overlap (Chapter 1).

Assumptions that 'foreign' women are loose and promiscuous compared to one's fellow countrywomen recur across numerous cultural contexts. For example, speaking of girls in Nevis, in the Eastern Caribbean, Debra Curtis observed that 'like many Nevisians, in response to the influx of immigrants, [they] are promulgating a sexual discourse that casts foreign women, including Guyanese and Dominican schoolgirls living on Nevis, as sexual others and as sexually promiscuous' (Curtis 2009, 40). Commenting on female anthropologists' experiences in the field, Margaret Willson suggested that 'nearly any woman outsider who cannot be controlled by the norms of the dominant society is typecast as loose: loose because she is truly independent, and because she is not corralled by the male-ordered society' (M. Willson 1995, 263). Similarly, in Italy, migrant women's stigmatization is both racialized and gendered, reflecting the assumption that once away from home and patriarchal control they become women of 'loose' morals (Merrill 2006; Zambelli 2018).

The figure of the 'Eastern European lap dancer' was thus crucial in recreational pole dancers' negotiation of their practice, embodying the epitome of the dishonourable woman onto whom they displaced the whore stigma. The deployment of this respectability tactic did not necessarily imply a negative judgement on women lap dancers. Nonetheless, it reproduced a racialized us/them boundary, based on which Italian women could claim to be respectable by default – that is, by virtue of their nationality. For example, Federica, a pole dance entrepreneur and instructor, meticulously described her students by their age, body size and gender – she did in fact proudly stress that among them there also was 'a male rugby player coming for the [intensity of the] workout'. True to the script unfolding before my eyes, my nationality question similarly appeared to unsettle her, and despite her absence of judgement, Federica, like many of her colleagues, conflated a woman's 'foreign' nationality with her work in erotic entertainment. So, when I asked if her students were Italians, she exclaimed

> Absolutely not! There are foreigners too. In this city, we have many Eastern European girls who came in search of fortune. Many of them started as night club [i.e. lap] dancers, so they come here to prepare their evening shows and learn technical tricks that can help them earn more money. But there is a bit of everything, and seriously, I have no prejudices against anyone.

In her work on British working-class women migrating to Tenerife and working as lap dancers, Esther Bott observed that the women articulated their gendered and class-based distinction by contrast with their Eastern European colleagues (Bott 2006, 38). They portrayed the latter as women who were to be 'feared for [their] abjection and ruthless drug-dealer boyfriend[s], pitied for [their] victimhood (having being trafficked against [their] will and beaten by [their] pimp), and resented for [their] desperation and willingness to sell sex and "do extras", thus degrading the work of lap dancers' (Bott 2006, 38). Among the recreational pole dancers that I encountered and/or interviewed, the figure of the 'Eastern European lap dancer' similarly embodied their despised female other, but in less vivid terms. Possibly, this variation in tone partly mirrors the different working spaces they inhabited. The women in Bott's research were all lap dancers who claimed their distinction from within a shared work floor, where they were at a high risk of being mistaken for their despised female other. Conversely, Italian recreational pole dancers relayed performing everywhere but *not* in night [i.e. strip] clubs. Their respectability tactics thus pivoted around their firm statement that pole and lap dancers did *not* share the same work floor; that they inhabited different spheres and that, therefore, they embodied different moralities.

As shown in the book's opening vignette, this process of discursive purification could be symbolically violent (Bourdieu 1989), as women like Zeza, who (had) worked as lap dancers, concealed their trespassing of this female respectability line. This likewise emerged vividly in my interview with Eleonora, to which I conclusively turn next.

The Journey to Respectability

I met Eleonora briefly at the end of an interview with a colleague of hers, who made the introductions. When she heard about my research, I had the impression that she looked down on me. I recall feeling small, almost ashamed under her defiant gaze. I took her demeanour as a sign that she considered it insignificant at best and contemptible at worst, for the proximity it implied between two practices – pole and lap dance – that the recreational pole dancers I was meeting consistently claimed to be incommensurable. Anticipating a refusal, I did not even venture into asking Eleonora whether she wanted to participate in my research. I was thus very much surprised when I received an email from her a few days later in which she did not simply volunteer but demanded that I interview her.

The evening we met, in a bar of her choice, I was feeling quite clumsy. Each of my ice-breaking attempts kept crumbling, one after the other, and I saw Eleonora growing restive at my futile attempts to sound even just a little bit funny. Eventually, resigned to my fiascos, I took the audio recorder out, put it on the table, turned it on, and asked Eleonora a self-presentation question just to get started: her age. 'I am thirty-nine', she replied dryly. 'Oh well, then we are almost peers!' I exclaimed, 'but we look younger. It must be because neither of us is married yet!' Admittedly, mine was another – the nth – attempt to round the researcher/researched edges, but it failed miserably like the previous ones. 'No! No! No', she exclaimed – her vigorous head shake conveying her impatience – 'the truth is: I started practising pole [dance] while I was into lap [dance].' And then Eleonora told me the story that she kept concealed to her colleagues; the story of how she entered one space and came out the other.

Born into a middle-class family, Eleonora left her parental home when she started higher education and had been 'totally independent ever since'. Whereas such a statement of economic self-reliance might sound unremarkable to many, in Italy, young people generally continue living with their parents until they move in with a partner (Saraceno 2004, 50). In recent years, several ministers have shamed Italian youth for doing so, within the framework of the wider neoliberal attack on aspirations to a decent, secure and stable job (Chapter 1).[8] Like many of her peers, Eleonora started her pathway to economic self-sufficiency by doing 'the typically poorly paid student jobs'. However, the money came in irregularly, and as a result, she was often on a knife-edge with rent. Eventually, she stumbled on an ad for a waitress position in 'a "sexy restaurant", where there were food and striptease shows'. While at work, Eleonora used to watch lap dancers' shows and started wondering about being on stage, where the financial return on a woman's work was much higher, and time-use more effective – as several scholars researching higher education students' engagement in erotic and sex work have observed (Roberts, Jones and Sanders 2013; Sanders and Hardy 2014; Sagar et al. 2015). So Eleonora eventually started lap dancing. 'I used to earn one hundred and fifty euros per night plus hotel and drink fees, and every time I moved to another city, I would negotiate at least four nights', she recalled, with a hint of nostalgia.

She then spoke at length of her acrobatic stripping experiences in night clubs all across the country. Our time together was flying, however, and I was keen to hear about her recreational pole dance experiences. As soon as I could, I thus asked if it was there, in night clubs, that she 'discovered' pole dancing. 'No. Meanwhile, it was *born*', she rebutted, 'it could have *never* been born in a gym.' Eleonora explained that at that time – that is, around the end of the 1990s/early 2000s – there were many Romanian women working in night clubs – as is still the case today (Chapters 3; 5): 'They were *bravissime*, they were monsters, because anyway, many of them were former gymnasts, and could do these *fantastic* things ... to the level of what is now considered [pole] sport, but they were doing it ten years ago, understand?' It was in night clubs that the early pole dance contests took place. 'Clubs would inaugurate the season and organise the contest – there was a sort of challenge', she continued, 'that's how it was born. Then obviously, the thing started to spread, and some people *c'hanno visto lungo* [they did it right].' Part of this farsightedness, this chapter has shown, involved the discursive erasure of the migrant women who brought their gymnastic skills with them and put it to use in night clubs: Eastern European women.

This end-of-century journey of pole dance from seedy night clubs to polished pole dance schools, and the concomitant shift of its female practitioners from dishonour to respectability, follows in the wake of other leisure activities with the performance of women's sexuality at their core. First introduced at the 1893 Chicago International Exhibition by a Syrian female dancer performing under the stage name 'Little Egypt' (Wynn 2007, 215), 'Oriental' or 'belly' dance became over time alternatively associated with 'spirituality, sensuality, femininity, and exercise' (Hanna 2010, 220). The mainstreaming of this practice unfolded within a colonial and then postcolonial space shaped by white Western men's orientalist fantasies about unveiling Arab women (Yeğenoğlu 1998). Akin to recreational pole dance today, 'Oriental' dance's popularity among white Western women might have thus reflected their longing to embody the mysterious, alluring woman whom men intensely desired for her sexuality. Today, in the contemporary Western sexscape, this figure is no longer mainly represented by the woman concealing her body behind a veil but by the woman who confidently displays her sexuality. 'I used to have so many students … this year I have only twenty-five', lamented Lola, an Italian 'Oriental' dance instructor, 'what sells now is zumba, burlesque, pole dance.'

Sine Nørholm Just and Sara Louise Muhr suggested that recreational pole dance instructors' 'anti-strip position' is an expedient that they use 'to brand themselves and their work as "clean"' (Just and Muhr 2019, 4). In this, it resembles how, in the 1980s, middle-class women sought access to the strictly male bodybuilding space by claiming their respectability against the 'stereotypical counter image of the stripper' (Boyle 2005, 146). In Italy, both the 'sporty' and 'sexy' school followers deploy these respectability tactics in different situations. Nevertheless, this chapter has shown that behind closed doors, many of them would acknowledge female strippers (i.e. 'lap dancers', in Italian 'vernacular') as pioneers and sources of inspiration. In a cultural context that the women depicted as particularly oppressive, they negotiated their access to this practice by deploying gendered, racialized and class-based othering processes, through which they claimed their own respectability. The release that Eleonora sought by offering me her story indexes the symbolic violence of these processes, which women ambivalently contributed to reproducing.

Conclusions

In this chapter, I have discussed how recreational pole dance instructors and/or entrepreneurs narrated their enjoyment and/or sale of this pleasure practice at a time when its market was still at its early stages but in rapid expansion. Women aspired to feel the pleasure of sexuality by emulating the culturally glamourized figure of the female stripper but feared being stigmatized as 'whores' for doing so. They managed this tension by deploying multiple respectability tactics.

The first tactic was outright concealment. The invisibility of the pole dance school in the opening vignette – no boards, no signs, no doorbell – suggests that there was some fear of attracting undue and perhaps even dangerous outsiders' attention. Recurrently, the women concealed their longing to feel sexy and desirable, on which this pleisure practice thrives, behind a wall of modesty. They would thus, for example, refer to recreational pole dance as a *disciplina* thereby seeking to share in sports' dignified, respectable status, or they would call the pole a 'vertical perch' instead. The second tactic was the women's appeal to 'nature'. Some instructors presented the practice as a gentle remedy helping women heal from their gendered insecurities by retrieving or building confidence in their heterosexual desirability – thereby contextually reproducing the heteronormative overlap between sex, gender and desire. The third tactic was women's self-presentation as vanguards of a particular type of modernity characterized by women's capacity to display sexiness freely and confidently in public. The fourth tactic was the women's claim of their embodiment of glamour and/or hard work – the latter signalled by their bruised body and their committed and engaged (versus opportunistic) relationship with the pole. The fifth tactic, which recurred quite systematically, implied the displacement of the whore stigma onto a racialized female other – the 'Eastern European lap dancer'. However, as some pole dance instructors acknowledged behind closed doors, it was precisely Eastern European women who first introduced pole dancing in Italy, from within night clubs. They are the real-life women whose (hetero) sexual appeal underpins the globalization of pole dance as a pleasure practice and, as my encounter with Zeza (Preface) and Eleonora suggests, and much scholarship confirms (Murphy 2003, 318; Egan, Frank, and Johnson 2006b, xxvii; Colosi 2010, 111–12; Price-Glynn 2010, 35), they are also the women that remain harshly stigmatized.

Caught between the yearning to feel the power and pleasure of sexuality and the danger of being stigmatized as whores, recreational pole dancers claimed respectability – i.e. a class-based inflection of patriarchal notions of female dis/honour – to enjoy more of the first while protecting themselves from the latter. However, by displacing the whore stigma onto another category of women, they contributed to reproducing the very same processes underpinning their own gendered subjection in a sexist social order.

In the next chapter, I continue following the journey of the whore stigma from where I left off. It is thus a chapter about women dancing with a vertical steel pole for work, in night clubs.

Notes

1. In September 2014 – i.e. two years after I started fieldwork – the Pole Dance Italy blog listed one hundred and twenty-five venues, out of which only nineteen (i.e. approximately 15%) lie in Italy's southern regions and main islands. Since the page is updated regularly, it no longer reports the data I collected then. For the current number and geographical distribution of recreational pole dance schools in Italy, see Valentina D'Amico (n.d.).

2. Bartky's concept of 'internalized oppression' starts from a comparison between workers and women's experience of alienation under capitalism and patriarchy, respectively. She posited that, while workers may try to resist capitalist-imposed 'fragmentation and loss of self' (Bartky 1990, 32) women do not only comply with but find pleasure in their 'sexual objectification' (Bartky 1990, 36–37). Women's internalization of the role of the object of male sexual desire leads to their adoption of practices to style themselves according to a particular regime of feminine embodiment and comportment (Bartky 1990, 65–68).
3. Among other things, the sporty schools supported the ongoing international campaign demanding the inclusion of 'pole sports' in the Olympics. In 2017, the International Pole Sports Federation was granted Observer Status in the Global Association of International Sports Federations, bringing it a step closer to achieving this goal (International Pole Sports Federation 2017).
4. 'Floorwork' encompasses choreographic dance moves that generally accompany the transition from one acrobatic trick to another; for example, walking around the pole while holding on to it and doing body or leg waves against it.
5. Laura Mulvey coined this term in her critique of women's representation in mainstream Western visual culture (1975), as women have been constrained to embody the object of male desire. 'In a world ordered by sexual imbalance', she posited, 'pleasure in looking has been split between active/male and passive/female. The determining male gaze projects its fantasy onto the female form, which is styled accordingly.' (Mulvey 1975, 19)
6. 'I know it when I see it', wrote US Supreme Court Justice Potter Stewart, when he explained how he came to his verdict on whether visual material (a movie) brought to his court was to be considered 'obscene' (Gewirtz 1995).
7. The meaning of 'vulgarity' in the Italian context is underexplored, except for Mainardi (2018), who discusses it in her analysis of Italian girls' digital and, specifically, Facebook culture. In her research, Mainardi observed that the girls' judgement of their peers' pictures showing breasts or cleavages as 'vulgar' reflected the girls' assessment that their peers circulated these images out of a 'commercial logic' – that is, 'with the purpose of gaining visibility through popularity' (Mainardi 2018, 195).
8. See, for example, La Stampa (2010); Corriere della Sera (2007). While in government, Silvio Berlusconi also infamously recommended a young *precaria* – i.e. a female member of the 'precariat' (Standing 2011) – to find economic security via marriage with a rich man, such as his son (Repubblica 2008).

Chapter 3

WOMEN POLE/LAP DANCING FOR WORK

Prior to undertaking this research, I had never stepped into a 'night club' (as Italians generically call female-to-male erotic entertainment venues) in my life. Frankly, I never thought I would, for several reasons. As a start, I should admit that back then I used to hold quite a prejudiced view of its customers – men who would pay women to entertain them but despise them being available to do so; men who would admit that they attended these venues only in the privacy of their privileged homosocial spaces. Second, as a woman, I would have not been welcome. While today, in many Western countries, parts of the erotic entertainment industry also cater to female customers (see e.g. Montemurro, Bloom and Madell 2003; Pilcher 2011; 2012; Barton and Mabry 2018), in Italy, this is not the case. Women are usually exclusively allowed in for special women-only events, such as on occasion of International Working Women's Day, for which exclusively male striptease shows are organized. Third, mainstream media representations stereotypically link these venues to illicit traffic of commodities and people, fuelling their perception as seedy and dangerous places. Disdain and fear thus blended in my outsider's perception of these sites, and when I decided to step into one for my research, I did not feel like going alone. So, when I eventually spotted a 'women welcome' night, I asked some female friends to come along with me.

The first time was at Charlie's (Preface). That night, women customers were not just welcomed but also seemingly actively sought after, since their entry (but not men's) was free of charge. Still, many cues signalled that the gender of the customer for whose pleasure the entertainment had been arranged was not theirs. Whereas any man stepping into Charlie's was readily approached by one or more female staff wearing a distinctive red bikini uniform, nobody, of any gender, greeted my friends and I upon arrival. As I walked around, I saw very few women whose attire did not immediately signal that they were on duty, and even they were never in each other's company but always accompanying a man. The staff were also all-women, except the male bouncers at the doors. Nonetheless, this exception to the otherwise strictly male-only entry rule allowed me to start building some research contacts from within. Indeed, that was when I met Zeza (Preface), and although our encounter did not subsequently flourish, our conversation had still brought to light some of the tensions and points of contact between recreational pole dance and lap dance.

That night, after Zeza's departure, I walked around in search of my friends, and I was pleased to find them at the bar counter sipping a drink on the house. I took it as a good omen, and I already looked back on my initial fears with some embarrassment. Moments after our reunion, I heard a female voice rising loud above my head. 'Gentlemen! Please welcome these three beautiful, young women!' exclaimed Nadia, the compère who earlier put me in contact with Zeza. Frozen, I turned in the direction of her voice, and there she was, emphatically gesturing with her hands and inviting us to get closer to her. In a matter of seconds, the crowd of men standing between us began to part, opening a narrow passage for us to get through.

Why did Nadia turn the lights on us? Was it mockery? For we surely were neither that 'young' nor that 'beautiful'. Was it my payback for her having put me in contact with Zeza? And if it was, what pleasure, what reward was there in this prank for her? While these questions crossed my mind, I also knew that I could not afford to withdraw from Nadia's game if I wanted to try and build some research contacts that night. 'Let us go', I told my friends. As we walked under the gaze of the men in the audience, I recall feeling both amused at Nadia's playfulness and embarrassed for being effectively outed as a 'bad' woman – as I was in a place where there could be no 'good' ones.

'Come on ladies! Do come along and have a seat!' continued Nadia – her sparkling voice accompanying us all the way until we reached the sofas that she was directing us towards. Moments before we did, I saw some commotion – a couple of female staff, recognizable by their uniform, had rushed in to ask some men sitting there to please stand up and move elsewhere. We were effectively being treated as 'special guests', and I found it odd and unexpected, to say the least. As soon as we sat down, Nadia had the next show started, and I leaned back on the sofa to watch it, relieved at my fall back into irrelevance. That feeling, though, did not last long.

'What are you doing here?' a female voice asked in my direction. As I turned my head, my eyes met those of a young woman leaning over me, hands on knees. I could easily imagine that she found my presence puzzling, for all the customers around us were male. 'I am a researcher, and I am doing a study on pole and lap dancing', I replied quickly, in a hushed tone, 'and you?' I politely asked her in return, expecting to hear no more or no less than what her uniform signalled. 'I do the lesbo show, but ... later', she whispered conspiratorially, 'when there are fewer people around'.

In hindsight, I reckoned that probably her straightforwardness was meant to be a quick check on my sexual orientation. There and then, though, I did not perceive it that way. Since stepping into the club, we had been systematically ignored by every staff member. I was also ready to bet that it was not a woman's gaze that she imagined to please when she decided to put on a 'lesbo show' for the night.[1] 'Ah, ok', I said, nodding. Then I smiled and turned my head back to the stage to watch the show.

'So, what is your research about, precisely?' the same woman asked me whilst taking a seat on the small table right in front of me. At that point, *I* started to find her presence puzzling. I wondered whether she was collecting information on me on the management's behalf (something that, as I relay later, I indeed experienced in another night club, where I similarly embodied the odd non-working woman). I thus decided to anticipatorily defuse any potential problem by describing to her my research in detail: the puzzle driving me to it, my research questions, my fieldwork design. 'But that is so interesting!' Miriam exclaimed at every pause I took – her excitement gradually dissipating my surveillance paranoia whilst reassuring me about the value of my research. 'So that is what I am doing here', I said, reaching the end of my tale and leaning back again on the sofa, 'and I came with them', I added, pointing at my friends sitting close-by, 'because ... well ... I just did not want to be hooked by ... you know, whomever!' I said, snickering.

Looking possibly ten years younger than me, surrounded as we were by men at least twice her age and older, I thought that she would smile along, but she did not. 'That is the difference between you and me', she said, looking deadpan into my eyes, 'I am paid *precisely* to be hooked.' Ashamed, I realized that my words had not only expressed my contempt for the male customers in the venue – a form of gendered stigma (Frank 2002; Egan 2006) that I have since learnt to no longer reproduce – but that they had unwittingly rebounded onto her. Mortified, I expected her to stand up and leave, but she did not. She rather took my hand in hers, softly traced the lines in my palm with her fingers and then asked me how old I was. I went along with this flirtatious ritual play, and as the script goes, I asked her to guess it instead. I told her when she could not, to which she exclaimed that I looked 'so much younger!' – a statement that, in a sexist and ageist country as Italy is, few women would not feel flattered by. We kept chit-chatting a bit more, then she stood up and, stretching her hand to take mine, she asked, 'Shall we have a drink?'

It was only *then* that I understood that I was to pay for the conversation we just had (women get commissions on the drinks that are consumed in their company). Suddenly acknowledging that after all Miriam probably had not found my research so very interesting, I felt as silly as a newbie and as embittered as a dejected lover. I also unexpectedly found myself in the 'customer' position, realizing only then that I had not sufficiently pondered whether I was comfortable with paying (another woman) to receive this type of emotional and potentially erotic service (I am, with the caveat that she is an adult and consenting to it as freely as an outsider can know). And after all, even if I was a means to her end, was she not a means to (my research and therefore to) mine? Look at where exactly you are reading about my encounter with Miriam.

With my head abuzz in these reflections, I followed Miriam to the bar and got a drink each, as she asked. I hoped that she would leave me and my raving thoughts alone, there and then, at the bar counter. Instead, she walked me back to the sofa. Seated in the same position, we chatted some more about something I could not later recall. A few minutes after we finished the drinks, she said goodbye and left.

****

This chapter's opening vignette offers a snapshot of an evening out in an Italian night club as seen through the eyes of a cis female researcher who fallaciously assumed that her gender was structurally at odds with a customer position. Throughout, I experienced veering between invisibility and hypervisibility, irrelevance and flattery, uniqueness and disposability. Ignored at first, my female friends and I suddenly became 'special guests' for whom some male customers were asked to leave their place and make room for us instead. This honorary position that we were granted that night represents one of the many articulations of women, commodity and modernity constitutive of the contemporary Western sexscape. A modern *white* Western woman is the glamorized female stripper whom recreational pole dancers long to emulate: an icon of female 'empowerment' and sexual liberation who confidently displays and takes advantage of the power of her sexuality. A modern woman is also someone who looks for and tries new sexual commodities to develop her sexual knowledge, diversify her sexual experiences and learn new techniques to give and take sexual pleasure (McCaughey and French 2001; Curtis 2004). It is likewise the woman who goes to strip bars to watch other women dancing erotically for the pleasure of whoever pays, thereby contributing to making the status of a venue shift from 'seedy' to 'respectable'. It was precisely because of this dignification and gentrification potential that we embodied as *female* customers that, I suggest, Nadia turned the spotlight on me and my friends that night.

The gentrification of parts of the erotic entertainment market is both a driver and an effect of the cultural and economic transformations characterizing the contemporary Western sexscape. In Western countries, such as the US, upscaling processes started amid the HIV-AIDS pandemic, as these venues promised '"clean" and respectable interactions [and] could alleviate certain fears about contamination and disease that escalated around prostitution' (Frank 2002, xxv). In parallel, the competition pressure arising from booming online pornography pushed 'live' erotic services to diversify (Egan, Frank and Johnson 2006b, xxi; Price-Glynn 2010, 31). Today, in parts of these countries,[2] the range of live erotic entertainment on offer is wide and multifaceted, catering to customers' differently racialized and gendered 'taste' (Bourdieu 1984) and desire. However, in Italy, these processes have not reached similar proportions (yet?). Generally, within Italian night clubs, the gender of the customer is always male, and the gender of the entertainer is always female. Italians generically call the latter 'lap dancers' (Eng. original), and although I have also been using this term to align with emic use and the imagination it evokes, it is nevertheless partly deceiving and partly dismissive of women's work in these venues.

The 'lap dance' is an 'exotic' or 'sensual' dance routine in which the exact nature of the contact between the viewer and the performer is unclearly defined. For example, Katherine Frank posits that this dance involves 'varying amounts of contact' (Frank 2002, xxiii), while for Rachela Colosi, workers perform 'between the customer's legs in close proximity to his body but not necessarily making contact with him' (Colosi 2010, 34). Notwithstanding this difference, at the core of both definitions similarly lies the direct, unmediated relationship between the worker and the customer. What I mean is that no vertical pole appears to be necessarily involved in the definition of this work practice. Nonetheless, it is precisely the women-and-pole imagery that dominates Italian night clubs' promotional materials, next to the announcement that there will be 'lap dance shows'. Undoubtedly, the pole circulates as a phallic signifier but at the same time this slippage impresses on the imagination (including mine, until I did this research) the overlap of 'pole dance' with 'lap dance'. In this overlap lies the roots of recreational pole dancers' always uphill battle in trying to disentangle their pleasure practice from erotic work and the whore stigma that is 'stuck' (Ahmed 2004, 120) on it.

Besides, lap dancers' performance of different forms and types of dance – on stage or in private, with or without the pole, from close or afar, partially dressed or naked, etc. – is only one component of women's work in night clubs. Indeed, as shown in this chapter's initial vignette, women also provide customers with conversation and companionship – that is, 'emotional labour' (Hochschild 2003).³ This is, for example, evincible from the spectrum of emotions I experienced through my interaction with Miriam: the initial feeling of being important (for I was sought after), bright throughout (for I was attentively listened to and told that my research was interesting) and eventually disappointed ('I was just another customer'), when the spell of the commodity I was (unwittingly) consuming dissolved. As some scholars have observed (Frank 2002; Egan 2006), women's income indeed depends on their ability to conceal that the pleasure that men purchase is a commodity strictly bound to time, money and place. As I show in this chapter, these very skills further exacerbate the women's gendered stigmatization at work.

Ethnographic scholarship on lap dancers in Italy is lacking, so I draw here from the existing works on women working as 'exotic dancers' – a category encompassing strippers, lap dancers and table dancers (Frank 2007, 502) – in some Western and specifically Anglophone countries (Frank 2002; Egan 2006; Egan, Frank and Johnson 2006a; Brooks 2010; Colosi 2010; Law 2012). Against the backdrop of the feminist sex wars (Chapter 4), these authors have argued that, although women's work contributes to reproducing the unequal gender relations of power constituting the condition of possibility of these venues, women's experiences are more ambivalent and nuanced than the sexual oppression/liberation binary can accommodate (Egan, Frank and Johnson 2006b). Building on this body of knowledge, in this chapter, I focus on a different aspect of the relationship between gender and power in this sexscape. Hence, I continue exploring women's negotiation of the tension between sexuality and status, focusing particularly on their participation in the reproduction of hierarchies of value among them.

The chapter starts with a discussion of some of the pressures and contradictions that women working as lap dancers in Italian night clubs cope with, as they are required to maintain a delicate balance between authenticity and commodity whilst facing some customers' requests to enjoy more than what is (at least officially) on offer. Next, the chapter discusses how the women negotiated the whore stigma in front of me – a cis female researcher, not their colleague, and hence, in their eyes, a likely straight, 'respectable' woman. It will present the most recurrent narrative repertoires – entrepreneurship, sacrifice and love – that women deployed to dignify themselves through or despite their work. While doing so, the chapter will highlight the processes of othering underpinning some women's respectability tactics.

Commodification Paradoxes

On a weekday afternoon, I drove to an interview to be held in a provincial, popular night club. Realizing I had missed it, I drove backwards and forwards a couple of times before deciding to park the car and find out whether, perhaps, the club lay somewhere hidden from street view. I eventually found it in the basement of a commercial building – impossible to detect unless by looking at the doorbells. As soon as I set foot inside, however, such structural invisibility flipped 180 degrees, as the club's interior design – white marble-like columns, silver chandeliers, mirrors in baroque golden frames – evoked an imperial atmosphere instead. At a closer look, I observed that such majesty coexisted with some arguably cheap decor, such as plastic *abat-jour* in the shape of women's legs in fishnet stockings, and clippings of naked women glued onto any horizontal surface on which a drink could be placed. In the centre of the main room there was a big floor-to-ceiling steel pole, which was surrounded by plenty of smaller ones. Each of the latter stood at the centre of a U-shaped sitting area that with just a pull of a brocade curtain could be turned into a lap dance *privé* (private lounge).

The person I was about to meet was Gianna: an Italian woman in her fifties who had been working in this night club as a human resource manager for over ten years, selecting, appointing and managing employee relations with the women working as lap dancers or aspiring to. Seated in that empty, well-lit room next to her, I felt as if I was paying a visit to a merry-go-round engineer a few minutes before the show begins. 'This is a companionate place, where you come to spend a night', she told me, her right arm comfortably draped across the back of the sofa we were sitting on, 'the customers coming here are almost all *our* customers'. Not simply, or even perhaps mainly, conveying a proprietary acceptation, her emphasis on the nature of the relationship between the club and its regulars elevated it above an indiscriminate, commercial and opportunistic one. Theirs, she suggested, was an intimate relationship: personal and familiar.

Gianna's words disoriented me at first, particularly because, as I told her, I was under the impression 'that customers always looked for the novelty'. What I meant was that I expected that *male customers* would be moving across different venues in search of the novelty, rather than *women workers* having to continuously change work sites. In hindsight, I realized that the fallacy in my reasoning reflected my own positionality, as I was looking at the night club first and foremost as a workplace for women rather than a leisure site for men. Rather, as Gianna readily clarified, providing that level of job security for women would have run against the club's investment in customer loyalty: 'the thing with novelty', she explained, 'is about ensuring an almost continuous turnover of the women'. In a similar way, it occurred to me, Italian female brothels used to change their workforce every *quindicina* (fortnight), as this fast turnover attracted men to come back for the promise of finding pleasure in variety rather than in a particular woman. The compulsory depersonalization of these commodified encounters made prostitution and marriage compatible and even complementary. Two weeks were, in fact, unlikely to lead to a romance so intense as to endanger a man's marriage – and, by all means, the latter was indissoluble, as divorce was legalized over a decade after female brothels were shut down by law (Chapter 1). Today, though, that rigid, heteronormative architecture of intimacy no longer exists, and the liquidity of people's intimate relationships (Bauman 2003) engenders particular risks for these businesses and the women working in them.

'How long does a contract with a lap dancer last on average?' I asked Gianna. She replied that it was difficult to say: 'Sometimes it lasts one night only. Unfortunately, this is not a simple job: *here*, you work if you are good [at it], if not, it is hard.' I asked Gianna to explain to me what criteria underpin her assessment of a woman's work performance as 'good', about which she said:

> If customers make her drink, if she drinks, if they ask her again … sometimes they [male customers] say, 'no, I do not want that one; she is too arrogant'. It depends. In the end, they do not have to do who knows what! They should be kind, nice, and let them speak, but many [women] are just self-interested, understand? All they do is just push men to spend money on drinks.

In Gianna's account, women's ability to promote male customers' alcohol consumption contradictorily qualifies them as good *and* bad women workers – an ambivalence that, in the Italian language, similarly characterizes the definition of the 'good woman' (Introduction). This paradox lies at the heart of lap dancers' position in the club, and navigating it requires mastery of the craft of providing male customers with an experience that feels authentically pleasurable *despite* its commodity status (read: my interaction with Miriam).

Unlike erotic entertainment venues in the US and the UK, where exotic dancers usually pay a house fee to perform in a club (Frank 2002; Colosi 2010; Brooks 2010), the lap dancers I interviewed relayed receiving an eighty euros fee per night. Their shift consisted of six working hours (10 PM–4 AM), meaning that their hourly remuneration was approximately a third higher than the minimum wage.[4] The club's fee covered the emotional labour that women put in maintaining a welcoming attitude to customers and a few shows on the main stage. Most of their earnings, however, came from commissions on the drinks that they got customers to consume in their company throughout the night – the higher the cost of the drink, the higher the commission they earned. This money flow is nonetheless disguised via its temporal displacement. Hence, when instructed by Miriam, I got us two drinks – one each – no money changed hands: the barwoman punched my 'drink card' (Eng. original) twice, prepared and put our drinks on the counter, and then handed two thin rubber bracelets to Miriam, who readily hanged them around her wrist. It was only at the exit, when a man looking more like a bouncer than a cashier asked that I show him my drink card, that I was made to pay my dues (Miriam must have also exchanged her rubber bracelets for cash at the end of her shift).

Women's income and the club's revenues were therefore inextricably tied to one another in what would appear to configure a 'win-win' scenario. And yet, Gianna's reprimand of the women who 'just push men to spend money on drinks' suggests that they were paradoxically blamed for doing their job, or more precisely, for 'doing *it* for the money' – as 'bad' women do. 'Especially when the club first opened, there were some heavy situations', Gianna recounted of her early days at work, when the club's management entrusted her with the task of putting things back straight. As a start, she searched and fired any 'homewrecker', thereby restoring the *proper* boundaries between the night club and the mundane life outside its walls:

> I have always told the girls that I do not want them to ever put feelings in what they do, like 'I make that one fall in love, so he comes every night, he drinks, and I am better off.' No. *No feelings*. [I have always told them that] This is your *work*, and you must tell him: 'This is my work, I am here with you as long as you want, but do not think that outside then … .'

Acquainted as I was by then with the feminist sex wars' debate on women's oppression and liberation through sexuality (Chapter 4), I found Gianna's focus on male fragility unsettling. Her words conveyed an image of lap dancers as cynical, greedy and predatory women, intent on taking advantage of vulnerable men, seemingly at the women's mercy and in need of protection from them. I cannot know whether and to what extent this portrayal of gender relations in the club may have been plausible. What I take from Gianna's words, however, is that some men do believe in the possibility of detaching the pleasure that they consume from the very marketplace where they purchase it. Danielle Egan, for example, suggested that some customers experience themselves as 'lovers', and their attempts at moving the interaction with the women outside of the club partly reflect their longing to resolve this ambiguity (Egan 2006, 67). A keystone in the scaffolding of the plausibility of this illusion – arguably, the main one – is women's skill at producing an interaction that feels so authentically pleasurable that it appears incompatible with its commodity status.

Women's ability to make men feel good about themselves, in whatever aspect and for whatever reason, is, in fact, the defining task of their work in these venues. Speaking of Tokyo's female hostess clubs, Anne Allison argued that the object of male customers' eroticized consumption is neither only nor necessarily mainly the woman, but rather customers' own 'projection' as 'powerful [and] desirable' men (Allison 1994, 22). Scholars who have researched the US context similarly underlined that exotic dance venues are 'special places' that are 'constructed specifically for men's unencumbered pleasure' (Egan 2006, 35). There, men can enact their aspirational masculinity and feel 'desirable, connected, and powerful' (Price-Glynn 2010, 68). These venues can also function as shelters and cocoons, offering men 'a sense of escape from those aspects of the self that felt oppressive in other spheres – old age, ugliness, or insecurity, a lack of social skills, or intimate failures' (Frank 2006, 131).

Yet, as Gianna's words suggest, women's craft, if left unbridled, is also potentially dangerous and disruptive. Now that marriages can easily be dissolved (except for the Catholic Church), that ability may, in fact, unleash destruction from within and without the club, unsettling the intimate and economic arrangements upon which male customers' everyday lives may rest. The stake is nonetheless higher than the sum of the individual men risking jeopardizing their marriages, financial assets, or both. If rumours spread that, akin to the Sirens in Homer's *Odyssey*, the women first seduce and then destroy the lives of the men following their voices, night clubs would lose their theatrical, merry-go-round quality and with it, most likely, a conspicuous part of their revenues too. 'These are delicate things, especially people's feelings. It takes nothing … [to hurt them? To spoil them? Gianna did not finish her sentence]. So, fixed-term girls need to be able to do this [to hold on to the boundary between life inside and outside the club], otherwise … [they will stop working with us].'

Paradoxically then, the management demands women to simultaneously conceal and remind male patrons that they are at their service only for the money they can dispose of in the club, and that their interaction ought to exclusively unfold within its walls. They must promote customers' alcohol consumption but not so much as to show that this is what they are paid for and have a direct stake in. It is from within this structurally ambivalent employment position that women must negotiate some male customers' demands to consume more than what is (at least officially) on offer.

Porous Boundaries

Strictly speaking, exotic dancing is not sex work, although at times the boundaries between the two can blur (Frank 2007, 502). Indeed, defining sex work is an inevitably elusive endeavour, partly due to the very complexity of defining 'sex' itself. People can subjectively experience (and arrange to purchase) sexual pleasure in many different ways. Some of these do not involve physical touch (think of camming and phone sex); others do, but they might not involve direct stimulation of a person's sexual organs (think of BDSM). In this book, I use Carol Wolkowitz's definition of 'body work' (Wolkowitz 2006) to trace the difference between these two occupations. Body work, which includes sex work, is a form of 'employment that takes the body as its immediate site of labour, involving intimate, messy contact with the (frequently supine or naked) body, its orifices or products through touch or close proximity' (Wolkowitz 2006, 147). Differently, these forms of intimate touch do not characterize exotic (including lap) dancing. On the contrary, they seem to be often prohibited – indeed, ethnographies of women working as exotic dancers in the US and UK were all set in venues enforcing strict no-touch policies. Scholars have rather portrayed the women's work in these sites as mainly consisting of the production and servicing of fantasies (Frank 2002; Egan 2006).

In Italy, the definition of what exactly constitutes permissible touch may vary from place to place, but what is certain is that the Merlin Law prohibits the sale of sex in any indoor establishment (Chapter 1). According to its all-encompassing definition of the crime of aiding and abetting prostitution, night club owners and managers can be charged not only if found to have wittingly organized an indoor sex marketplace but also if they 'tolerate' the presence of sex working women independently attending their venue for soliciting purposes.[5] Nevertheless, some scholars have suggested that Italian night clubs 'can conceal forms of prostitution' (Serughetti 2013, 277) or observed that some women do, in fact, sell sex within their premises or annexes (Palmisano 2010, 51). In these circumstances, these sexual services take the name of 'extras', and their provision contravenes the definition of licit work in the clubs. In my fieldwork, I observed that 'extras' lingered as an absent presence, as they were simultaneously everywhere and nowhere – that is, they were always elsewhere.

One evening I organized to go with a group of female friends to a renowned night club in the hinterland that had advertised a 'women welcome' policy during weekdays. The club lay in a remote industrial area, and, again, finding its precise location was not easy – an emerging pattern signalling how, akin to the female brothels of the past, such venues in Italy continue to be ambivalently conceived as sites of male privilege and social pollution. Their remoteness affords men discretion and privacy (as they will unlikely be seen by anyone but other men in the act of doing the same) while containing their purportedly harmful impact on the 'health' of the social body.

I parked the car in front of the warehouse-like building hosting the club – another resonance, this time with recreational pole dance schools (Chapter 2). The sight of a group of women unaccompanied by not even one man evidently puzzled the male bouncer at the door. Admittedly, a women-only group was unlikely the type of clientele that the club meant to attract with their 'women welcome' marketing message. Speaking from the US context, some scholars have suggested that the club's imposition of a male 'escorting' rule is aimed at preventing female customers from competing with working women for male attention, and impinging upon the latter's revenues (Brooks 2010, 25; Barton 2017). During my fieldwork, I learned that in Italy this gendered constraint also served other purposes. It was, in fact, enforced also as a rule of order to prevent entry to customers' potentially 'angry female partners', and as a precautionary measure to keep sex working women out, thereby defusing the risk of a charge for aiding and abetting prostitution. Against this backdrop, the bouncer could have justified our denied entry that night based on a claim that we looked like 'trouble'. Instead, despite some visible hesitation, he eventually handed us a drink card each. We walked in and up the first floor, to where some loud pounding music was coming from.

A cocktail waiter intercepted us as soon as we stepped into the room. Gently, he invited us to sit at 'our' table – a corner one, the farthest away from the stage – and offered us the first of a couple of rounds of drinks on the house, which were probably meant to keep us happy but seated – that is, out of the way. As he poured some wine in our glasses, he started interrogating us: who were we, what were we doing, why we did not alert them beforehand of our arrival. 'Had we known it', he said, not without a hint of reproach, 'we could have arranged some men for you, who would have made an "almost complete" performance'. In response, I explained to him that I was a researcher, that part of my research was on women pole and lap dancing and that my friends had simply come along with me for company. Seemingly satisfied with my answer, he excused himself and left us sipping our drinks. Shortly afterwards, the night club manager came to talk business with me. He led me downstairs to show me a room with plenty of poles, which – he said – he was ready to rent out for a good price should I know anyone interested in using it for teaching or training purposes. 'Sure', I said, feeling a bit dazed, 'I will keep that in mind.' I later reckoned that his proposal was not so odd as it first appeared to me. A few recreational pole dance entrepreneurs I interviewed indeed mentioned having entered into similar arrangements, which had helped them keep their start-up costs low in their early days.

Then, the club's manager invited me to follow him back upstairs, where he literally placed me face-up in front of 'one of his girls, who is very good at it'. He whispered something in her ears, after which she performed a couple of 'basic' pole dance tricks – 'basic' not because they were easy but because I saw them taught in recreational pole dance beginners' classes (by the way, where did she learn them?). Then, the lap/pole dancer went back to a low-intense strut around the pole, not quite subtly suggesting that it was time for me to leave and let her entertain a 'real' customer instead. Moments afterwards, the manager – who kept holding my right arm tight throughout, as if in fear I would suddenly flee and roam around unbridled – led me back to 'our' corner table, from which I promised that I would not stand up if not to leave for good (and so I did). There, I saw my friends chatting with some young men sitting at the table next to ours – a football team, as it turned out – and I joined in their conversation. Asked why we were there that night, I briefly explained my research and then turned the question back at them. 'You see that guy over there?' one of them said in response. Then, pointing at his peer seated at the end of their table, who was embracing a woman sitting on his lap, he explained, 'It is his birthday; she works here, so he brought us all here to celebrate it.' We continued talking about football and my research, and shortly afterwards I saw the couple stand up and leave, hand in hand. 'Did you see that? Poor guy', one of his peers said, shaking his head, 'he is in love with her, but she treats him like an ATM. She takes him to the *privé*, and each time he pays fifty euros.' 'What for?' I asked. 'Just a private dance', he sighed, 'but elsewhere you can have extras if you pay … .'

In my interviews with the women working at the time as lap dancers, I did not ask about the potential circulation of extras in their workplaces. As gatekeepers mediated my access to them, I did not feel that raising this question would have been particularly meaningful. At best, I would have doubted the truthfulness of their answer – as the women may have had a strong inclination to deny the existence of such practices, since affirming otherwise would have implied admission of illicit acts to a nosey stranger as I probably was in their eyes. At worst, I would have irritated my gatekeepers (who would have certainly come to know about my question) and maybe lost their consent for my research. Still, references to 'extras' abounded, albeit only as reprehensible acts that some despicable, 'other women' performed.

Working 'Clean'

Mirca is an Italian woman of approximately my age, whom I met through contacts made in the recreational pole dance community. At the time of the interview, she was in an ordinary 9-to-5 white-collar job. Previously, she worked as an acrobatic stripper in a wide range of venues both in Canada and in Italy. Akin to Eleonora (Chapter 2), Mirca looked back at her high earnings of those years with evident nostalgia. It was, however, a case of not all that glitters is gold. In fact, she relayed that, in Italy, she was always on alert every time she had to choose which night clubs to perform in:

> [In Italy] I worked in clubs where you do not have to do ... whatever, because *there*, club owners do not want women who do not make extras ... . So if you do not work with this [she pointed both hands at her vulva], it is better to move fast because once people know you, they do not even invite you for a drink. Because unfortunately here it is not like in [North] America, or in the UK, where clubs are chock full only to watch ... Italians are ... Italians are *sick*. Not only do they want to touch you, but they would want to do everything, and they invite you for a drink only to ask if you would get out of the club with them or if you would give them some extras inside.

Mirca's scornful tone as she evoked the memories of male customers' inappropriate sexual propositions conveyed the extent to which the memory of being in that position upset her still. I asked her if the management knew about the recurrence of these undue demands, about which she said:

> Some owners pretend that they do not know anything, so, for example, when you tell them 'I only come if I can work clean', they will say 'Do not worry, come! Everything is clean here', but eventually it is not clean at all! And you know that already when you see that there are dark curtains and bouncers passing by without looking inside ... . Whereas other places enforce such tight control that customers cannot even get close to you, and any strip show, any dance truly needs to be performed from a distance: *there* nothing happens for real, and if someone is caught doing something, he will be kicked out.

In Mirca's words, to work 'clean' means to provide no extras. By contrast, these sexual services and the women providing them are implicitly qualified as 'dirty'. Following Mary Douglas' concept of dirt as 'matter out of place' (Douglas 1966), the 'dirt' of the 'extras' may be seen as a consequence of it being in the wrong place, from where it unsettles the boundaries between night clubs and brothels, lap dance and sex work, licit and illicit trades. Alternatively, this 'dirt' status could be taken as a normative judgement on the act itself and, by extension, on the women performing it. The concept of 'dirty work' was first coined by Everett Hughes to describe jobs and tasks that society classifies as disgusting, degrading and debasing (Hughes 1958). Albeit generally deemed necessary for the good of society, the people performing them are stigmatized (Hughes 1958; Goffman 1963). This category includes erotic and sexual services, which feature as 'morally tainted' occupations, considered 'somewhat sinful or of dubious virtue' (Ashforth and Kreiner 1999, 415). Nevertheless, dirty jobs are also deemed functional and necessary for the common good, since the people performing them take on themselves the symbolic and/or material 'dirt' that would otherwise spill over and pollute the rest of the social body. Significantly, the Italian term *puttana* evokes 'the Latin putida ("stinking or rotting", giving us words like *putrid*), connecting to a long European tradition of associating sex workers with sewers or drains' (Smith and Mac 2018, 22 – see also Chapter 1). The 'dirt' in these particularly gendered jobs, I suggest, is the whore stigma, which is embedded in the women's employment contract. It is the flip side of the power of their intense (hetero)sexual desirability, making the return on their labour considerably higher than most 'clean' jobs.

Dirt, however, is neither absolute nor monolithic matter. Indeed, Mirca's management of the whore stigma, which is attached to women lap dancers' peculiarly gendered occupation,[6] reproduces a hierarchy of cleaner and dirtier jobs and, with it, of more and less honourable women. She thus reacted to this polluting danger by seeking to displace the whore stigma onto another category of women: women who, by selling sex from within or without the night club premises, 'become' prostitutes.

These respectability tactics recurred among the women who were working as lap dancers at the time of their interview with me. For example, Fiona, a Romanian woman in her late twenties, recounted that when 'somebody' offered her work as a lap dancer in Italy, she initially refused because back then she would 'not even [have dared to] undress in front of my mother!' She eventually accepted the offer and started travelling to Italy on tourist visas to work in night clubs (Chapter 5). When I asked Fiona what she liked and disliked in her job, she said:

> Ok, as my mother used to say: 'You are young, let yourself be seen.' So, I like dancing, I like meeting people, I do not consider myself ugly, and I like to show it. That is it, basically. The things that I do not like are that sometimes there are people who do not see lap dance for what it is, but they see things as if we are *puttane* – excuse me for this term. And, obviously, that bothers me because I am not here to do certain services, but [I am here] to dance, entertain the person, and let the person have fun, but not like *that*. Those are the things that bother me: when I am treated as a sordid person. That is it.

Like Mirca, Fiona's tone betrayed a noticeable crescendo of rage as she recounted the above. Her irritation, I suggest, indexes the pressures that she has to handle in maintaining a distinction that does not appear to hold equally in many male customers' eyes. By their demands, in fact, the latter seemingly consider her to be a woman who does provide 'certain services' (i.e. extras) and who is, therefore, a prostitute.

Against this background, the supportive mother figure that she initially deployed to dignify her work choice could impress a straight, respectable woman as I must have been in her eyes. Being the same person who raised Fiona to be so modest that she refused to stand naked even in front of her, the mother's advice to use her beauty smartly could not be unseemly, could it? However, in Fiona's workplace, the boundary that she draws between clean and dirty interactions and people seemingly dissolves. There, she is employed to be available to men on demand, whereby her subjection to the whore stigma is embedded in her very employment contract. As already observed for Mirca, though, Fiona's displacement of the stigma onto women selling sex contributes to reproducing the affectivity of this disciplinary device, sparing no woman. This, as I show next, evoked a panoptical gaze (Foucault 1977) from which the women could never find a safe enough shelter.

'Just an Image'

I interviewed Lina at the beginning of her shift, at an early hour when she and her colleagues still outnumbered customers by far. Italian, she started working as a lap dancer several years before while in higher education. Initially, she covered her living expenses through a weekend pub job. During one of those nights, she was approached by

> the man who would have become my manager for a while. He told me: 'You are a beautiful girl. If you want, you can make much more money than you make here.' And so, he introduced me to this world, which until then I had only seen on TV. So, I tried it, and I started to see this job's positive side – [high] earnings – which is why everyone does it. And I stayed on.

Lina's tone was flat as she described her decision to work as a lap dancer as a smart choice, akin to a 'high risk – high gain' investment. Her words echoed the particular Western, neoliberal discourse locating rationality in the market and savvy in the entrepreneurial, risk-taking and flexible self (Brown 2005; Pollack and Rossiter 2010), which finds its female declination in the figure of the modern 'sexual entrepreneur' (L. Harvey and Gill 2011).

Lina continued: 'Already with the money that I was earning during weekends (which was a lot), I thought, "you know what? I will try to buy a house!" So, I studied during the day, and at night, I came here to pay off the house loan.' Lina smiled and shrugged her shoulders as if to say that, while she was herself flabbergasted at the exceptionally high economic return on her lap dancing work, taking advantage of the chest of gold that she seemingly effortlessly embodied was 'normal' – not 'deviant' – behaviour. Indeed, her capacity to have access to a house mortgage on her own and at such a young age was remarkable. Achieving that, in fact, required matching an elusive, almost magic formula consisting of having (1) landed a permanent job at a time of increasing job precarity (Istat 2012, 124–26); (2) parents who can help with or entirely put forward the initial deposit and act as guarantors at a time of increasing erosion of private assets (Istat 2012, 144–46), and (3) an ideally opposite-sex partner also in permanent employment, for the extra financial stability guaranteed from being in a dual-earner relationship.[7] As a result, very few young people are 'mortgageable', and Lina was one of them. At that point, I asked Lina her age – just to gauge how exceptional her achievement was. 'Thirty-five', she said giggling, 'and now I am buying another one!'

Scholars have observed that sometimes some lap dancers (Colosi 2010, 64–65) and sex workers (Chapkis 1997, 104) tactfully inflate their earnings to provide outsiders with a socially acceptable and rational justification for their choice to perform a stigmatized job. Yet, during my fieldwork, I observed that this sought-after normalizing effect appeared to function only to a certain extent and up to a certain threshold. So, although I expected Lina to appreciate my congratulations on her truly stunning achievements, the awe I admittedly clumsily expressed ('Wow! That is really loads of money!') triggered the opposite reaction. 'Unfortunately, this is not a normal job', she lamented, displaying a suddenly sombre facial expression. Then she relaxed her arms, which had been hugging her shoulders partly to keep herself warm in that chilled night and partly, perhaps, because she was being defensive. Concomitantly, Lina's eyes invited me to follow her hands as they moved down her body and the revealing costume holding it. 'It is not easy to have a private life', she uttered disconsolately, 'I speak for myself – and I am Italian – but it is difficult to find a boyfriend who allows you to be [dressed] like this in front of strangers.'

As Lina's abrupt tone switch suggests, balancing her use of sexuality for work with her status as an honourable woman required continued adjustments and shifts between multiple discursive repertoires and subject positions. In this process, her work revenues switched from constituting the worthy materialization of her smart, entrepreneurial self to a hard coin that she was earning at the cost of romance. Her remark on her nationality possibly indicates that she associated Italian-ness with open-mindedness and, more particularly, with that peculiar Western modernity characterized by market and sexual freedom intertwined. This interpretation may appear to be at odds with recreational pole dancers' self-identification as modern *despite* being Italian (Chapter 2). Yet, status definitions are always relational and situated. Hence, recreational pole dancers claimed their status as modern vanguards living in a bigoted country by comparing Italy to the contemporary beacon of Western modernity – that is, the US. Conversely, Lina's implicit referent likely was her migrant colleagues' countries of origin. These were generally post-socialist Eastern European countries, whose purportedly, relatively 'backwards' status is linked to their belated arrival into Western capitalist modernity after the 'end of history' (Fukuyama 1992) was (prematurely) proclaimed.

Nonetheless, Lina's words suggested, work and romance appeared incompatible even among the 'modern' Italians. 'But, as with many other things, how you make them should matter, shouldn't it?' she continued, arms crossed hugging her shoulders as if closing the ranks again in self-defence. 'There are people who work with the mind and people who work with the body. Here, we do not work with our bodies. Surely, the fundamental thing is our image; but to concede the body is something else.'

Taken literally, the boundary that Lina drew between lap dancers and 'people' who 'concede the body' – that is, people selling sex – is tenuous. In fact, workers cannot separate their labour from the body, which enables them to perform it in the first place: '[a] worker cannot send along capacities or services by themselves to an employer. The worker has to be present in the workplace if the capacities are to be "employed", to be put to use' (Pateman 2002, 33). Likewise, Lina's performance of the woman whom men enjoy watching, being in the company of and talking with – that is, the commodified 'image' that she provides them – is inescapably embodied. Yet, based on Wolkowitz's concept of body work (Wolkowitz 2006), her reasoning is sound: then, lap dancing is not sex work (unless a woman's performance of extras dissolves the boundaries between the two) but a service job like many others. Lina and many of her colleagues actually claimed that their job was better than some of these, because it could 'do good' for people (Frank 2002, 118–19; Price-Glynn 2010, 137). Hence, when I asked her its pros and cons, Lina shrugged her shoulders and said that she did not find any of the latter:

> It is like any other service job, isn't it? You are in contact with people. Everyone comes here for a reason – some customers occasionally come to have fun and get to know a girl; others come more frequently because they are alone all day long and need some company ... you often become a kind of psychologist,

more than a dancer. So, you try to entertain them both vividly with a dance break and by staying close to the person by giving him some comfort.

There and then, Lina's sympathy for male customers surprised me, for never before had I thought of night clubs as a space of emotional support and consolation. In hindsight, I realized that my reaction again betrayed the gendered stigma that I entertained for male customers and that likewise emerged during my dialogue with Miriam, in this chapter's initial vignette. However, what disoriented me the most was the effects of Lina's words on my position in the feminist sex wars' debate on boundaries in sex work (Chapter 4). 'But don't you end up taking a bit of their sadness home?' I asked her, in a gut expression of empathy. '*Nooooo! Noooo! Not at all!*' she repeated vehemently, almost shouting, as if the words I pronounced were an anathema. Simultaneously, she made a step back – as if wishing to distance herself from me, my words and the proximity these evoked – and explained that:

> As soon as I am out of here, I am no more interested in that! Any psychologist or doctor does the same. And anyway, a person who is very sick should go to the hospital. If you come here, all I can do is to tell you, 'You did the right thing; look at my two boobs, so you recover!'

Then Lina laughed wildly but briefly. Perhaps she thought she might have come across as coarse instead of smart. In fact, immediately after, she shook her body lightly, as if in the act of pulling herself together, and she added that she was '[j]ust joking, you know'.

Surely, Lina's comparison with other service workers, particularly those positively valued for their social utility, allowed her to occupy another position from where to claim her 'normality', as a worker and a woman, and, eventually, her humanity. Nonetheless, even that altruistic position was difficult to maintain, as it mirrored back to her an image of undesired intimacy with the men in the club.

The Power of Love

The tension between the women's work and romance that surfaced in Lina's interview recurred in the narratives of many of her colleagues. Women who did not have dependent children, like herself, appeared to handle it dispassionately: since their work obstructed their capacity to establish stable intimate relationships, the latter could wait until achievement of a satisfactory level of economic security. For others, however, its management was less straightforward.

Like Fiona, also Zeina – another Romanian woman, in her early thirties – started working in Italy as a lap dancer before her home country joined the EU:

> I finished high school in Romania, and I was looking for a job, but I could not find any. You know how it is like; it is the same everywhere. Everybody looks for people with some work experience, but you do not have any when you have just finished high school. So, nobody gave me a chance. One day, a friend told me, 'If you want to go to Italy, you can do lap dancing, and they will pay you so and so.' So, I said, 'Fine, I will go'. I was young, I was only eighteen, and I stayed with a very nice girl. I was lucky because some bad stories also happen.

Back in those days, as a Romanian citizen, Zeina could migrate to Italy for work reasons only if she had secured a contract prior to entering Italian territory.[8] Landing an employment contract, however, was already arduous enough an objective to meet for a freshly graduated woman in her home country, let alone in another country of which she did not even speak the language (yet). Against this backdrop, the market for female-to-male erotic entertainment, with its structural quest for 'novelty', offered her the opportunity to take on a temporary, irregular, precarious and stigmatized job that nonetheless was quite well-paid:

> In the beginning, everything was okay – [work brought me] fun, money, evenings out – even though I could not speak any Italian! Then, I met my husband (now ex-husband), but after three months, I had to go back to Romania because my [tourist] visa expired. I kept coming to do this job anyway because I loved him. Eventually, we got married, and he made me stop working. But things turned out for the worst, and so I returned to this job.

Italy's migration laws initially kept Zeina between a rock and a hard place. While she was able to keep coming back on tourist visas to cultivate her blooming romance, she could only afford to do so by sticking to her lap dancing job. Marriage with an Italian citizen allowed her to let go of this irregular and stigmatized occupation – although, more truthful to her words, this looked less a choice of her own making than her husband's. In fact, in this switch to the wife and (soon-to-be) mother position, Zeina lost her economic independence. When her marriage ended, she went back to the same job, as only this occupation allowed her to play both a caring and breadwinning role in her newly female-headed household – which now also included her mother, whom she brought from Romania to help her with childcare (Chapter 5):

> How much would I earn if I worked in a factory, a thousand Euros a month? I would never make it. Never. ... First of all, if I worked during the day, the money would not be enough; and secondly, I would not be able to spend the whole day with my son. So, I work while my son sleeps, and I stay with him during the day. My mother takes him to the kindergarten in the morning, and when he comes back, I am already awake.

Zeina's readiness to go back to working in a stigmatized but highly paid and cost-effective job for the love of her minor and adult dependents put her in the dignified position of the breadwinning single mother *and* daughter. Notably, the value in such a position appeared to be self-contained – it did not, that is, rest upon the displacement of the whore stigma onto another category of women. Zeina, however, regretted not having 'a family'. I thought that she did have one by the household arrangements she just described, so I asked her to tell me more about this lack. Listlessly, Zeina acknowledged that yes, of course, she did have a family, 'but it is not like sleeping every night at home with your husband ... it is a bit different, isn't it? I am happy because my son can always see me, and I can offer him and my mother anything that they want ... anything. But I lack that thing that girls here cannot have ... .'

The meaning of Zeina's words, I contend, exceeds their face value as a mourning for the romance that she could not live fully due to her job. Instead, their contrast with her deeds suggests that the 'thing that girls cannot have' is not one but two things: (1) having a stable intimate relationship with a man whilst (2) maintaining one's economic independence (also from him). I thus take Zeina's words as a firm statement of self-reliance from within the intersecting structural constraints that her gender and nationality have thrown upon her.

I was about to close the interview and thank her for the (working) time that she had generously given me when I suddenly saw her eyes light up and follow something happening right behind my back. As I turned, I saw a group of young men walk down the stairs and then head towards the club's doors. One of them smiled at Zeina, and they seemed enthralled by each other. As soon as they slipped through the door, she unexpectedly offered that, actually, she did

> like this job. It is never dull. Never. You also find nice people; it is not [true] that everyone [male patrons] here is a bastard and ignorant. You also find people with interesting experiences, who come here, let us say, to forget some bad ones; normal people you meet during stag parties. Actually, I had an affair with a guy who came to the club. All the customers say, 'Ah, you are made of stone, you girls are very cold.' But it is not true; we also have feelings. If I see a handsome guy, I can fall in love [with him] even if I am here; it is a very normal thing.

'But *work* is *work*, isn't it?!' I partly asked and partly exclaimed, feeling disoriented again, as my mind kept returning to the role that metaphors of separation play in workers' resistance to capitalist-imposed alienation from their labour (Wolkowitz 2006, 25–26) and sex workers' rights advocacy (Chapter 4). 'Work is work, but it can happen. Trust me: it can happen', she said with dreamy eyes,

> because also young men come [to the club]. Maybe he ended up here by chance, with his friends, and you immediately see that he is not a regular, that he is a decent guy, beautiful, who speaks well … it is normal that you fall in love. And this makes this job even more complicated, because if you fall in love with a man who comes here, then it is over … . If he comes in and I am working with someone else, I cannot continue, I lose my mind, and I cannot work anymore [she smiled]. Love exists in this job too. It exists. And this is beautiful. Yes.

Rather than signalling a problematic overlap between the spheres of work and intimacy (Chapter 4), Zeina's admission that she felt love at work afforded her a dignified subject position from which to resist the gendered stigma that she is arguably paid to endure. Hers is not a tale of redemption, akin to a 'Pretty Woman' fantasy (Egan 2006, 64), where a Prince Charming comes to the rescue of the 'bad' woman.[9] In a workspace that mandates her alienation from her feelings, Zeina's statement is a surrender to the power of love; a form of resistance taking the shape of a claim of inalienable sovereignty over them. It is a claim to be a 'normal' (i.e. not 'deviant'), full-fledged human. Akin to Filipina migrant women working as hostesses and entertainers in Japan, whose 'professions of love' for their regulars conveyed 'a sense of humanity, countering the stigma associated with their work in bars' (Faier 2007, 149), Zeina's capacity to feel love at work dignified her as a worker, a human and a woman – in no particular order.

Keeping Afloat

Notwithstanding the stigma, the economic security that lap dancing jobs afforded women seemingly constituted an anchor in stormy waters. Akin to Lina, Eleonora (Chapter 2) and other women I encountered and/or interviewed, also Milena – a Spanish woman in her late thirties – started working in female-to-male erotic entertainment whilst in higher education. After graduation, she 'stopped and got normal jobs', particularly white-collar occupations. In between them, she sometimes tapped into her erotic entertainment experience to buffer unemployment. However, the 2007–08 financial crisis had a devastating impact on the Spanish labour market, and like many others, she lost her job to the company's downsizing.

> So, one day, I looked in the mirror and told myself, 'You can still do it, you still have the body for that, you can!' When you go back to this job as an adult who has studied ... I have a degree, I had nice jobs ... but eventually, I am not crying out and about. I earn my money.

Milena thus resumed performing erotic shows across Europe, while, back in Spain, her mother cared for her child (Chapter 5). Still, she observed with some concern that this time her career switch appeared to be less temporary than at other times in her life. By then it was already a few months since this had become her only source of revenue – an unprecedented situation, reflecting the depth of unemployment at the time.[10]

Milena's erring between 'normal' jobs and 'non-' indexes the 'constant entrepreneurialism or on-the-make-ness' newly characterizing the life of many in several Western late capitalist countries (Berlant 2010).[11] This haunting precarity engenders a spiralling race to the bottom, pushing some people to move in multiple directions just to keep afloat. While Milena was describing her temporary work arrangements in gentlemen's clubs in the UK and France, I wondered what made Italy – a country that was similarly engulfed by the economic crisis[12] – an appealing destination. She answered my question before I could put it into words. 'In Spain, you cannot do this job now because there is prostitution', she said. Then she turned and directed my attention to a group of young women standing at the bar counter and chatting with some male customers. The women's looks – green and blue hair, tattooed arms, face piercings – stood out to me as quite unconventional vis-à-vis their colleagues in the club that night, and yet were quite ordinary among their peers outside of its walls. 'You see those Spanish girls who are here tonight?' Milena asked me,

> Some have finished their higher education but cannot find a job; others maybe need one more year to finish. So, they come here to work for a month and make some money. Instead, in Spain, the only option to earn money fast is prostitution. If a man in Spain pays fifty euros to fuck, why would he spend that money only to watch a naked woman dancing?! However, here in Italy, there is a chance to get fifty euros only to strip.

Some scholars have discussed the impact of the financial crisis on the Spanish sex market. Like in Italy (Chapter 1), a few news outlets also reported that women who had never sold sex before started doing so, in a context characterized by deteriorating working conditions in the erotic and sex markets

(Piscitelli 2020, 285). 'Now there is internet [pornography], but not fifteen years ago', Milena continued, 'in these clubs you would earn loads of money! It was impressive. But now, nothing. People outside [the erotic entertainment market] think that we earn a lot, and they cannot believe it is not true. Obviously, we earn more than supermarket cashiers, but … people have priorities, and this is the last one of them.' In order to navigate this downward spiral, Milena and her Spanish colleagues set themselves on the move to negotiate a better economic return on their labour – better in some respects but not all. Indeed, when seen from another perspective, the Italian female-to-male erotic entertainment scene was far from ideal. Whereas in London and Paris Milena's work was 'more respectable, and nobody touches you even slightly', in Italy, she said, lowering her voice to almost a whisper, 'customers come to have fun in a more … sexual way. And they are older!' she exclaimed, laughing. She also found her colleagues' average profile to be quite different: whereas in the UK they mainly consisted of higher education students, like she herself once was, she observed that

> For many in Italy, it [lap dancing] is a job for life. Here girls do not bother studying and doing other things afterwards or finding another job. Here they are concerned with finding a man with money [she laughs]. They have no beginning, no end, no purpose – like 'I do it for this reason.' No [it is like]: 'I do it as a job as long as I can, and when I no longer can, I marry an old man.'

Milena's words conveyed some scorn for colleagues lacking in vision and ambition. Underneath her self-dignification narrative, there echoed some disapproval for women remaining forever economically dependent on men – whether as erotic entertainers or (house)wives. Her self-reliance and resilience against all the odds were so valuable to her that she made sure that I got that right before parting ways. A customer had come out to look for her – impatient for her prolonged break in my company – and she held him off by saying that she was just on her way. As soon as the club's doors closed behind his back, she asked me, 'What message do you want to get across with your research?' Admittedly, I was then still quite too far out in the woods to be able to offer something even tenuously bright, torn as I was between too many conflicting narratives and theoretical positions. 'There is so much moralizing around sex work …', I vaguely uttered, 'for example, I would like to show that it can be a rational response to poverty and insecurity and … .' 'No, no, no', she reprimanded me, gently but firmly, 'it is not just about poverty. Many women choose to do this job because they have a precise goal to achieve in two- or three-years' time. They know that this job is tough, but they also know that they will do it only for a while.' Then she smiled, said goodbye and went back into the club – back to work.

Conclusions

In this chapter, I have discussed how women who worked (or had worked) as female-to-male erotic entertainers in Italian night clubs negotiated the tension between sexuality and status, which lies at the core of their employment contract. Women worked in contexts where their ability to commodify pleasurable feelings for male customers' consumption was simultaneously valued and feared. It was both a 'resource', generating high revenues, and a 'curse' (Zambelli 2018), as it intensified their subjection to the whore stigma. They were despised for being women who were 'only after the money'; expected to be ready to provide 'extras' on-demand and criticized for being 'too cold' and with 'a heart of stone' for maintaining – as their job required – strict boundaries in their interaction with male customers. Against this backdrop, the chapter illustrated some of the most recurring narrative repertoires that women mobilized in front of me – an outsider, a straight woman and a 'nosey' female researcher – to handle these pressures and claim dignity and value through or despite their work.

Some women's respectability tactics resembled recreational pole dance entrepreneurs and/or instructors' (Chapter 2). They normalized their occupation via its desexualization, suggesting that theirs was an ordinary service job, with an added healing potential. Many claimed respect by more or less explicitly stating that they were doing 'nothing wrong', thereby alluding that others did: colleagues selling 'extras' and, more broadly, sex working women. Effectively, therefore, they sought to displace the whore stigma onto another category of women who are similarly, albeit perhaps more fatefully, stigmatized for their commodification of sexuality. However, this tactic was not the only one at the women's disposal. Some women managed the whore stigma by stressing their constrained choice in contexts characterized by high unemployment and restrictive migratory regimes, while others claimed value in their breadwinner position. In so doing, some occupied a self-contained dignified subject position – one that did not rely upon nor reproduce othering processes. Others found pride in their rejection of a fate of economic dependency from a man.

Unlike recreational pole dancers, the women working in this sexscape were both Italian and migrant. Perhaps the mixed nature of their work environment prevented the fissure of their respectability and self-dignification narratives along racialized lines. After all, the women were all subjected to similar work pressures – albeit from different social locations (Chapter 5).

In the next chapter, the journey of the whore stigma reaches the last sexscape included in this book, where work the women whom recreational pole dancers and lap dancers most dreaded to be identified with. It is, then, a chapter about sex working women and sex workers.

Notes

1. Having a threesome with two women seemingly recurs in contemporary accounts of heterosexual men's top fantasies, see, for example, Sarah Young (2018).
2. Even within these countries, in fact, the spatial distribution of these erotic entertainment venues is highly uneven, reflecting local geographies of heterosexism and homophobia (Hubbard 2000b; Kitchin and Lysaght 2003; Hubbard et al. 2008; Bailey and Shabazz 2014).
3. In her ethnography of flight attendants, Arlie Hochschild coined the concept of 'emotional labour' to describe 'the management of feeling to create a publicly observable facial and bodily display' (Hochschild 2003, 7). Other scholars have subsequently described the key characteristics of emotional labour as consisting of (1) the requirement of 'face to face or voice to voice contact with the public'; (2) the requirement for workers 'to produce an emotional state in another person (i.e. client or customer)' and (3) employers' capacity 'to exercise a degree of control over the emotional activities of employees' through 'training and supervision' (De Castro, Agnew and Fitzgerald 2004, 109). The concept of emotional labour has engendered extensive bodies of sociological and psychological research on service occupations; for a review, see Alicia Grandey, James Diefendorff and Deborah Rupp (2013).
4. In Italy, in January 2015, the minimum hourly wage was 8,5 euros.
5. Art. 3.2 of the Merlin Law criminalizes 'whoever owns or administers a house or another venue and rents it out with the purpose of opening a tolerance house'; Art. 3.3 criminalizes 'whoever is the owner, manager or person in charge of a hotel, furnished house, boarding house, bar, club, dance or show venue, or their annexes, or any other venue open to or used by the public and habitually tolerates the presence of one or more persons who undertake prostitution within that venue.'
6. Even though men and non-binary subjects also work in the erotic entertainment industry, women still constitute the bulk of the workforce in this sector. Moreover, male-to-female strippers do not experience the same kind of stigmatization that their female colleagues face. In fact, under some respect, men's performance of sexuality in front of a group of desiring women positively confirms and reproduces their male identity. Therefore, the same behaviour that is labelled 'promiscuous' and 'deviant' for women may constitute a valued element of their 'hegemonic masculinity' (Connell and Messerschmidt 2005).
7. At the time of the interview, same-sex unions were not recognized by law (Chapter 1), so they unlikely counted as stable partnerships for mortgage assessment purposes.
8. The Treaty of Accession between the EU member states and Bulgaria and Romania (2005; entered into force on 1 January 2007) allowed the temporary restriction of the latter's citizens to the EU labour market for a maximum transitional period of seven years (European Commission 2011). Not all EU member states enacted these intra-EU mobility restrictions, but Italy did, and they were still in place at the time of my fieldwork.
9. The reference here is to the American romantic movie *Pretty Woman* (Marshall 1990), starring Richard Gere and Julia Roberts in the roles of the wealthy businessman and the sex worker, respectively. During the movie, their relationship transitions from work, based on Julia's paid performance of his girlfriend for a week, to romance.
10. In the last trimester of 2012, Spain's unemployment rate rose 'to 26%, or 5.97 million people. This figure, which is the highest since the mid-1970s, follows Spain's prolonged recession and deep spending cuts' (BBC News 2013).

11. The perception of this condition as 'new' and 'unprecedented' reflects the post-Second World War prosperity and employment stability characterizing for some decades the life of many people in Western countries. However, such makeshift self-entrepreneurialism has always been part of the livelihood strategies of marginalized population groups such as, for example, refugees (Field, Tiwari and Mookherjee 2020) and people working in the informal sector (Evangelista et al. 2020).
12. In 2012, Italy's official unemployment rate was 10.7%. Additionally, there also were 11.6% 'so-called "discouraged" workers – that is, people who were not actively looking for work' (Jones 2013).

Chapter 4

WOMEN SELLING SEX

When I approached the association that I would eventually volunteer for in their street sex working women's outreach service, I was fresh from my readings on the Western feminists' 'sex wars'. Against the radical feminist and abolitionist position that women in prostitution are structurally victims of sexual violence and exploitation (see e.g. Dworkin 1993; Farley 2004; MacKinnon 2011; Bindel 2017), I aligned with sex workers and sex radical feminists' position that adults who consensually sell sex are agentic subjects, albeit from within constraining conditions not of their choosing (see e.g. Chapkis 1997; Kempadoo and Doezema 1998; Doezema 2001; Agustín 2007; Weitzer 2010; Kotiswaran 2011; Grant 2014; Smith and Mac 2018). Nevertheless, my engagement with this debate was exclusively theoretical, and in hindsight, I had to accept that, unexpectedly (to me), my position at that time was quite liberal and contractarian. I used to overemphasize individual agency over structures, and as a result, I could not reconcile my notion of 'choice' with the compellingly hard material constraints under which most people sell sex for a living (Smith and Mac 2018). However, once I got into the field, I could not help but develop a more grounded and nuanced synthesis of these positions.

I met Luisa at 8 PM in the parking lot where the mobile outreach van was stationed. In her sixties, she was a senior volunteer with strong contacts among the sex working cis and trans women. Since the women were overwhelmingly migrants (Chapters 1; 5), our main objective was to share practical information on how to access sexual and reproductive health services based on their nationality/citizenship (i.e. EU or non-EU) and migration status (i.e. un/documented).[1] Luisa arrived carrying the work tools that we needed for the night – boxes of safer sex items, hot tea and coffee thermoses and the mobile phone that a colleague would call to check in with us at regular intervals to ensure that we were safe. We put the material within easy reach on the back seats. Luisa switched on the phone, I turned on the van engine, and we started our night shift.

While I had never stepped into a night club before undertaking this research (Chapter 3), the streets where people negotiate the sale of sex are public spaces that anyone can potentially walk or drive through at any time of the day or night. In some sense, then, they are accessible, perhaps even familiar spaces. However, they transfigure once we look at them as work sites. As we reached the city's outskirts, the web of arterial roads and secondary streets connecting motorways, industrial zones and agricultural fields that in the daytime was abuzz with factory and agricultural workers had turned into an outdoor sex marketplace. There and then, any cis or trans woman stationing on the side of the street was quite likely at work. The luckiest ones were under or in the proximity of a streetlight – making women more visible to potential customers; allowing them to screen the latter better in the initial approach stage, and more broadly enabling them to practice higher levels of street-savvy. There were, though, more women than streetlights, so some were stationed in the shadows, and their silhouette emerged so late that, at times, we could no longer stop the van safely and had to make a U-turn to reach them. Few enjoyed the privilege of stationing on a pavement – those streets were made to be traversed by motor vehicles only, not to walk along or stand by.

The night was as cold as an ordinary winter night can be, with a looming threat of frost. In some respects, however, it was quite an exceptional one. It was the 23 December – the night before Christmas Eve – and compared to the usual bustle, this semi-urban landscape suddenly looked emptied of women and cars. Perhaps in the festive season men were spending more time at home with their families and more money on gifts to them, rather than going out to buy sex for their only pleasure. If that was the case, many women were likely and purposefully staying at home as well – lest they risked being out all night in that freezing cold to earn hardly the money to pay the taxi back to their accommodation. As we drove in the dark, I noticed longer-than-usual stretches of road between a working woman and the next. Suddenly, I sensed all the dread of standing on those streets and the compelling nature of the needs underpinning such a difficult, hazardous and constrained choice.

We spotted Stefania at the crossroad where she was normally stationed. This consistency, which may have reflected her relatively senior status on the street, enabled her to nurture relationships with potentially regular customers – as the men would know where to find her if they so wished. On this particular night, Stefania was with a new colleague, Ileana, who was Romanian like her and also seemingly as young (early twenties). Stefania cheered us up with more spark than usual, as if we were friends coming to pay her a visit after a long absence. Excited, she leaned through the car window to show us a picture of her and her husband's new puppy, and we complimented her on its cuteness. Then, Luisa asked whether her husband had found a job 'at last'. Stefania shrugged her shoulders and said that he had not. Evidently, her sex work revenues supported the livelihood of them both, and I knew that Luisa and other volunteers considered such spousal arrangement as evidence that theirs was no 'genuine' marriage and that it somewhat disguised some forms of sexual exploitation. That was both possible and impossible to know from our outsider position.[2] Still, I took note that Stefania's husband was Romanian himself, and in Italy's highly gendered and racialized labour market, there were few jobs that he could realistically aim for, while the construction sector that typically employed many Eastern European male migrants was at a standstill following the 2007–08 crisis.

After the new puppy, Stefania started chatting about the many Christmas gifts she was receiving from her regulars: white gold and yellow gold earrings, necklaces, Swarovski. 'And it is just the beginning!' she giggled. Then she spoke of something else, but I was not really listening, for in my mind I began wondering why Stefania was throwing one conversation starter after another, like on a rushing stream. Perhaps, I thought, we were an entertaining distraction in the emptiness of a slow and cold working night. Meanwhile, Ileana stood silent throughout our chatter, her eyes steady on the street and the few vehicles passing by.

At some point, I saw a car approaching from the rear-view mirror. It stopped just a couple of meters behind our van. Two men sat in the front seats, and that was all I could see. I thought that one of the two women would go and speak with them, but they did not. Instead, Ileana moved closer to Stefania and turned her back on them. Shielded by her colleague, Stefania leaned in the window and asked us to please stay until the car left because they were scared. She explained that she recently got spooked after seeing a man unexpectedly jumping from a car. 'You have to be very careful at Christmas time because people have little money, and we are at risk of robbery', she explained (ICRSE 2020, 16).

I cannot say how much time went by before that car made a U-turn and left, but it felt awfully long. After all, we were four women out at night, in the middle of nowhere, and even if we had called for help, realistically it would have taken too long to arrive to spare us an assault. Throughout, Stefania did not stop one minute chatting with us. However, her tone and tales had turned gloomy. She lamented that her father kept spending all her remittances on alcohol and said that he was physically abusive with his wife – her mother. Disconsolately, Stefania added that the latter had tried a few times to leave him but eventually stayed, fearing that she would be labelled 'a *puttana*' had she deserted the marital home (Pheterson 1996, 15). I did not know, nor did I ever ask, whether her mother knew that she sold sex (also) to support them. Other scholars, however, observed that there is often a tacit 'do not ask do not tell' agreement between the women and their families (Andrijasevic 2010, 102).

As soon as the sinister car left, the women moved away from our van and regained their street visibility. Stefania retrieved some of her cheerfulness and started teasing Luisa. Since they had become 'like mother and daughter', why not make that tie official? 'So you can then put your inheritance in my name!', she exclaimed. We all laughed loudly, yet there was something in Stefania's joke that did not entirely sound like one. As economic necessity drove her to that dangerous work and place, and a wish to 'help' women in her position drove the associations' volunteers there, what would effective 'help' look like?

Both women kept switching their eyes from us in the van to the street whilst moving sideways to keep warm on that freezing winter night. 'And if I meet a man richer than my husband, I will marry him', Stefania proclaimed, 'for love passes through one's belly, right?' She then told us of a recent conversation she had had with one of her regulars after one of his recurrent professions of love for her. 'Are you rich?' she asked him. He was bewildered. 'He said, "Are you asking it for real?!" and I told him, "Yes, I will not marry you if you are not rich."' Then Stefania gave Luisa and me a frank look, stretched her arms wide open and shrugged her shoulders, as if to say there was nothing left to be said, that it was very much normal to think this way, and she was just being honest in saying it out loud. 'What does marriage consist of, after all?' she added. And as her question worked its way inside me, it shifted shape into belly cramps.

****

Stefania and Ileana are two out of an unknown number of Italian and migrant cis and trans women selling sex in Italy – outdoor or indoor, regularly or occasionally, as a primary or side occupation. As such, they embody the archetype of the unchaste woman that most recreational pole dancers and lap dancers dreaded to be identified with. This chapter, then, discusses how women whose sale of sex structurally subjects them to the whore stigma claim value and dignity through or despite their work. Doing so requires delving deeper into the analysis of the relations of power among women, for which this chapter's opening vignette provides an entry point.

Class profoundly shaped the position of the four women in it. As a start, Luisa and I – the two non-sex working women – enjoyed a privileged position affording us to be in the van, rather than outside. Moreover, albeit unpaid volunteers, we still occupied a self-ascribed 'helping' position akin to the 'new employment sphere' that middle-class women created for themselves over two centuries ago 'through the naming of a project to rescue and control working-class women' (Agustín 2007, 8). 'Rescue' coincided with the discipline of women into docile female subjects who would be good servants and, as such, functional to the reproduction of the social order and the prosperity of the family and the nation (Skeggs 1997). Against this background, Stefania's tease that Luisa should adopt her so that she can become her heir puts in stark relief the gap existing between the soft 'help' that we (the women in the van) could offer and the compelling material needs pushing the women to be out on the street.

From a gender perspective, though, the differences between the four of us were less vivid and rather blurred along a continuum of degrees of subjection to the whore stigma and experience of its hazardous effects. In fact, in the particular situation portrayed in this chapter's opening vignette, we were all exposed to the threat of male violence. Moreover, the law would have unlikely been on our side had an incident happened. Under the gaze of the state enforcement apparatus and the media, we would have surely been put on the block for 'having taken it on ourselves', being as we were women out at night 'alone' – that is, without men – and in a remote and deserted place. Victim blaming in Italy is, in fact, recurrent and almost endemic (Zambelli, Mainardi and Hajek 2018; Hajek 2018).[3] Moreover, albeit physically absent, the thought of Stefania's mother was haunting – her resignation to endure life with her abusive husband attesting to the vicious and polymorphous productivity of the whore stigma.

However, there was another way in which class may have shaped the subjectivities of the four women in the vignette, and it lies in the different views that we held on the relationship between intimacy and money. Stefania's tease that Luisa should adopt her reflects how kinship plays an increasingly pivotal role in the intergenerational transmission of wealth or destitution (Piketty 2014). Nevertheless, it was her 'view from the belly' on marriage that struck me the most. Looking back at my intimate relationships with men, I could not recall having ever attributed any importance to their financial assets, nor marriage. So, when Stefania bluntly stated that it was not romance but money that made marriage both possible and desirable to her, I suddenly realized the extent to which my indifference to this contract indexed (also) my economic privilege. In that epiphany, I recognized within me the workings of what Viviana Zelizer famously conceptualized as the Western cultural norm positing that intimacy and the market belong to two 'separate spheres and hostile worlds' (Zelizer 2005, 20).

As this chapter shows next, this normative, albeit imaginary separation plays a central role in feminist debates on the nature and regulation of prostitution, involving scholars, activists and sex workers (the three being sometimes overlapping categories). Its deconstruction matters, I contend, to find ways to resolve the tension between women's sexuality and status in ways that do not reproduce the patriarchal division of women into 'good' or 'bad', which the whore stigma regulates and reproduces. Subsequently, the chapter discusses these tensions empirically, drawing from the field notes annotated during my nights out on outreach service and the interviews with self-identified current or former sex workers. Against the normative view of work and intimacy as two discreet spheres, it will foreground the meanings and effects of their 'connectedness' (Zelizer 2005) and the role of boundaries in the women's lives.

Separate or Entangled Spheres?

The Western cultural norm juxtaposing love and money, emotions and calculus, intimacy and the market reflects what Viviana Zelizer epitomized as the 'twin ideas of "separate spheres and hostile worlds": distinct arenas for economic activity and intimate relations, with inevitable contamination and disorder resulting when the two spheres come into contact with each other' (Zelizer 2005, 20–21). This view gained strength in the nineteenth century in the context of the dramatic social transformations brought about by rising industrial capitalism (Zelizer 2005, 24). Against the cold, impersonal instrumentality of the market, where men sold their labour, the home was imagined as a space of respite and nurture (Wilson 2012, 41) – a shelter from commodification (O'Connell Davidson 2014, 518), wherein relationships were based on reciprocity rather than self-interest. Hence, intimacy signified both a space (i.e. the home) and the affects producing and involving its subjects through acts, emotions, attachments and orientations. However, as Marxist feminist political theorists (Federici 1975; Bhattacharya 2017) and economists (Folbre 1994; Elson 1998) have amply shown, the imagery of the home as a site of rest and leisure reflected a particularly gendered experience of consumption. It was, in fact, premised on the structural invisibilization of the work that women put into making it available as such. The signification of women's care work as an 'effortless' expression of their 'natural' dispositions rather than a pool of economically significant activities was a keystone in the scaffolding of this normative view.

The home was also discursively constructed as the shell of 'respectable' sexuality, which ought to be heterosexual, reproductive in purpose and gratuitous. Prostitution was intrinsically at odds with this imagined separation, as the sale of sex symbolically and materially transgressed its containment within the sphere of intimacy and the home. The ensuing social disapproval for this trade, however, was unequally distributed. In a context where the cultivation of men's heterosexual orientation clashed with female chastity norms, a class of abject female workers (McClintock 1995) emerged to meet the needs of the former – in times of war and peace alike – without spoiling 'good' women's virtue (Chapter 1). Some men also exchanged sex acts with other men in more or less explicit return for money, gifts and/or other types of rewards, but these 'sexual-economic exchanges'[4] were dangerously dysfunctional in the moral and political economy of heteronormativity. Thus, there lacked the material conditions for the development of a class of male prostitutes. Today, people selling sex are prevalently women (Smith and Mac 2018, 4), and they remain highly stigmatized for their work.

Female prostitution occupies a central position in the Western feminist debates on the role of sexuality in women's oppression and liberation (Chapkis 1997) – that is, the so-called 'feminist sex wars'.[5] At their core ran the juxtaposition of sexuality as fundamentally dangerous due to the patriarchal structures under which women lead their lives and as 'a domain of exploration, pleasure, and agency' (Vance 1984b, 1). Pornography and prostitution were the wars' two main battlefields, and the latter became 'a central trope. The prostitute [came] to function as both the most literal of sexual slaves and as the most subversive of sexual agents within a sexist social order' (Chapkis 1997, 12).

Radical feminists and abolitionists conceive the prostitution of women as the 'cornerstone' of 'institutionalized sex [sic] inequality' between men and women (MacKinnon 2011, 273). They posit that sex should express mutual desire only (MacKinnon 2011, 281) and conceive its commodification as intrinsically harmful for women, contributing to the material and symbolic reproduction of an oppressive patriarchal order. For Carole Pateman, the social contract that Western political theorists imagine as being the foundational covenant marking the shift from the state of nature to organized societies is a 'sexual contract' sanctioning women's structural subordination to men (Pateman 1988). To be a man in 'modern patriarchy', she argued, means having the right to appropriate women's domestic and sexual labour through contracts of marriage (providing both) and prostitution (providing the latter only). Although Pateman acknowledged both contracts to be sources of livelihood and economic security for women (Pateman 1988, 132; 195), she maintained that the symbolic value of prostitution ought to override its material significance: 'When women's bodies are on sale as commodities in the capitalist market, the terms of the original [sexual] contract cannot be forgotten; the law of male sex-right is publicly affirmed, and men gain public acknowledgment as women's sexual masters – that is what is wrong with prostitution' (Pateman 1988, 209). The marriage contract, though, is spared similar indictment, notwithstanding its material and symbolic role in the reproduction of the very same oppressive patriarchal order.

From the opposing perspective, sex radical feminists reclaimed the 'whore' as the most powerful symbol of political subversion. Differently from 'domesticated women [who] don't dare put a price on their time', they conceive the 'whore' as fully cognisant and in control of the value of her time and sexuality (Pat Califia quoted in Chapkis 1997, 30). For sex libertarians, the women '*rule*; they are in total control', and men's use of money is 'a confession of weakness [because] they have to buy women's attention' (Camille Paglia quoted in Chapkis 1997, 22).

Hence, although for sex working people prostitution is first and foremost an economic activity, the feminist sex wars pivoted on its symbolic value instead and specifically its impact on the reproduction or subversion of the gender relations of power between men and women. Prostitution was thus mainly discussed 'as a site of metaphor' more than 'an actual workplace' (Smith and Mac 2018, 2). On this abstract plane, notions such as 'choice' and 'coercion' could stand in a relation of mutual opposition. Nevertheless, as foregrounded in this chapter's opening vignette, women's entry into either prostitution or marriage cannot be detached from compelling material concerns – although the latter may be concealed behind a discursively purified intimate sphere (Zelizer 2005). By claiming the primacy of the material over the symbolic, then, sex workers demand that their work is recognized as a form of labour that ought to be performed in safety and dignity (see e.g. NSWP 2013; ICRSE 2020; TAMPEP 2021). The use of the term 'sex work' (versus prostitution) semantically realigns this activity within the totality of 'work' (by which I mean a person's exchange of labour for money); work that most people across the globe undertake under the coercion of need rather than in fulfilment of their 'free choice' (Doezema 1998). Perhaps, in an ideal world of perfect equality people would be able to choose their occupation based on preference and ability (Phillips 2013, 154). However, in the world as it is, the very possibility of this choice is rather often 'a significant class-marker' (Smith and Mac 2018, 40).

The normative, imagined separation between intimacy and the market, therefore, reflects the position of a particular (versus universal) and privileged subject. This trope is also harmful to women, in more than one way. Historically, it is indeed women who have been and largely remain disproportionately in charge of performing the work that sustains its imagination by providing unpaid care work within their household and paid care work in someone else's (Ehrenreich and Hochschild 2004).[6] Women also constitute the largest group of people who transgress it by selling sex, and who have borne the brunt of the stigma attached to this trade. As the rest of this chapter and the next (Chapter 5) will show, for the migrant cis and trans women I met on the street, these two spheres were intricately entangled, making their imagination as separate a phenomenological impossibility (Zambelli 2019). Against this backdrop, I now move on to discuss how sex working women and sex workers claimed value through or despite their work.

Bittersweet Fruits

'Work is not going well. Actually, it is not going', commented Stefania, when the colleague in outreach service with me that night asked her how she was doing. 'Every day, I have more and more expenses', she pensively continued, 'I am consumed by this a lot when I have so many things to pay, and I cannot sleep at night.' Her work revenues ought to sustain both her nuclear family in Italy – her unemployed husband – and her family of origin in Romania, where high inflation rates had eroded her family members' salaries and pensions' purchasing power. 'Today, my brother sent me a text that made me cry', she continued, 'he said they have not eaten in the last two days.'

In Stefania's words, the market and intimacy are intensely interconnected spheres that she cannot afford to imagine as separate. Anguish, love and exploitation blended in her account of the burdensome, everyday material and emotional responsibilities she has to endure as the breadwinner for her multilocal and transnational family. Several scholars have highlighted the ambivalent needs, demands and desires informing the relationship between sex working women and their families. Prompted to the job by economic deprivation, their revenues support a large web of dependents (Brennan 2004, 123) but are also a gateway to higher consumption (Oso-Casas 2010, 53; Oso 2018, 113–14) and may engender some family members' abusive expectations (Piscitelli 2020, 289). Livelihood concerns thus interplay with status and social mobility aspirations, deepening the women's reliance on sex work.

Women's emotional and economic ties to their family members ambivalently appeared to be a source of additional strain they had to endure and pride for the fruits that their hard work allowed them all to enjoy. Stagnating unemployment, high inflation and the presence of minor and adult dependents often constituted the dire backdrop against which women narrated the reasons why they were in Italy selling sex on the street. The forcefulness of the material needs pushing them to that place and position, and the lack of viable *and* financially equivalent alternatives, recurred in the conversations we had while on the mobile unit. For example, when I met Ana, she had just arrived in Italy on a tourist visa. After I presented the mobile unit services, she disclosed fear of contracting a sexual infection and asked whom to approach for a health check. Perhaps it was the sudden intimacy of this conversation between strangers that prompted her to say that she frequently cried at night repeating to herself that she was a prostitute. 'I do not like it here', she said. Then, possibly in anticipation of a question or objection that she thought that we – the privileged women in the van – might have raised, she immediately added that she knew that she 'could try to work as a *badante* (live-in care worker)', but she was 'doing it [selling sex]' for her kids, whom her mother cared for back in Albania (Chapter 5), her home country.

Like Ana, many sex working cis women coming from Eastern European EU countries were engaged in forms of circular migration, akin to Filipina migrant women in Japan's hostess clubs (Parreñas 2010), migrant cabaret dancers in Switzerland (Dahinden 2010) and Brazilian women selling sex in Spain (Oso-Casas 2010, 52). In their narratives, the cycle of work and consumption appeared to be by and large spatially split between 'here', where they sold sex on the street, and 'there', where their remittances sustained the livelihoods of their minor and adult dependents and to where they kept returning, time after time. 'There' was, therefore, the primary place to which they remained affectively oriented and where they projected their social mobility aspirations through the assets that they were working hard to accumulate. This cycle also followed a particular rhythm: women migrated to Italy to earn money *fast* then returned to their home (country) to partake in consuming the fruits of their labour as *slowly* as possible before going back to Italy to work when economic necessity dictated again.[7] And yet, this apparently neat spatial and temporal division of work and the home was never entirely so. Instead, these two spheres were profoundly interconnected through the transnational circulation of money and emotions, responsibilities and rewards, expectations, fulfilments and new demands.

EU and Italian migration laws and the costs of travelling from/to one's home (country) shaped the rhythm of women's movements across borders. Most third country nationals (i.e. non-EU) likely were undocumented migrants, who would refrain from crossing the border as much as possible. Conversely, EU citizens could and did flexibly and cyclically move in and out of Italy as much as they could afford to. This latter mobility pattern appeared to be more accessible to women from an Eastern European EU country than to women from a Latin American country holding a Spanish (and hence EU) passport, many of whom relayed having been away from their home (country) for several years seeking to accumulate as many assets as possible before making the reverse journey.

Mercedes is a Paraguayan trans woman who left her country amid the 2007–2008 financial crisis, searching for a way out of rising unemployment rates and deteriorating living conditions. She migrated to Spain, where she married a Spanish man, thereby legally obtaining the right to reside in the country and, subsequently, to move freely across the EU (Chapter 5). When we first met, it was already several years since she had left home. 'Because I am here suffering not for … [nothing]: [but] for my children', she vehemently uttered. Like many of her peers, Mercedes looked at her home country as the place where she will eventually return to reap the fruits of her work (Oso 2016). In her case, however, the circularity of her migratory project was not just spatial and temporal but also deeply performative and embodied. Before going back, she gravely stated, she would 'turn back to male. I will remove *everything*', she stressed, pressing her hands down on her breasts. When I asked her why she was planning on doing that, she explained that 'they [her children] would not understand it'. I could not tell in that brief exchange what emotions she projected with regards this prospective bodily transformation that would erase these embodied signifiers of her trans woman identity. Pain and sacrifice nonetheless marked her position both here, in Italy (and in street sex work), and there, in her home country.

Against this backdrop, women's fulfilment of their breadwinning responsibilities for their family members provided them with a dignified position – as it was for their love that they coped with such difficult, hazardous, precarious and stigmatized job. Their attachment to a better life thus constituted a form of 'cruel optimism' – a term expressing 'a relation of attachment to compromised conditions of possibility' and a subject's projection of continuity onto 'an enabling object that is also disabling' (Berlant 2006, 21). For Lauren Berlant, 'the conditions of ordinary life in the contemporary world … are conditions of the attrition or the wearing out of the subject' (Berlant 2006, 23). Women's endurance in sex work, I contend, was an embodied statement of their capacity to bear with the hardships that life threw at them. As such, the fruits borne through their hard work were bittersweet: they were costly but worthy. Arguably, though, the shame that the whore stigma reproduced prevented them from *commanding* respect for their breadwinning role.

I would like to suggest that women's projection of continuity onto these bittersweet fruits of their labour offered them a means to cultivate dignity and self-respect as *workers*, expressing materialist ethics that is self-contained, as it neither rests upon nor reproduces anyone else's othering. This ethics, therefore transcends the necessity to displace the whore stigma onto any other category of women. I am nevertheless aware that this interpretation is both partial and situated (Haraway 1988; Harding 1992) and contingent upon the specific context, scope and limitations of my research. Hence, it complements rather than refutes other scholars' observations. For example, speaking of non-EU Eastern European migrant women who worked in third-party controlled prostitution in Italy, Rutvika Andrijasevic observed that they 'worked with the "victims/whores" binary, as they identified other women as "whores" and themselves as not-prostitutes' (Andrijasevic 2010, 113). They embedded their engagement in sex work in a narrative of familial sacrifice in the face of economic necessity (Andrijasevic 2010, 119), contextually passing the stigma on to women selling sex for 'economic gain' (Andrijasevic 2010, 114). Andrijasevic's work was based on in-depth interviews with women who were already out of sex work and under some form of social protection and/or assistance based on their status as sex trafficking victims (Andrijasevic 2010, 19). Differently, my suggestion is based on observations and brief conversations with women who were still in (street) sex work. Perhaps in those circumstances the women I met had no interest in claiming 'respectability', as we – the women in the outreach van – were too fleeting a presence in their lives. I like to think, however, that our contingent irrelevance was not the only reason explaining this difference I observed. I want to suggest that some women may have found it futile and eventually counterproductive to seek shelter under the very same patriarchal norms condemning them for being where they were – at work.

The night I first met Aleksandra, a Serbian woman well known to the association, she had just returned to work in Italy after an extended stay at home. She relayed that she had hoped to stay away longer, but as her mother fell sick, part of her savings went to cover this emergency health expenditure. She then shrugged her shoulders and shifted her eyes away from us and back to the street – the workplace enabling her to pay for the medical treatments that restored her mother's health but to where she would have rather postponed returning for a little longer. Her tone and posture betrayed her disappointment, but her deeds attested that she was putting her relational self above her individual self – and there was value in her positioning as a loyal, reliable and accountable family member.

As we spoke, a big car – an SUV – stopped right behind our van. Like Stefania and Ileana in the chapter's opening vignette, Aleksandra gave it a glance and kept talking with us. 'You know the hazards when you start this job', she said pensively as soon as the vehicle left, 'but I do not want to stop before I realize my dreams: buying a house, opening a shop back home.' Another car stopped shortly afterwards, and this time Aleksandra said goodbye to us, for it was one of her regulars. The choice of which men to work with and which ones to discard is one of the key strategies that women adopt to stay safe at work in any sex market segment (UK Network of Sex Work Projects 2008). Working with men whom women know does not erase the risk that the latter may turn violent against them, but it nonetheless mitigates its likelihood. Regulars are also reliable sources of income and 'help' in difficult times (Piscitelli 2020, 286–87).

Once back on the road, the volunteer on shift with me told me that Aleksandra was first trafficked into Italy and managed to escape. Back in Serbia, however, she could not find any job, so she returned – but this time alone and on her terms.

Pliable Boundaries

Kyla is an Italian woman in her early fifties and a self-identified sex worker. It was her trust in the person vouching for me that opened the doors to her home, which was also her workplace. As I walked up the stairs to her flat, I wondered whether her neighbours knew about her job. They possibly did, I thought, due to the hustle and bustle of unknown men moving in and out of her apartment. I also wondered whether their cognizance was a good or a bad thing; if it made her feel safe; if any of them would step in and help if she required some, or if it was rather a cause of tensions and disputes.

At that time, Kyla worked as an 'escort' – an English term that Italians use to broadly refer to any sex working woman who does not sell sex on the street. A woman's classification under this label may offer shelter from the intersecting stereotypes projected onto the latter (Chapkis 1997, 96; 103). For Kyla, however, her self-identification as an escort did not reflect nor reproduce this othering premise, because it was right on the street that she first started selling sex.

Flash-back thirty years before: Kyla was working at a car factory, she was married to a man with a job that paid more than their bills, and they had three children. One day, when she lay bruised on the floor – like many other days before – she decided that it was time to leave her abusive husband. At that point, however, her wage was insufficient to make ends meet. 'How do you cope when you have three [children]? How can you? They have to go to school!' So, she started moonlighting, combining daytime factory work with night-time street sex work:

> I used to drive one hundred kilometres from my home to avoid any kind of ... [possibility to be recognized]. I would go with my rattletrap to the truck parking space near the highway, and I would do anything with them [truck drivers]

for fifty thousand Liras – or was it fifty euros?[8] I would do whatever. I stood there still, in the car, and they would arrive. There is an unspoken code that says that if a girl is there, she is there because … [she sells sex] and it is very dangerous, because you are surrounded by men.

Prevalently male, long haul truck drivers have a reputation for being frequent sex buyers.[9] For street sex working cis and trans women, they are simultaneously good and bad customers: they are good because many demand their services, but they are also bad because their transience runs against one of the women's key safety measures, which is to work as much as possible with known men. In Italy, male truck drivers are also widely stereotyped as aggressive and dangerous men on the street. Against this backdrop, Kyla's decision to sell sex alone at night in a truck parking space indexes both the compelling nature of the material needs pushing her to that dangerous place and position and her courage and determination to get by against all odds. 'And when you start to understand that this body can give you more than by saying "goodbye, thank you" [as shop assistants do], or by breathing acids in a factory …', she said, narrating her decision to resign from the latter workplace and sell sex only. Nonetheless, acknowledgement of Kyla's agency should not obfuscate the intersecting structural constraints under which she exercised it (Smith and Mac 2018): intimate male partner violence, capitalist exploitation of her labour and lack of appropriate public welfare support for a single working mother.

Over time, Kyla gradually moved indoors, where she could enjoy safer work conditions and higher returns on her labour. Work remained hard nonetheless, as the following attests:

> I used to work in this little house with the *maîtresse* [mistress] and three or four revolving girls. Once, there was this very rich, eighty years old man. I did it. It was only a … [oral sex, as she gestured]. Horrific, horrific! Lowering his trousers; seeing the panty girdle; the colour of his back; these hands that looked like my grandfather's … I cried on that occasion. It was dark, and I cried while doing it. It was shocking, one of the worst things I have ever done in my life. [I got] two hundred euros, of which one hundred went straight to the *maîtresse*. It was fifty-fifty. Always, for every meeting. Quite a lot, right?! And in fact, I resisted only three months there.

Under Italy's prostitution law (Chapter 1), this place where Kyla used to work would be classified as an illegal brothel. Its existence, though, was not at all exceptional. Already in the late 1980s – that is, approximately thirty years after brothels were officially shut down – Carla Corso (one of the two cofounders of *Comitato*) relayed they still existed, albeit under the guise of 'activities of massage, fortune-telling' (Corso 1991, 225). Nevertheless, their illicit status engenders particular hazards for the women working in them. For example, Kyla had no leverage to negotiate better pay and, more broadly, she and everyone else working there were vulnerable to blackmail (ICRSE 2020, 34). 'We had the police coming', she said, 'Do you think they ever paid? No!'[10]

At the time of the interview, Kyla had been working independently for several years, running her own website and keeping an eye on how customers assessed her work on online escort forums (Serughetti 2013, 289–96). 'You should know that there is a forum where customers meet to judge whether she [the escort] is really whom she claims to be, how she makes it [sex], how is the house …', she explained to me. Then, Kyla went silent. Suddenly upset, she told me of a customer who publicly complained, in this forum, about her 'disquieting house'. 'How can this be disquieting?! As if I had coffins on display! … You can say what you want, but there are ten thousand [men] more who find it *bellissima*', she proclaimed as if addressing him there and then. Then, standing up, she said, 'I show you my bedroom if you want. Do you want to see it? My office?'

The relationship between the spheres of work and intimacy, which Kyla's description of her 'bedroom' as her 'office' touches upon, lies at the core of the feminist sex wars. For radical feminists and abolitionists, sex should only express mutual desire (MacKinnon 2011, 281), and its commodification is considered to be intrinsically harmful to women and a form of rape (Barry 1995; Jeffreys 1997). 'Dissociation' – the splitting of bodies and selves – is thus both a means that women adopt to survive prostitution and the outcome of the sexual violence that is intrinsic to it (Farley 2004, 1106–8; MacKinnon 2011, 286–87). Women's capacity to enjoy sex with a partner of choice is also seen as radically compromised (Farley 2004, 1106).

Conversely, women's capacity to separate their work persona from their selves is key in sex workers' labour and human rights' advocacy (NSWP 2013; Grant 2014; Smith and Mac 2018; ICRSE 2020), which a broad and composite constellation of scholars and international organizations supports.[11] People selling sex are seen as agents who can uphold 'healthy' – that is, functional – boundaries between their work and intimacy spheres. Rather than set in stone, though, these are reimagined as pliable and subject to their ability to craft them in time (e.g. by setting a work routine), space (e.g. by delimiting work to a specific room) and on the body (e.g. by excluding the use of specific body parts) (Chapkis 1997, 77; Day 2007, 42; Robillard 2010, 537; Smith and Mac 2018, 44–45). Therefore, the relationship between prostitution and harm is conceptualized as phenomenological and borne of the risky, exploitative and precarious conditions under which it is often performed.

I followed Kyla to her bedroom. When she opened the door, I was struck by the contrast between its refinement and the humble decor of the kitchen that we had left behind. At the centre lay a king-sized bed with a white mosquito net tied to its sides; the furniture was in thick olive wood, and there were candles everywhere. As both a perfect host wishing to make her guest 'feel at home' and a worker wishing to rebut an unfair performance complaint, Kyla invited me to sit and try her mattress. For a moment, I hesitated to take her up on her offer, as I thought that doing so would have constituted an infringement of her intimacy. But was that space intimate, there and then? Does intimacy belong to a physical space, or does it contingently arise through the practices and imagination of the people who constitute and evoke it?

As I sat on Kyla's bed with these questions buzzing in my head, I suddenly saw the image of myself refracted across the four corners of the room. 'Wow! You have many mirrors', I distractedly observed, disoriented at the meaning of their presence. The woman-with-mirror imagery evoked in me a disturbing association with female narcissism and the male gaze (Mulvey 1975; Bartky 1990; Meyers 2002), which I could not reconcile with the impression that Kyla had left upon me until that moment. In fact, those mirrors had nothing to do with that: 'They [mirrors] accelerate orgasm. When I am naked and on top of one of them [male customers], the only thing I ask is: "Will you let yourself be kissed?" This is something that you always need to ask because a man does not necessarily enjoy kissing; maybe he enjoys everything but the kiss.' 'Yeah, I understand. I likewise do not like kissing somebody if we are having sex only', I conspiratorially uttered, realizing too late that I had taken up her customers' position. Kyla's was my first in-depth interview with a sex worker, and while at it, I often felt naïve in front of the tastes, roles and rules that she was disclosing in front of my eyes. At that very moment, though, I thought I knew perfectly well what she was hinting at. That was *Pretty Woman*'s rule number one:[12] never to kiss a customer, because a kiss is too intimate to be commodified.

In her discussion on whether prostitution and surrogacy should be considered as legitimate economic activities, Anne Phillips conceptualized sex workers' refusal to kiss their customers as a defence in front of what, drawing from Mary Shanley (Shanley 1990; 1993), she described as the risk of 'forfeiture of self' (Phillips 2013, 150). 'Any paid employment sets requirements on the body, but the level of bodily regulation and control associated with prostitution or surrogacy considerably exceeds the norm' (Phillips 2013, 152). This excess thus underpins her judgement of these practices as intrinsically coercive: 'The point about both prostitution and commercial surrogacy is that you have no choice. You have to manage your emotions if you are to survive emotionally intact' (Phillips 2013, 152).

In sex workers' narratives, however, the meaning of kissing emerges as more nuanced. For example, Christina Parreira (2021) observed that it was central in the sex work stigma management strategies of the women working in some Nevada brothels. Women providing the 'girlfriend experience' situated kissing within the framework of their dignified offer of 'a holistic experience of mind and body', while women offering the 'porn star experience' found it to be '"too intimate" to be on the market' and reclaimed their capacity to reserve it for their 'sexual partners outside of work' (Parreira 2021, 181; 182).[13] Kyla's approach to kissing was again different, as it appeared to be quite tactical and situational. 'No, no, my dear', she said smiling whilst shaking head vigorously to signal that I got it all *so* wrong,

> a kiss is a way to accelerate a man's orgasm! Because if you look at him in a certain way, you captivate him … and when you give him a kiss in a certain way (and by the way: I never kiss a customer the way I kiss the one I love) you hear the typical sentence 'no! No! Stop! Stop!' So, instead, you go faster, 'Yes! Yes!' And it is over.

Admittedly, I initially found Kyla's instrumental description of kissing disappointing – as if something precious had been forever lost in this epiphany; as if the same act could not be a sign and vehicle of intimacy with some people and a means to an end with others. But then, I thought, are not cultural productions – movies, theatre plays, etc. – full of people kissing each other because they are paid to do so? Are those kisses not also commodified? Undoubtedly, the social value attached to kissing varies radically when it is performed by lovers, models, actors or sex workers; while the people themselves performing it will also invest it with different meanings based on context, circumstances and social locations. It thus follows that sex acts do not have any intrinsic meaning either: different people performing the same act will attribute it different meanings depending on whom they perform it with, when, where, how and why. Nor does their more or less frequent commodification erase sex workers' capacity to feel pleasure, including while at work (Kontula 2008; Doezema 2013).

Deeply absorbed in Kyla's tales, I suddenly jumped at the puff coming from behind my back (I am easily startled by the tiniest noise when I am concentrating on a task). 'Do not be scared!' she burst out laughing, pointing to an air fresher in a corner plug, 'they are everyone's terror! I have one in each room. They mark the time when I am with a man, each half an hour. It is crafty because you never work with the clock; it is a sign of disdain … .' Concealment of the act of managing the time-bounded nature of her services is a trick of the trade allowing Kyla to command higher prices than colleagues working in other segments of the sex market, such as the street. There and then, though, this episode brought me back again to the debate on boundaries in sex work.

Did Kyla turn the air fresher on before my arrival to discretely manage her time with me, as she does when she is with her customers? Then, I thought, this might mean that she did not *authentically* enjoy being in my company. Still, commodification and pleasure can and do coexist. Indeed, in contemporary Western late capitalist countries, pleasure *is* the promise projected onto consumption (Appadurai 1996, 82–83).

If, conversely, Kyla did not purposefully put on the air fresher before my arrival and had had it on all the time, then it may have been a clue that she held no boundary between her space and time on and off work. But after all, do we not constantly live keeping an eye on time – that very time that capitalism commodified (Appadurai 1996, 79)?

And how long does it take for a sound to dissolve? This last question came to me later, while reflecting on this episode from the position of a woman born and raised in a flat adjacent to a Catholic parish. Every day, from as far back in time as I can remember, its thunderous bells have been unfailingly ringing every half an hour, from 6 AM until midnight, marking a particular rhythm of work, rest and devotion for its community of piety and everyone else – devotees of other religions, atheists, agnostics. They also ring several times a day over weekends and at least once every weekday to call devotees to Mass; to announce weddings and funerals and to mark religious festivities. One day, though, I must have stopped hearing their sound. I do not know when and how it occurred – I just did. If I want to hear them again, I must intentionally attune myself to retrieving their sound from the midst of my everyday soundscape. The noise of Kyla's air fresher was incomparably lighter than those church bells. Ultimately, whether she did or did not count the puffs spent in my company, she graciously gave my research and me an entire morning, even if I only asked for an hour of her time. In similarly flexible ways, I would imagine she manages her time on and off (sex) work counting or ignoring the puffs and switching the air fresher on or off as she needs.

'How much do you usually work in a week?' I asked Kyla before saying goodbye. 'As much as I need to', she said, 'if I worked based on the requests I receive, I think that I would make [a lot of] money, but I am not bound to it.' It was perhaps out of fear I would not believe her restraint that she carefully explained on which occasion she had been gifted the few expensive items on display in her flat and by whom. 'I have all the time I want, and this is my luxury. Few people have time. I have nobody telling me "No" to any of my life plans.' As she said that, she smiled and stretched her arms wide open as if to say that there were no limits to her freedom. Yet there were – because any worker knows that one's time off work is not free of charge but is paid for through one's labour.

Of Means and Ends

'When we started to speak out, we were in the aftermath of the battle to obtain [the right to] divorce, abortion; all the key struggles for women's self-determination', recounted Pia Covre as she looked back at the time when she and Carla Corso co-founded *Comitato* (Chapter 1):

> It was very clear to us that our sexuality was ours and that we could use it as we wished: for love, within the family, to make sacrifices if necessary, but also to obtain benefits – something that, anyway, was not so different from marital relations, since back then many women used to get married to improve their social and economic status. ... We argued for years that whatever a woman did with her body was a personal, private decision, regardless of whether she wanted to have sex for money, gifts or for free. I thought that this was a very feminist concept of self-determination. Instead, we immediately clashed with feminists supporting the old concept that exchanging sex for money reinforced the patriarchy and was a form of violence against women. Even today, abolitionists repeat this.

In the extract above, Pia foregrounds the different understandings of self-determination characterizing the relationship between women sex workers and feminists in Italy. 'The personal is political' and 'I am mine' were some of the key second wave Western feminists' rallying cries of the time that were forged during the battles to retrieve women's control over their bodies from the patriarchal institutions of the family, the nation state and the Church. Likewise, in its founding manifesto, *Comitato* claimed women's 'right to use and manage our bodies as we wish, in the factory as well as in the street' (Comitato per i diritti civili delle prostitute 1983). Yet, sex workers' early engagement with Italian feminists was fraught with tensions (Corso 1991, 221), reproducing on a local scale the feminist sex wars' debate on the role of sexuality in women's oppression and liberation. As Pia's words suggest, feminists' claims of women's sexual and bodily autonomy stopped short of questioning the hierarchies of value underpinning the normative separation between intimacy and the market. Hence, while women's use of marriage for social mobility purposes is concealed and/or condoned, women negotiating their use of sexuality from without this contract are condemned as accomplices of patriarchy.

If, as I argued throughout this chapter, women's entry into either marriage and/or prostitution cannot be abstracted from livelihood needs and social mobility aspirations, then understanding a woman's decision to sell sex requires a feminist materialist framework. This ought to consider how women's social location mediates their access to different labour markets and the exchange value of their labour. Before deciding to sell sex on the street for a living, Pia relayed having worked 'as a hairdresser, [and as a waitress] in restaurants and bars', adding that she 'did not mind these jobs'. However, the problem was that

> they paid too little and too badly for too many hours' work. So, one day I calculated how much I earned, how many hours I worked, and how much [free] time I had to enjoy life, to do the things that I liked … and I thought that it did not add up: I was spending all my time working and when I had a day off I had no money to have fun, to buy the things I wanted … to go to the theatre, to the cinema, on holiday … and it did not add up because I was not earning enough.

Pia's words aptly foreground late capitalism's structural tension between its consumerist-fuelled growth and the lack of decent jobs through which access to consumption can be democratized. Her gender implied subjection to another, intersecting axe of oppression, so that even if sex had been by then disconnected from the imperatives of marriage and reproduction, its enjoyment continued to unfold on an unchanged patriarchal terrain. Indeed, Pia recalled that, while working as a waitress, the restaurant's male customers would invite her out, but then 'they would expect to *averla* [to have 'it', i.e. have a vaginal intercourse]' at the end of the dinner. As this expression suggests, Italians commonly portray heterosexual intercourse as an uneven exchange between men and women, resulting in men's appropriation, and arguably destruction, of the women's patriarchal-defined honour. Another example is the expression '*gliela ha data*' (she gave 'it' to him), describing a woman who has vaginal intercourse with a man, where 'it' may refer either to her vulva or her virgin status. This language, then, forcefully suggests that sex acts circulate as gendered symbolic capital that men accumulate, thereby becoming more manly, while women lose, becoming subjected to the whore stigma. 'They thought that I was an easy girl', Pia bitterly continued. At the crossroads between her experience of work exploitation and her stigmatization for using her sexuality on her own terms, Pia thought,

> 'Well, wait a moment: why do I have to *dargliela* [to give 'it' to him, i.e. to have vaginal intercourse] for free? I do not like it. And [to do] that only because he offered me a dinner? No, that is not right.' But when I was offered money, I thought: 'well, if I can turn this into making him pay me the equivalent of a month's salary, well, why not?' And so, I did my math and realized

that the numbers added up much better because I could earn a month's salary just by going out [on the street] once a week. Why bother working the whole month? So, I balanced myself on my needs. To me, this is a job. I have decided [to do] it; I have chosen it as an occupation – I do not say 'work' because it does not have the canon of traditional work. I have done it freely, by myself, independently, and I have decided what I wanted to earn, how much time I wanted to commit, how much free time I wanted, and what I needed to live.

Akin to Kyla, who left her factory job because the salary she received was not a living wage for a single mother, Pia acknowledged the constraining circumstances under which she decided to sell sex for a living. Against this background, both women claimed value in achieving a better balance in the structurally unequal relationship between capital and labour. Importantly, Pia's materialist ethics implied her cultivation of moderation in the *pleasures of the market* – rather than the pleasures of the flesh, as the ideology of respectability dictated (Foucault 1984; Mosse 1996). The risk is to otherwise succumb to the bondage of consumerism, as Carla Corso aptly described in the extract below from her memoir:

We [Pia and her] met a woman in Rome ... who had two or three of these flats where she kept many young girls coming from the south [of Italy], and she would coerce them, she bonded them to her, by means of the same system of the [pre-Merlin Law] brothels, meaning by getting them into debts; since these girls had never owned anything before, she would first of all have them buy a car and anything else they wished. Then they [the girls] had to work to pay her back in instalments everything they bought, eventually entering into the spiral of consumerism and remaining bonded to her. (Corso 1991, 225–26)

Carla spoke of women selling sex to finance this lifestyle consumption. Nonetheless, her analysis has broader applicability, hinting at the role of loans, mortgages, credit cards and other financial instruments in sustaining the everyday materialities of the social world as we create it. What Pia values, then, is her capacity to find and hold on to a balance between means (work) and ends (consumption) that feels right to her. This materialist ethics thus dignifies the subject in the act of earning the means to access the pleasure that capitalism falsely promises to everybody. Simultaneously, it offers a way for women to claim dignity and value outside of the patriarchal binary dividing them into 'good' and 'bad' based on their use of sexuality.

In 'a world characterised by weak [economic] growth and high return on capital', where income gaps are widening, and the concentration of assets is worsening, long-term inequality in the distribution of wealth is rising' (Piketty 2014, 46). During the interview, Pia spoke passionately about the relationship between work and dignity in the feminist debate on prostitution. 'I do not understand why using my sexuality for an objective that I consider to be fair or appropriate would not be "respectable,"' she said. Against the backdrop of the burning contradiction between a consumerist-driven capitalism and the unequal distribution of the opportunities to access the promise of pleasure fuelling it, she affirmed:

> So, either they [abolitionists] give us all decent and well-paid jobs … but if [not, and if] I want to enjoy a certain living standard and … some particular commodities – [those] that you constantly put forth in your society – then you also have to put me in the position of being able to obtain them through what you say is decent, and if you cannot, then you have to put me in the position to do my work decently: because eventually, this is what it is.

Pia spoke of sex work specifically, but surely, the inequality bells she rang reverberate loud and travel much further across the world of work.

Conclusions

In this chapter, I have discussed how women who are structurally stigmatized as 'whores' due to their sale of sex claim value through or despite their work.

Against the normative Western view that the market and intimacy are and should remain separate and hostile spheres (Zelizer 2005), which underpins the radical feminist and abolitionists' position on prostitution, the chapter foregrounded these spheres' complex entanglement in women's lives (see also Chapter 5). In the narratives of the migrant cis and trans women I met while on the mobile outreach unit, the sale of sex was a difficult way to pursue multiple goals. It enabled them to fulfil their breadwinning responsibilities, nurture their intimate ties with their family members 'here' and 'there', sustain their own and their relatives' social mobility aspirations, and buy for themselves as much time off work as possible. Their (sex) work revenues thus sustained their intimate and familial relations, which, in turn, contributed to keep the women (sex) working.

Interconnectedness (Zelizer 2005), however, does not mean *overlap* – a term conveying the pathologizing assumption that people selling sex can never uphold 'healthy', functional boundaries between their work and intimacy sphere. I have shown that for some migrant sex working women this separation reflected the circularity of their migration, as their move between Italy and their home (country) corresponded to their move in and out of sex work, respectively. For sex workers like Kyla, who regularly turned her home into a workspace, this boundary was temporal and affective, as it relied both on her time management skills and on the different meanings that she attributed to the same act (e.g. kissing) when performed with a customer or a partner.

I have thus argued that the radical feminist and abolitionist position on prostitution reflects a privileged position that fails to account for the compelling material predicament under which most (but not only) women sell sex. Surely, no sex working woman I have met on the street or sex worker I interviewed worked under 'free choice' conditions. Some women sold sex to rise above the economic stagnation characterizing their home countries. Kyla started doing so due to the economic precarity in which she fell at the crossroads between intimate male partner violence and capitalist exploitation of her labour. For Pia, sex work constituted a means to increase the return on her labour and enjoy more time and money off work.

I have also suggested that the women in this sexscape did not appear to be invested in managing the whore stigma by displacing it onto another category of 'other women'. Some, I have argued, found dignity and value in their projection of continuity onto the bittersweet fruits of their hard and hazardous labour. Others found both in the achievement of a better balance in the structurally unequal relationship between capital and labour. I have thus argued that the women's positioning as workers offered them a dignified subject position – for it was this precarious, hazardous and stigmatized work that gave them the means to pursue the ends which they valued. This materialist ethics, I contend, disallow the resolution of the tension between women's status and sexuality through the whore stigma, feeding into a feminist politics of liberation from intersecting structures of oppression.

Notes

1. The association's volunteers would also be available to accompany women to medical visits and support them with translation (if necessary), thus ensuring that they received fair treatment.
2. In his research in the UK and Italy, Nicola Mai reported that the 'working partnership' and the 'fiancé contract' were the two most recurrent types of arrangements between migrant women selling sex and their male partners (Mai 2013). He described their differences as follows:

   > The first foresees a greater degree of autonomy for women, who are usually considered as 'work partners', able to keep half of their earnings and to have a social life with and/or without their male agents. According to the 'fiancé contract', all the money earned by selling sex is handed over to the prospective husband, to save up for a shared future life. When men adhered to one of these two patterns, women did not feel exploited, and vice versa'. (Mai 2013, 115)

3. For example, recently, one of the most influential men in the country posted a video where he ferociously defended his son, who is under investigation over a charge of rape, by undermining the victim's credibility (AP news wire 2021).
4. Paola Tabet coined the concept of the 'sexual-economic exchange' to describe a continuum of social relations between men and women implying an economic transaction, ranging from marriage to prostitution (Tabet 2004; Trachman 2009). This concept reflects a feminist materialist view of gender relations of power as co-constitutive of class relations: women provide services to men, including sexual, and men pay or compensate them in connection to their 'possible sexual use of the woman, to her sexual accessibility' (Tabet 2004, 8). While this formulation appears to sit within a sex/gender binary framework, the concept of the 'continuum' may be applied, as I do here, to an analysis of the economy of value distribution in different intimate and economic arrangements across multiple axis of differentiation, including gender and sexuality.
5. The 'sex wars' started on occasion of the organization of the Scholar and the Feminist conference IX: 'Towards a Politics of Sexuality', which was held in 1982 at Barnard College (New York City). A review of the extensive body of literature produced since on this subject exceeds the scope of this book. In addition to the edited collection *Pleasure and Danger: Exploring Female Sexuality* (Vance 1984b), constituting the conference proceedings, some resources for a sex-positive perspective include Rubin (1984; 2010) and Wendy Chapkis (1997); for a recent engagement with the history and legacy of the sex wars, see the Special Issue on the journal *Signs: Journal of Women in Culture and Society* curated by Suzanna Danuta Walters (2016).
6. Today, care work remains globally undervalued and underpaid (Zimmerman, Litt and Bose 2006; Razavi and Staab 2010; Boris and Parreñas 2010b; Baines, Charlesworth and Daly 2016; S. Butler 2016).
7. During a public meeting organized within the framework of the VI Congress of the Radical Association *Certi Diritti*, Andrea Morniroli, currently the spokesperson for Italy's National Antitrafficking Platform, spoke of the emergence of a bracket of 'seasonal' migrant sex workers moving across national borders according to their needs. Intervention in the roundtable '*Regolamentare la prostituzione. Come ridare dignità e sicurezza alle persone che scelgono di prostituirsi. Gli interventi locali possibili senza dimenticare la lotta alla criminalità ed alla tratta degli esseri umani*', (Regulating prostitution. How to give dignity and safety back to people who choose to prostitute themselves. Possible local interventions without forgetting the fight against criminality and human trafficking) 5 April 2013, Naples.
8. On 1 January 2002, the euro became the official currency of twelve (now nineteen) European Union member states. Two months afterwards, the Italian Lira ceased to be legal tender. However, it kept circulating for ten years side by side with the euro – hence, Kyla's uncertainty about the currency in which she priced her labour at that time.
9. Across Europe and the US, '[t]he trucking industry is dominated by men' (M. Gibson 2020); in Italy, women are only three percent of the total number of truck drivers (Di Rosa 2020). Research on the connection between male truck drivers and the consumption of commodified sex is extensive, albeit strictly linked to the unfolding of the HIV pandemic outside of Western countries, including the Baltic region (World Bank 2003), Uganda (Gysels, Pool and Bwanika 2001), South Africa (Makhakhe et al. 2017), India (Singh and Malaviya 1994) and Brazil (Malta et al. 2006).
10. Human Rights Watch 'documented that, in criminalized environments, police officers harass sex workers, extort bribes, and physically and verbally abuse sex workers, or

even rape or coerce sex from them' (Human Rights Watch 2019). Kathleen Deering et al. (2014) have undertaken a thorough review of the correlates of sexual or physical violence against sex workers globally, including when perpetrated by the police. Speaking of her research with sex workers in China, Tiantian Zheng has also observed the abuses they are exposed to at the hands of 'corrupt law enforcement officials' due to incarceration fears (Dewey and Zheng 2013, 28).

11. Among the many recent scholarly works, see Nicola Mai et al. (2021) and Lucy Platt et al. (2018). In 2021, on International Sex Worker Rights Day (3 March), a coalition of over two hundred and fifty scholars and researchers from the US and across the globe signed a letter demanding the decriminalization of sex work (Decriminalize Sex Work 2021). Many international organizations also hold a pro-sex workers' rights position. See for example World Health Organization et al. (2013) and Amnesty International (2016).

12. At the beginning of the movie *Pretty Woman* (Marshall 1990), Richard Gere (Edward), a wealthy man, asks Julia Roberts (Vivian), a sex worker, 'What do you do?' – meaning, what sexual services does she offer. Vivian responds that she does 'Everything. But I do not kiss on the mouth.'

13. Elizabeth Bernstein described the 'girlfriend experience' as consisting of the performance and consumption of more than just sex – including foreplay, cuddling and the establishment of a 'reciprocal erotic connection' (Bernstein 2007, 127). The 'porn star experience' is less clearly defined (Parreira 2021, 170). Abbe Horswill and Ronald Weitzer define it as a service in which the 'provider will exhibit certain stereotyped pornographic behaviour, such as talking dirty and displaying a willingness to please her partner' (Horswill and Weitzer 2018, 151).

Chapter 5

SEXSCAPES IN THE MATRIX OF DOMINATION

As I moved through the sexscapes discussed in the previous chapters, I gradually noticed the uneven distribution, position and visibility of the women working within them. For example, recreational pole dance entrepreneurs, instructors and students (Chapter 2) were almost exclusively white Italian cis women, while women working as lap dancers (Chapter 3) or selling sex on the street (Chapter 4) were overwhelmingly white cis women from Eastern European countries. This chapter aims to foreground the 'matrix of domination' (Collins 2000) of which these patterns of segmentation are an expression. It will focus particularly on the legacies of the racist and sexist colonial tropes informing white Western colonial constructions of women's sexuality and the effects of Italy's migration and prostitution laws.

The chapter starts with a discussion of the racialization of the recreational pole dance space as prevalently white and Italian. Next, it moves to night clubs, linking the observed prevalence of white cis Eastern European women in the lap dancing workforce to a political economy of migrant labour exploitation and male customers' racialized desire. Subsequently, the chapter introduces the concept of 'exotic value' to discuss the changing relationship between women's heterosexual desirability, race and space in their erotic and sex work experiences. In the last section, the chapter analyses the segmentation of the street sex market at the crossroads between Italy's prostitution and migration laws, showing how migrant women navigate it by differently assembling their 'intimate labour' (Boris and Parreñas 2010a).

The Racialized Boundaries of Pleisure

Some scholars who have researched women's recreational pole dancing in Western countries observed that its practitioners are prevalently white (Whitehead and Kurz 2009, 231; Holland 2010, 92; Griffiths 2016). The roots of this stratification pattern have nonetheless remained underexplored. During my fieldwork, I similarly noticed that recreational pole dance entrepreneurs, instructors and students overwhelmingly consisted of 'white' Italian cis women – with the caveat that the use of this racial descriptor to classify Italians is fraught with contradictions (Chapter 2, and later). Italian was the only language that I have heard being spoken in these spaces, and I did not notice the presence of any woman who did not look white *to me* – that is, based on my own 'racial grammar' (Bonilla-Silva 2012). The market for this pleasure practice was thus markedly racialized. Explaining this outcome, I argue, requires an exploration of how race enduringly affects the tension between women's sexuality and their status.

Under the white European gaze, Black women have been consistently imagined as subjects 'naturally' endowed with excessive sexuality (Gilman 1985; hooks 2001) and as the female other of white 'respectable' women (Introduction). These racist and sexist tropes persist today, positioning women differently in the discourse and politics of sexuality. This became apparent, for example, during the anti-rape protests that went under the name of 'Slut Walks'.[1] 'As Black women', a public letter stated, 'we do not have the privilege or the space to call ourselves "slut" without validating the already historically entrenched ideology and recurring messages about what and who the Black woman is' (Black Women's Blueprint 2016, 10).

In the wake of this analysis, I contend that the racialization of the recreational pole dance as white reflects the 'duress' (Stoler 2016) of the racist and sexist tropes informing the white Western colonial imagination of Black women's sexuality. For women enduringly imagined as always already 'improperly' sexual, in fact, the promise that this practice holds for some women to feel 'sluttier' (Chapter 2) might be less of a pull and more of a deterrence factor.

A Political Economy of Whiteness

Akin to what has been observed by scholars who have researched exotic dancing in contemporary Western countries (for the US, see Frank 2002; Egan 2006, 39; Price-Glynn 2010, 5; Brooks 2010; for Canada, see Law 2012; for Switzerland, see Dahinden 2010, 336), white women prevailed in the lap dancing workforce of the night clubs where I undertook fieldwork.

Most came from Eastern European countries from within and without the EU, and while I occasionally encountered some Arab women, I never saw any Black women doing lap dancing work. This racialized employment pattern forcefully emerges from the interview extract below, where Gianna, a night club HR manager (Chapter 3), describes the club's workforce composition – albeit using strongly derogatory language:

> In the beginning, lap dancers were only and exclusively Italians. Around 1999, there was the invasion of Russian women; they came here, and they were all *entreneuse* or ... well, you know: each nationality has its own things. Russians came to look for a husband and money: I have seen girls getting married, having children, and then sending their husband to hell and keeping everything – flats, cars ... aaah, Russians were really fearsome! Then there was the period of *extracomunitari* [non-EU citizens],[2] but that was a mess because if they did not have visas, you could not make them work. Then came the Hungarians [women]: they were beautiful, and they were not like the Russians, who would take one [man] and spoil him of everything. Hungarians were okay, but the problem is that many drank a lot, and then they would become unmanageable. With the Romanians [women] the decline began because ... Romanians [women] are pretty gypsy: they do not have the Russians' [women] refinement, or the elegance of the Hungarians [women]. Maybe they lose their mind for a phone top-up ... just like that. Like them [the Hungarian women], they [Romanian women] are also here to find a husband, but they do not mind if he is rich or poor: the important [thing] is that they find one because they say that all Romanians [men] are assholes, and Italians [men] are much better because they respect women, whereas Romanians do not. Lately, after having almost completely disappeared, Italians [women] are coming back [to work as lap dancers] – you know, it is [due to] the economic crisis.

The picture emerging from beneath these derogatory intersecting racist, sexist and classist stereotypes is that of a predominantly white Eastern European female workforce. The roots of this market segmentation, I suggest, lie in the interplay between a political economy of migrant labour exploitation and male customers' racialized desire.

Migration laws play a crucial role in producing migrant women as a docile and cheap workforce that is structurally subjected to the double bind of exploitation and deportation (De Genova 2002; O'Connell Davidson and Anderson 2007; Anderson 2012). The differential wage that Italian and migrant women received for their labour emerged clearly in the interview with Mirca – an Italian woman who worked as an acrobatic stripper in Italian night clubs (Chapter 3). Mirca recounted that she used to earn 'two or up to three hundred euros [per] show', whereas 'most clubs paid foreign girls only twenty-five euros'. Part of this pay gap may be attributed to the different ways in which Italian and migrant women are more likely to find employment in Italian night clubs. Eleonora (Chapter 2), another Italian former acrobatic stripper, received cachets as high as Mirca, and she relayed having always worked 'without an agency, without a manager, without *anything* – always on my own'. When I asked her whether she had ever received any pressure to avail herself of a third-party mediation,[3] she vehemently denied this because 'you tell them to fuck off in a second! These environments are so much on the ropes that … they do not mess up with an Italian woman, because they know that you go to the police and have them shut down in a second.'

I did not ask Eleonora whether she used to work on a contract basis; nonetheless, considering these venues' structural quest for 'novelty' (Chapter 3), informality was possibly widespread. What her words make clear, however, is that she – and everybody else – knew that she could seek help from the state's law enforcement apparatus if she so wished. That last resort bargaining threat, however, is structurally unavailable to women without a regular work-and-migration status (the hyphenation underlining that these were mutually entangled). In fact, in my fieldwork, I observed three elements similarly characterizing the migration trajectories of women coming from non-EU countries: (1) use of third-party mediation to move and find work; (2) entry into the destination country on tourist visas; (3) informal work thereafter. These three factors emerge clearly in the extract below from the interview with Fiona, a Romanian female lap dancer (Chapter 3):

> Years ago, Romania was not in the EU, so you had to work through a manager who would arrange a tourist visa for you. You had to prove [to the Italian Embassy] that you had three thousand euros to support yourself for three months, and you had to stay [maximum] three months in Italy, and then [spend minimum] three [months] in Romania. He [the manager] would talk with the clubs and send you to work there. He would give you a driver and a house – and in the beginning, when you leave for a new country, that is an ideal situation. He sent me to many different clubs because you had to change fast – *carabinieri* [police] checked clubs frequently, and since I had a tourist visa, I was not allowed to work. Then Romania entered the EU, and it became easy [to work in Italy].

As I explained earlier (Chapter 3), I did not ask the women who were working as lap dancers at the time of the interview questions concerning their relationship with the manager who mediated their migration and employment. Still, it is reasonable to assume that had the EU external borders been open Fiona and her non-EU colleagues would have been less in need of this figure to try and find a job in Italy and more likely to have migrated autonomously (Agustín 2007; Andrijasevic 2010; Mai 2013; 2018), as many EU citizens – including myself[4] – have been doing for decades within the framework of the intra-EU freedom of movement regime.

Migrant women's informal employment in Italian night clubs offered some advantages to both sides of this labour market – without implying that these were in any way comparable. Women worked every other three months, and although this imposed alternate cycle of work and unemployment was unlikely ideal, it offered them access to a job they unanimously assessed as economically rewarding. From the club's management's side, these short-term collaborations fitted well with their structural quest for 'novelty'. Thanks to this arrangement, they could dispose of a vast reserve army of docile foreign workers structurally constrained to accept worse employment conditions than domestic ones, thereby enabling the continuous turnover of the staff with no strings – that is, no labour rights attached.[5]

While women's nationality, and specifically their status as non-EU nationals, structurally placed them as a docile and cheap workforce, we need the analytic of race to understand why the women featuring in Gianna's disturbing account above overwhelmingly came from countries with a predominantly white population. Far from a coincidence, this pattern suggests that such workforce composition must have also reflected the club male customers' racialized desire. Its roots may be traced back to the racist and sexist hierarchies of women's heterosexual desirability reproduced throughout Italy's colonialism. Italian colonial novels emphasized the purported 'instinctual and animal-like character' of black African women's sensuality and contrasted it to the 'charm and sophisticated seduction skills' of Arab women (Stefani 2007, 104). Nonetheless, whiteness was firmly at the top of this hierarchy, as clearly evincible from the differential price attributed to women's sexual services in the Italian colonial brothels. For example, in Libya, in the 1920s, men paid the lowest price to purchase sex with local women and the highest with French women (Schettini 2019, 14) – who were both white and foreign and thus arguably more 'exotic' than Italian women.

Today, this combination of whiteness and exoticism, which I discuss more in depth in the next section, was similarly observed by Tuulia Law in her study of female strippers in Canada. Law explained the prevalence of Eastern European (and particularly Romanian) women as an effect of their positioning as 'acceptably exotic' (Law 2012, 139–40). In male customers' eyes, she suggested, they represented the Orient (Said 1979), embodying the stereotypical image of a sensual, intellectually limited and sexually available woman (Law 2012, 139). Nevertheless, they were 'still white – other but not too other' (Law 2012, 138).

Experiencing and Commanding 'Exotic Value'

In her ethnography of exotic dancing in the US, and drawing from Adam Green's notion of 'erotic capital' (Green 2008), Siobhan Brooks introduced the notion of 'racialized erotic capital' to describe 'a form of capital that is related across bodies', which 'gives bodies value based on a socially constructed ideal model of beauty/attractiveness held by the dominant culture, that is recognised and accepted by the general public' (Brooks 2010, 6). Ideal models vary across time and place, and in the contemporary US, dominant standards of beauty 'often include someone who is White, young, and/or has a lean body' (Brooks 2010, 7). Race is thus crucial in this definition, and so is the body onto which it is projected, as Brooks links (a woman's) racialized erotic capital to 'variables such as weight, skin color, speech patterns, gender presentation, and hair texture' (Brooks 2010, 7).

The prevalence of white women in Italian night clubs' lap dancing workforce would appear to be consistent with Brooks' concept of racialized erotic capital. Yet, in my fieldwork, I observed that race circulated as a more ambivalent, situational and fluid signifier. To capture this complexity, I therefore put forward the concept of 'exotic value', which departs from Brook's conceptualization in three ways. Firstly, 'exotic value' encompasses both elements that are socially appreciated-qua-normative (and vice versa), and elements of denigration. As Anne McClintock posited, in fact, '[f]or centuries, the uncertain continents – Africa, the Americas, Asia – were figured in European lore as libidinously eroticized' (McClintock 1995, 22). The people inhabiting these exotic lands were marked by 'monstrous' sexual attributes, appetites and behaviour (McClintock 1995, 22), but they were also considered to be 'exceptionally attractive or beautiful' (Nagel 2003, 19). Under the white European gaze, they were marked at one and the same time as despicably pre-modern *and* intensely sexually appealing. I suggest that, today, 'exotic value' encapsulates the projection of (men's) racialized desire *and* contempt for some (women's) purported racially and/or culturally defined 'backwardness'. Secondly, (a woman's) exotic value is not a fixed property of the racialized body but it is fluid and situational – because race is itself a 'floating signifier' (Jhally and Hall 1996). Thus, and thirdly, some (women) may try to manipulate their exotic value to increase the return on their labour. I illustrate these three characteristics by drawing from the interviews with Mirca (Chapter 3 and this Chapter), a former acrobatic stripper, and Roberta, a sex worker.

Mirca first worked in female-to-male erotic entertainment in Canada, where she lived a few years as a temporary economic migrant. When she returned to Italy, she stayed in the job for a while, but she soon realized that work there was very difficult ... because in Canada, I was 'the foreigner'. In fact, girls there hated me because, even if I did not do or say anything special, customers used to give me so much money! And now, after having worked for so long in Italy, I understand ... what the fuck! [she laughs] When a man sees you like a fresher, he assumes that you are naïve and that you do not know how things work. Indeed, many asked me to go out with them, but I never did.

In the above extract, Mirca's explanation of the differential value of her erotic entertainment services in Canada and Italy pivots around her status as a foreign or a local worker, respectively. While I do not intend to diminish the value of this interpretation, I would contend that race also contributed to producing this outcome – a suggestion requiring an exploration of the exotic value of her specifically *Italian* nationality.

The whiteness of Italians has always been a contested, precarious and unstable property (Giuliani and Lombardi-Diop 2013; Giuliani 2019), reflecting Italy's uncertain inclusion in white Western modernity. In a context where sexuality functioned as a racialized signifier of class (Introduction), white North-Western Europeans imagined the south of the continent as a land plagued by sexual excess and economic underdevelopment. In the eyes of their (prevalently male) travellers, the territories that will become the Kingdom of Italy were 'both "Africa" and *terra vergine*, a reservoir of feudal residues, sloth, and squalor on the one hand and of quaint peasants, rustic traditions, and exotica on the other' (Moe 2002, 3).[6] They were imagined as lands of 'warm weather, cheap wine, relaxed company and sex' (Gundle 2007, 2). Male travellers found local women to be 'highly-sexed' (Gundle 2007, 4) and so they found local men: between the end of the nineteenth and the beginning of the twentieth century, the south of Italy was depicted 'as a paradise and an erotic oasis for self-identified homosexual [men]' (Rinaldi 2019, 90). These tropes accompany the history of modern Italy up to the present time.[7] For example, after the Second World War, in the eyes of the British and US audiences, the dark-haired, dark-eyed and olive-skinned Italian sexy stars such as Sofia Loren and Gina Lollobrigida were perceived as 'exotic', as they were seen as the embodiment of 'a certain raw earthiness that seemed natural and unspoilt' (Gundle 2007, 142). In the early 1950s, the renowned US sexologist Alfred Kinsey considered Italy his 'sexual Eden ... a country of sexual freedom and lack of inhibition' (quoted in Morris 2013, 29). In more recent years, Italian fashion brands, such as Dolce and Gabbana, have been relentlessly deploying the erotic power of Italians' racialized sexuality to market their products on the global stage.

I would thus contend that, in the eyes of Canadian male customers, Mirca's Italian nationality did not simply signal her 'foreign' status but also effectively turned her into an exotic female subject. Indeed, as a migrant woman coming from a not-fully-modern elsewhere, male customers reportedly expected her to be both naïve and sexually available. These intersecting racist and sexist stereotypes turned her into a particularly sought-after dancer. Once back in Italy, however, Mirca's exotic value dissipated, and the ordinariness of her local worker status decreased the request for her erotic entertainment services and, with it, the economic return on her labour.

Mirca's experiences foreground how race affects the value of women's erotic labour. Nevertheless, women are not just passive receptors of their ascribed exotic or domestic value; some do seek to manipulate race to increase their work revenues. For example, Law relayed that whilst working in Canadian strip clubs she purposefully stressed her 'Finnish heritage' (Law 2012, 143). Egan spoke of Margarita, an exotic dancer who used to play the role of '"*la mujer latina*" [the Latina woman] ... donning an accent (even though she was born and raised in the United States), dancing to salsa, speaking to [customers] in Spanish' (Egan 2006, 108). Similar observations were raised regarding women working in the sex market. Chapkis relayed how Cheyenne recounted describing herself to potential customers over the phone 'as half Native American and half Black. That way I appeal to the guys who want something "exotic" but want it packaged more like the girl next door. When I just say I'm Black, I get skipped over again and again' (quoted in Chapkis 1997, 105).

Women's capacity to manipulate their exotic value also emerged during my interview with Roberta – an Italian cis woman in her early thirties and a self-identified sex worker. When we first spoke, Roberta had been working for a few years for an international intermediation agency offering temporary sex-related jobs across and beyond Europe. She would, for example, alternate working as an actress in porn productions and as a sex shop assistant; as an escort for men on business or holiday trips and as a brothel sex worker in northern European countries such as the Netherlands and Germany, where these establishments are legal. At that particular moment, Roberta had just returned from one-month-long employment in one of these, in Switzerland, near the Italian border. When I asked her who her colleagues were, she said there were approximately fifty – mostly from Eastern Europe, a few from Western Europe and 'two African women'. Evidently, and consistent with what I earlier observed regarding Italian night clubs, the women selling sex in this establishment were overwhelmingly white. 'How did work go?' I asked her. 'Ok, normal', she replied, 'there [were] tons of Italians [men] to whom I disguised myself as an Eastern European [woman]!'

Roberta's tale highlights how she intentionally reassembled her race and nationality to increase the value of her heterosexual desirability in the eyes of her fellow countrymen. In her experience, her exotic value was a flexible asset that she could mould to her best advantage. In so doing, she switched from the unglamorous, ordinary position of the local worker (as so she may have been in the eyes of the brothel's many Italian customers) to the more attractive and economically rewarding position of the foreign and specifically Eastern European woman.

Segmentation Patterns in Street Sex Work

Different constellations of race, nationality and gender did not affect only the women's labour exchange value but also their presence and distribution in the sex market. This segmentation emerged starkly in the street.

The prevalence of migrant women on the Italian street sex market reflects the outcome of intersecting structures of discrimination, at the crossroads between the country's ethnonationalist affective economy (Chapter 1) and its prostitution and migration laws.[8] Some scholars have observed that, in many Western countries, the geographies of street sex work have dramatically changed as a result of the ongoing process of sex working people's forced displacement towards the margins or outside the borders of the city (see e.g. Hubbard 2000a; Hubbard et al. 2008; Ross 2010). Similar processes have taken place in Italy over the past three decades. For example, in my hometown, there are no more sex working women on the sides of the main street I lived off, and more broadly, the sex working population is no longer in plain sight within the city. It is, though, as soon as one moves outside of its perimeter. Such displacement, undertaken in the name of 'propriety' and 'decorum', operationalized the ethnonationalist drive to clean the streets to make the nation look 'respectable' (Chapter 1). At the same time, it exacerbated the sex working population's exposure to safety risks and police surveillance. As I have discussed elsewhere (Zambelli 2019), the Italian prostitution law does not forbid a woman to sell sex in a property that she owns. Nevertheless, this homeowner position is structurally unavailable to migrant street sex working women, who would instead have to rent a property to work indoors.[9] However, striking a tenancy agreement requires proof of financial stability and other types of guarantees that may be hard to obtain. Indeed, many women I encountered while on outreach service relayed living in peripheral and yet expensive motels. Inevitably, these high living costs reduced their earnings and remittances, requiring that women work more to live up to their own and their families' needs and aspirations (Chapter 4).

Race affected deeply migrant women's position in the street sex market. Whilst on outreach service, and influenced by the news reports on Nigerian women's sex trafficking to Italy,[10] I expected to encounter many black African women on the street, but I did not – though a senior volunteer told me that there were usually more at work during the day. This asynchrony may have been partly determined by the spatial distance between the women's home and their work sites. It seemed, in fact, that many lived and worked in different cities, so their work patterns may have been dictated by public transportation, which in those semi-urban and provincial areas usually runs from dawn to dusk only. Despite their relatively minor presence compared to white Eastern European cis women, black African women's position in the street sex market was lower. While the first were stationed on the main arterial roads, the latter were to be found on secondary streets only, which likely were less remunerative work spots due to the lower volume of cars passing by (Kulick 1998, 144). The price of the cis women's standard sexual service was also markedly different: while white Eastern European women received thirty euros, black African women were paid only a third of this money (ten euros).[11] This unequal remuneration reflects the higher economic value of whiteness, which other scholars have consistently observed across different segments of the US sex markets (see e.g. Brents and Hausbeck 2010, 20; Lever and Dolnick 2010, 190; Koken, Bimbi and Parsons 2010, 228; on the porn industry, see Miller-Young 2010, 220).

Race interplayed with gender in affecting the women's position further. Migrant trans women were overwhelmingly citizens of Latin American countries and they worked on the outskirts of the city and in particularly remote areas, such as industrial zones that were completely deserted at night-time (except for the cars of their potential customers). While I have never encountered a cis Italian woman selling sex on the street (Chapter 1 and next section), I did encounter a few Italian trans women – a difference which partly reflects trans people's marginalization from the labour market.[12] However, different from their migrant colleagues, Italian trans women worked in the city, in a few known places where they would wait for potential customers seated in their own car – an infrastructure affording them a safer work spot while indexing their relatively privileged position compared to their migrant peers. In his study of *travestis* in Brazil, Don Kulick relayed that they intentionally avoided 'point[s] of female prostitution', because 'they know that many of the men who stop for them will be expecting a woman ([whereas] at the other points of prostitution where travestis work, the majority of men who stop know they are stopping for a travesti)' (Kulick 1998, 146). Based on my fieldwork, I would suggest that discretion also mattered. In fact, the remoteness and/or deserted quality of the places where the trans sex working women were stationed enabled customers to find them easily and discretely, thereby being able to negotiate the purchase of sex away from prying eyes. To be seen doing so, in fact, would otherwise call into question customers' masculinity, with potentially disruptive consequences on their lives.[13] Notwithstanding their spatial containment, trans sex working women commanded the highest price for their standard sexual service. Ranging between fifty and eighty euros, it was two to three times what was paid to white cis Eastern European women (thirty euros) – which, in turn, was three times what black African women were paid (ten euros). This price pyramid suggests that trans women were highly desirable and sought after. Nevertheless, this appreciation does not align with their status in society, of which they are pushed at the margins.[14]

Assembling Intimate Labour in Migration

For the migrant cis and trans street sex working women I met on outreach service, the performance of 'intimate labour'– a category that 'places in a continuum the discretely examined categories of care, sex, and domestic work' (Boris and Parreñas 2010a, 3) – seemingly constituted the condition of possibility of their migratory projects (Zambelli 2019; Gutierrez Garza 2019). The women's concentration in these occupations reflect both the latter's gendered character and entrenched economic inequalities between countries, which contribute to driving migration from economically poorer to economically wealthier countries.

Historically, in Western countries, care work has been constructed as a typically female and, *therefore*, a socially and economically undervalued activity (Chapter 3).[15] When, after the Second World War, increasing numbers of women entered into the labour market, they struggled to juggle the double burden of paid work and unpaid care work, engendering what has been defined as a 'care crisis' (Parreñas 2004). It was increasingly women living in economically impoverished countries that, towards the end of the last century, set themselves on the move towards and beyond Europe to respond to this crisis (see e.g. Ehrenreich and Hochschild, 2004; Constable 2007; Moukarbel 2009). At the same time, women's migration produced a similar 'care deficit' (Hochschild 2000; 2004) in their own households, which their female kin – daughters, sisters, mothers – compensated. It is this transnational reconfiguration of women's paid and unpaid care work that the concept of the 'global care chain' (Hochschild 2000; 2004) describes.[16] In Italy, the demand for migrant care workers is high. In part, this reflects the widespread cultural preference for home-based versus institutionalized elderly services (Vietti 2010). It does also ensue from the very same political economy of migrant labour exploitation discussed earlier in this chapter with regards to women working as lap dancers. As the number of work visas issued yearly is consistently lower than the demand,[17] many women enter, stay and work in Italy as undocumented migrants, thereby increasing their structural exposure to exploitation and abuse.

The sale of sex is also a highly gendered occupation (Chapter 1), and it is again migrant women that make up the majority of the sex working population in Western European countries (see e.g. Mai 2013, 108; TAMPEP 2015; ICRSE 2020, 4), including Italy. During my outreach service, I observed that these different forms of intimate labour interplayed in multiple and complex ways in the lives and livelihoods of the women who were selling sex on the street.

As a start, care work, and more specifically to work as a *badante* (live-in care worker), appeared to be the only viable alternative occupation to selling sex that the migrant cis women I met could conceive (Zambelli 2019). Age further segmented this gendered and racialized labour market. 'They told me "You are too young": they are afraid that I do certain things', said Nunzia, a Nicaraguan sex working woman, who explained to me why she thought she could never work as a live-in carer in Italy. Women's age thus appears to function as a respectability marker, affecting their sex or care work patterns accordingly. Indeed, whereas most migrant sex working cis women were in their twenties or early thirties, recent research has shown that approximately 90 per cent of the women working as *badante* in Italy are older than thirty-five (Zucca 2016).[18] Nevertheless, *badante* work did not necessarily appear to constitute a better alternative to (street) sex work. For example, Nunzia said that even if she were offered a job she would not accept it: 'to be locked inside [the home] all day long, every day … to be on duty 24 hours, also on Sunday … and the pay is too little: nine hundred euros a month! Okay, they give you food but … it is too bad to be locked [in], and they [the employers] take advantage of you.' The average working conditions in this sector are in fact poor, and often outright exploitative. Recent research has found that, on a regular contract, women are paid four euros per hour, but many reported working more than the contracted hours (Marchetti 2016, 108), as well as widespread evidence of negative physical, emotional or psychological consequences.[19] Among migrant street sex working women, Nunzia's words were uniquely straightforward. Some of her peers did sometimes ponder over the possibility of shifting to *badante* work, particularly when sex work felt harder or more hazardous than usual – perhaps because either they themselves or some colleagues had a security incident or felt at heightened risk of contracting a sexually-transmitted disease. Yet, none ever said more than they could if they wished – a silence that may have partly indexed their hesitation to discuss their unreadiness to drop one job for the other in front of the two 'respectable' women comfortably sitting in a van.

These two occupations were also not necessarily mutually exclusive. For example, I occasionally encountered sex working women who said that they usually worked as *badante* but made recourse to street sex work either to buffer unemployment between two care jobs or top-up their care work revenues based on need. In her late forties, Ulla, a Ukrainian woman naturalized as Spanish, was one of them. After losing her job to the 2007–08 financial crisis, she moved from Spain to Italy to work as a *badante* for an elderly couple; additionally, she often had to care for the couple's grandson while his mother was at work. Nonetheless, Ulla's wage was too little to support herself and her own son, who was in higher education. 'I come out only when I do not have enough money to make it to the end of the month', she said when we – the women in the van – commented that we had never met before.

The multiple articulations of care and sex work in some of the migrant sex working women's lives may and did also cut across borders. When I first met Katarina, a Romanian woman in her late twenties, the volunteer with whom I was on service that night greeted her warmly, commenting that it was a long time since they had last seen each other. Katarina smiled – she seemed pleased to meet a friendly face, although she would have probably preferred to be elsewhere. It was in fact with palpable sadness that she told us that she had just come back from home, in Romania, where she spent over a year with her mother and her little child. Eventually, they ran out of the money that she had accumulated by (street sex) working in Italy, so she had to return for more while her mother took over childcare in her absence.

Katarina's division of intimate labour with her mother evokes the global care chain model (Hochschild 2000; 2004). Indeed, her migration similarly engendered a care deficit, which her mother has been compensating for by taking on childcare responsibilities for her grandson. However, it also partially deviates from it because the nature of the intimate labour performed at different levels of the chain varied. Katarina, in fact, did not migrate to sell to another family the everyday care acts subtracted from her own, but to sell sex. This transnational and intergenerational organization of women's sex and care work, that recurred among the migrant women selling sex, configures one of the possible articulations of what I would call a 'global intimate labour chain'. This all-encompassing term includes global care chains and other potential transnational assemblages of intimate labour in migration, such as those involving women working as lap dancers (e.g. Milena, Chapter 3).

Entry into different types of intimate contracts constituted one way through which migrant sex working women assembled and held together these global intimate labour chains. While some sought to strike a formal employment contract as *badante*, others aspired to marry an EU citizen – both cases implying the possibility for women to reside in Italy legally and continue selling sex (as they expressed the intention of doing) without fearing deportation (ICRSE 2020). Moreover, possession of a work contract would have increased the women's chances to secure a tenancy agreement independently and thereby start selling sex indoors, which some looked forward to for the safer and generally better working conditions they may have enjoyed.[20]

The women's interest and opportunities to enter either one of these contracts appeared to be nonetheless unevenly distributed, reflecting – I suggest – gendered and nationality-based constraints as well as differences in the temporalities of their migratory projects. Among non-EU Eastern European cis women, many of whom were engaged in cycles of circular migration from/to their home country (Chapter 4), a care work contract appeared to constitute a more sought-after means to their end, as it could provide them with flexible status on demand. Arguably, however, it was also potentially easier to be dissolved than a marriage contract. Possibly, next to the structural gendered violence discussed earlier in the chapter (i.e. homo- and transphobia) making trans women's employment as *badante* unlikely (and thus potentially implausible and suspicious in the eyes of the Italian migration authorities), it was in fact the longer durability of a marriage contract that made it more appealing to Latin American sex working (trans) women. The costs that they incur when migrating to Europe are indeed high, involving much indebtedness (Kulick 1998, 171–72) and often, the pursuit of their migratory project implies spending long, continuous periods away from their home country. A marriage contract would thus offer the women a durable legal status throughout the period they stay in the EU/Italy to sell sex. However, entry into such a contract was difficult and expensive. Mercedes, a Paraguayan trans woman (Chapter 4), recounted having paid a Spanish man tens of thousands of euros to marry him and still he kept asking her for more money, in the awareness that she had no choice but to pay if she were to reach the minimum temporal threshold, after which she could have obtained an independent residence permit.

The multiple uses of marriage with an EU/Italian citizen also emerged from the interviews with women working in night clubs as lap dancers. For example, Zeina (Chapter 3) used to work in Italy on tourist visas until she married an Italian man, through whom she acquired the right to reside and work in Italy legally. Fiona (Chapter 3) similarly recounted that her sister moved to Italy years before 'to do this job', which she left only when 'she eventually got married [in Italy] and established her family'. With these observations, I do not intend to suggest that the nature of these intimate unions was instrumental. I am saying, however, that in the context of a tight border regime and a gendered and racialized labour market, marriage appears to be a primary means through which women in this social location may be released from their structural position as 'bad' women.

Conclusions

In this chapter, I have foregrounded how race, class, gender and age affected the presence, visibility and position of women across the three sexscapes discussed in the previous chapters: the recreational pole dance school, the night club and the street.

White women prevailed everywhere and occupied a structurally privileged position vis-à-vis Black women. The recreational pole dance school space was almost exclusively inhabited by white Italian women for reasons that, I have suggested, reflect the legacy of racist and sexist constructions of sexuality linking Black women to sexual excess. In night clubs, the lap dancing workforce predominantly consisted of migrant white Eastern European cis women, at the crossroads between a political economy of migrant labour exploitation and male customers' racialized desire. Cis white Eastern European women similarly prevailed on the street, and they were paid three times as much as Black African cis women, while other conditions remained equal.

However, whiteness's social and economic value was not monolithic but internally fragmented based on gendered, racialized and class-based stereotypes. It could signify a woman's endowment of sound or loose morality, domestic or exotic value. I have described the latter as constituted by elements of appreciation and denigration for (women's) purported racially and/or culturally defined 'backwardness'. Exotic value, that is, encapsulates the erotic power of the hypersexuality of the 'pornotropics' (McClintock 1995, 22) and contempt for the backwardness of people coming from an 'anachronistic space' (McClintock 1995, 30). Its value is situational and fluid: it varies based on the 'racial grammar' (Bonilla-Silva 2012) of the (male) beholder of the gaze and (women's) race manipulation skills and possibilities.

Trans women occupied the margins of these sexscapes, mirroring their broader marginalization in society due to high levels of homo- and transphobia. Whilst acknowledging that the relationship between a person's appearance and her gender identity is neither fixed nor univocal (J. Butler 1990),[21] I find it plausible to suggest that trans women were largely absent from the recreational pole dance space. However, they were present on the street, where the higher prices they commanded compared to cis women across race indexed their advantageous position at a cusp where the demand for their services was significantly higher than the offer. At the same time, their spatial concentration in a few secluded or deserted places suggests that their potential customers wanted to find them easily but discretely, away from prying eyes.

As already discussed in Chapter 4, for the migrant street sex working women, the spheres of work and intimacy were intricately entangled, in multiple ways. Working as *badante* was the most readily and perhaps only alternative occupation that most thought they could realistically have access to. Nonetheless, this possibility was unevenly distributed based on women's age and gender. Racist and sexist stereotypes presenting young migrant cis women as 'disrespectable' female subjects (Zambelli 2018; 2019) impinged upon their possibilities to be perceived as fit for this job, while transphobia possibly contributed to making *badante* work unlikely available to trans women – the latter being a tentative suggestion requiring further investigation. At times, sex and care work could be seen to function as complementary occupations. For example, the sale of sex could constitute a flexible means for some women usually working as *badante* to buffer unemployment and/ or boost their revenues and/or remittances on demand. In many migrant women's lives, sex and care work were also transnationally and intergenerationally assembled in ways that I have suggested defining as 'global intimate labour chains', encompassing the performance of different assemblages of intimate labour at different levels of the chain. Among non-EU migrant cis and trans women, the possibility to enter into an intimate contract constituted one of the most valued ways through which these labour chains may be organized and held together, as they held the promise for women to legalize their residence status and thus possibly improve their living and working conditions.

Notes

1. For a history of the SlutWalk Movement and an analysis of its transnational and intersectional dimensions, see Joetta Carr (2018).
2. Literally, the term *extracomunitari* (extra-communitarians) would describe nationals of countries that are not part of the European Community – now European Union. However, in common parlance, Italians use it with a derogatory connotation to exclusively refer to migrants racialized as 'Black' (Komla-Ebri 2002).
3. Note that I felt in the position to raise this question with Eleonora because she no longer worked in night clubs at the time of the interview, and I did not rely on gatekeepers to contact her.
4. When I was in my early twenties, I decided to improve my language skills by taking on a job in an English-speaking country. I jumped on a plane and landed in Ireland, having no prior labour arrangements. That was possible because my Italian nationality

granted me the freedom to move, seek work and reside anywhere in the EU. Many peers of mine did the same (albeit more frequently heading towards London) and thousands of EU citizens have continued to do so until 'Brexit' i.e. when the UK withdrew from the EU.
5. Still, in some circumstances, a woman's Italian nationality circulated as a precious asset, signalling her purported endowment with higher 'cultural capital' (Bourdieu 1986) than migrant women. For example, Eleonora relayed that some night clubs 'look[ed] for the Italian [woman] because they need[ed] culture – someone who can speak properly and entertain a certain kind of table with people who have money but who also want to have some high [service] quality'.
6. On the role of the literature of the Grand Tour in fostering these racialized representations of Italians, see Silvana Patriarca (2005, 386).
7. On the persisting construction of intra-European difference through sexuality, see also Jill Dubisch (1995, 35–36).
8. The quantification of the street sex working population and the proportion of migrants in it is nevertheless difficult to obtain. As the sale of sex in Italy is not considered 'work' (Chapter 1), it is structurally confined to the informal economy. Therefore, the precise characteristics of this labour market remain largely unknown and unknowable.
9. Conversely, women who migrate intending to sell care but later transition to selling sex appear to be able to perform the latter indoors, as Ana Gutierrez Garza shows in her ethnography of Latin American women in London (2019). Possibly, their capacity to do so reflected the women's prior possession of a tenancy agreement based on their regular employment as care workers – although this tentative interpretation requires further investigation.
10. Among many other news articles, see Lorenzo Tondo (2020) and Annie Kelly (2016). Scholars who have researched the representations, practices and experiences of Nigerian women in Italy at the crossroads between migration, sex work and sex trafficking include Irene Peano (2013) and Nicola Mai (2016).
11. On the street, cis women's standard sexual service went by the name of *bocca-figa* (mouth–pussy), consisting of fifteen minutes' oral stimulation of a man's penis followed by vaginal intercourse. Women relayed that many men asked for unprotected sex, for which they were ready to pay a lot more than the standard price.
12. The US-focused report by Erin Fitzgerald et al. (2015) discusses the relationship between social exclusion and trans people's engagement in sex work. On the structural discrimination of visibly trans people on the Italian labour market, see Porpora Marcasciano, Cathy LaTorre and Monica Pasquino (2013); Monica J. Romano (2019).
13. The case of Piero Marrazzo, an Italian male politician whose political career stopped immediately after being outed for his relationship with a trans woman very much corroborates this suggestion. In 2009, the then governor of the Lazio region (which includes Rome) was blackmailed by four *carabinieri* (later found guilty of this crime) based on their purported possession of video footage portraying him with a trans woman. In a few days, Marrazzo suspended himself from all his public responsibilities. To date, he has not resumed his political career.
14. Quantitative studies on the experiences of discrimination of LGBTQI+ people in Italy are limited. Among these, see Carlo D'Ippoliti and Alexander Schuster (2011); Fabrizio Botti and Carlo D'Ippoliti (2014); Beatrice Gusmano, Anna Lorenzetti and UNAR (2014). According to the Trans Murder Monitoring Index, throughout 2008–2021, Italy has recorded the highest number of victims in the EU (Transgender Europe 2022).

15. In this book, I adopt feminist economists' definition of 'care work' as a field encompassing all activities aiming at social reproduction (e.g. from childcare to house chores), whereby I include domestic work(ers) under the rubric of care work(ers). In fact, in real life, it may be difficult to separate these two figures. For example, a *badante* is generally expected to clean, cook and perform a series of domestic chores; she might also be asked to care for her employers' grandchildren (see the case of Ulla later in this chapter).
16. Scholarship in this domain is extensive. Some recent critical engagements with the concept of the global care chain are found in Nicola Yeates (2004); John Borneman (2017); Helma Lutz (2018).
17. Every year, a *decreto flussi* (flows decree) establishes the number of migrants that will be issued a work visa, per economic sector, based on figures provided by the Ministry of Labour. The *decreto flussi* is an economic planning measure for migrant labour that was first introduced with Law n. 40/1998 *Disciplina dell'immigrazione e norme sulla condizione dello straniero* (Regulation of immigration and norms on the condition of the foreign person).
18. In his research, Gianfranco Zucca reported that one-fourth of the women (25.7%) were 55 years or older; over a third (36.9%) were in the 45–54 age range; a quarter (25.9%) in the 35–44 age range, and women younger than 35 were 11.5% of the total.
19. The research by Francesca Alice Vianello shows that, since taking up the job, more than half (52.9%) have suffered from back pain, a third (31.6%) from insomnia and over a quarter (27.5%) from anxiety or depression (Vianello 2016, 131).
20. In her research on street sex work in San Francisco, Montreal and Toronto, Frances Shaver reported that work on the street 'is much riskier than other venues in terms of legal intervention, police arrest, and experiences of violence' (Shaver 2005, 310).
21. Gender is not only performative (J. Butler 1990), but a person's performance of 'woman' does not necessarily imply identification as such – see Don Kulick's study on Brazilian *travesti* (Kulick 1998).

Conclusions

Midsummer 2013 I was in Rome participating in a protest organized by the International Committee on the Rights of Sex Workers in Europe (ICRSE), following the back-to-back murders of two sex workers in Turkey and Sweden (ICRSE 2013).[1] The demonstration took place in twenty-nine cities across the globe, and in Italy, it was coordinated by the *Comitato* (Chapter 1). That was the first time I attended a sex workers' rights demonstration but the nth time I had taken to the streets to publicly display my dissent. Throughout my life, I have participated in uncountable numbers of protests – local, national and international; in Italy or wherever I was living; against neoliberal policies, wars, racism, violence against women, homo- and transphobia and more. The scale of the solidarity we collectively displayed in the act of marching side by side varied between hundreds of people and hundreds of thousands (sometimes, over a million). Never before, however, I had attended an in-person protest where I could determine the number of fellow participants with some sense of precision. I could this time: in front of the Swedish Embassy, where we first convened, we were hardly twenty, including myself. I thought that had the initiative taken place on the weekend perhaps more people would have been in the position to join in and show their support in person. Perhaps. Nonetheless, this low attendance gave me a hint of the marginal position that sex workers' rights occupied in the Italian political scene of the time. The contrast between the stillness of the Embassy – laying in a quiet, residential neighbourhood, with very few people and vehicles passing through – and our attempts at being seen and heard as we shouted slogans, held signs and distributed leaflets could not but increase this perception.

We stopped the demonstration after an hour approximately, and we agreed to reconvene in front of the Turkish Embassy, in the afternoon. I had lunch with a group of fellow protesters, including Pia Covre, the co-founder of *Comitato*, and then we travelled there together. None of us knew the exact location, so I asked for directions from the people standing around us on the bus. A man of approximately my age responded to my query and then asked me where I was from. People of colour living in white-majority Western countries will likely find this question a disturbingly familiar expression of 'everyday racism' (Essed 1991), which reflects and reproduces the underpinning assumption that they are 'bodies out of place' (Puwar 2004). Surely, my accent betrayed my status as a stranger to the city, but more than manifesting the man's curiosity about my 'real' origins, I perceived his question as a wishful hook-up conversation starter. I replied out of politeness, reciprocating his help with directions, but then I turned my back on him to convey that I did not wish to continue chatting. My body language, though, went completely unnoticed. 'And so, what are you doing here?' he asked from behind my back, raising his tone to make sure that I would hear him.

Annoyed, I considered ignoring him, but I did not want to look rude. After all, we were not too far from our destination, so I turned back to him to answer. As I did, I noticed that the man was wearing the T-shirt of a charity supporting inmates' rehabilitation. Guessing that he must have thus been sensitive to social justice struggles, I decided to turn that undesired conversation into an opportunity to manifest and perhaps elicit solidarity for the cause that I was standing up for. 'I am in Rome to attend a demonstration supporting sex workers' rights to fair and safe working,' I stated plainly. My answer must have taken the man by surprise, for he remained silent, as if hit by a shock wave. 'Yes, indeed. It is true. That is work,' he pensively said after a few seconds, 'but what does your identity card say?'

Next to the carrier's picture, full name, citizenship and home address, the Italian identity card includes additional personal information, such as physical descriptors (height, hair and eye colour), civil status (although lately, this question has become optional) and occupation. Evidently, it was this last piece of information that the man was looking for: was I a sex worker, a 'bad' woman, a 'whore'? And if I was, was I in or out of the closet? Did I, that is, make myself known as one to the state? In the past, under Italy's system of state-regulated female prostitution, any woman selling sex was compelled to register herself as a prostitute (Chapter 1). Today, however, this is no longer neither required nor possible, as under the Merlin Law, the sale of sex acts is not considered 'work'. The inscription of 'sex worker' or 'prostitute' on one's identity card would thus be a bureaucratic impossibility. That historical nuance, though, unlikely was the kind of answer that the man was after. In hindsight, I realized that I should have called out his male entitlement to raise such an intrusive and morally laden question in public. There and then, though, I just felt on a battlefront from which I did not want to withdraw, lest I be shied into shame and submission. So, I did want to answer, but how? After all, I have never sold sex in my life, and I cannot deny having felt the instinct to say that – to say, that is, that I was 'only an ally'. But was that not precisely the refusal to reproduce the boundary between women in and out of sex work just one such way to stand in solidarity with sex workers?

As I kept juggling these questions in my mind, the man repeated his, making me feel as if I was a defendant under vice squad interrogation. Eventually, I decided to simply state the profession that was recorded on my identity card: 'consultant'. That was the employment category that I was regularly assigned while working in international development, which was still my main occupation when I last renewed my document. It was, that is, 'the truth'. Not for this man, though. 'A-ha! *Suuure*. A *c-o-n-s-u-l-t-a-n-t*,' he said disparagingly, effectively insinuating that it was a code word instead.

I was flabbergasted. I could not have – and in fact, I had not imagined – that my word could be twisted in such a way so as to tautologically confirm this man's assumption about what I was doing for a living and, *therefore*, what *kind* of woman I was (and vice versa). I remained literally speechless and so, silence fell between us. I looked at him expressionlessly, and he raised no further questions, suggesting that he must have been satisfied with the outcome of his voyeuristic truth search. Shortly afterwards, we reached our destination and got off the bus. Once on the street, Pia observed, amused and conspiratorial, that the man had taken me for a sex worker. 'True!' I exclaimed, reciprocating her smile. Inside, I was still ruminating on the meaning of that exchange and my positioning in it, but instinctively I felt good about my conduct. In retrospect, I suspect that there and then, more than my political consciousness, it was Pia's silent and trusting presence close to me that kept me grounded, preventing me from effectively claiming my 'respectability' in front of that man. Today, I look back at this episode as a watershed moment in the moulding of my subjectivity – of which I am grateful and proud.

****

This book has been an (auto)ethnographic journey into women's negotiation of selves in a strongly patriarchal and heteronormative context, such as Italy, where the division of women into 'good' or 'bad' is entrenched and forceful. More precisely, the book explored the workings of the 'whore stigma', which regulates the tension between women's sexuality and their status by operating simultaneously as an instrument of social control and subjectivation. Women's ascription into the 'whore' category implies their dehumanization and intensifies their vulnerability to gender-based violence of any type and form and at all levels.[2] From an early age, women are disciplined into conforming to patriarchal chastity norms to avert the whore stigma and its hazardous effects. However, in the current Western sexscape, (white) women's confident display of sexuality has been resignified as evidence of their empowerment, liberation and modernity, unsettling the tenability of this rigid binary division. The book thus explored how, in Italy, Italian and migrant women negotiated their use of sexuality from within a continuum of 'sexscapes of pleasure', entailing their heightened exposure to the risk of stigmatization as 'whores'. To this purpose, the book brought into mutual conversation the narratives of recreational pole dance entrepreneurs and/or instructors, who invest and/or teach other women how to pole dance for their pleasure; lap dancers working in night clubs; street sex working women and sex workers and the author's subjectivity, as reflected in this writing. In so doing, it offered multiple contributions to existing scholarship on gender, sexuality, race and migration in Italy and in Western Europe, across several disciplines.

First, the book offered an ethnographic enquiry into straight, white cis women's gendered subjectivation through sexuality in a Western European country, which is a research subject that is infrequently investigated ethnographically in the scholarship currently circulating in the English language. With the exception of Beverly Skeggs' highly influential ethnography on working-class women in North-West England (Skeggs 1997), I had to move outside the geographical boundaries of white-majority Western countries – thereby returning to anthropology's traditional areas of enquiry – to find ethnographies discussing non-sex working women's negotiation of selves through sexuality. I found particular inspiration in the works of Debra Curtis on young girls in Nevis (Curtis 2009) and Rachel Spronk on middle-class women and men in Nairobi (Spronk 2012); however, there is a tremendous body of anthropological scholarship on gender and sexuality in the Middle East, Africa, Latin America, Asia and Oceania, making the mere thought of deciding whom to/not to reference daunting. By turning the anthropological gaze back to Western societies and 'up' (Nader 1972) onto straight, normative subjectivities, therefore, this book positions itself in the wake of ongoing efforts to decolonize Western academic knowledge production, and particularly anthropology (F. Harrison 1991; Allen and Jobson 2016).

More specifically, the book offered an ethnographic exploration of how women negotiate dignity and value in spaces where they use their sexuality for pleasure and/or for work, thereby intensifying their exposure to the whore stigma. To this purpose, the book offered two novel theoretical contributions. First, it introduced the concept of pleasure to describe activities such as recreational pole dancing that women practice in their leisure time to enjoy their own projection as intensely (hetero)sexually desirable – as the glamorized figure of the female stripper is – mainly in front of their circles of significant others, friends and family (versus paying customers and spectators). Second, the book reconfigured the concept of the 'whore stigma' by combining its original definition as a patriarchal instrument of social control (Pheterson 1996) with a Foucauldian interpretation of its functioning as a disciplinary device of subjection. By following the journey of the whore stigma across the non-/sex working women binary, the book brought back centre stage its nature as a gendered rather than exclusively occupational stigma – while acknowledging that these two dimensions overlap in the lives of women selling erotic and/or sexual labour. In so doing, it contributes to recent sociological scholarship on sex work stigma (Bjønness, Nencel and Skilbrei 2021) and stigma power (Link and Phelan 2014; Tyler and Slater 2018; Tyler 2021).

While processes of straight, white cis women's gendered subjectivation in Western countries are ethnographically underexplored, there are conspicuous bodies of scholarship addressing them from within media and cultural studies, psychology, political theory and socio-legal studies. Since the outburst of the feminist sex wars, however, Western feminist debates on women's engagement with sexualized cultures and/or sex work have primarily focused on its impact on the reproduction or subversion of the gender relations of power between men and women. Therefore, this book's second main contribution has been to direct attention elsewhere and specifically at the power relations that women reproduce among themselves, across different social locations and intersecting axes of social differentiation. In fact, '[w]hore stigma makes central the racial and class hierarchy reinforced in the dividing of women into the pure and the impure, the clean and the unclean, the white and virgin and all the others. If woman is other, whore is the other's other' (Grant 2014, 77).

The book indeed foregrounded the centrality of gendered othering processes in non-sex working cis women's negotiation of selves (Chapters 2; 3). Many recreational pole dancers and lap dancers used a range of respectability tactics to claim their dignity and value. For the most part, their deployment implied the displacement of the whore stigma onto a category of 'other women', which they depicted using intersecting gendered, class-based and racialized stereotypes. Recreational pole dance entrepreneurs and instructors (Chapter 2), most of whom were Italians, claimed their respectability against lap dancers, whose patriarchal-defined female dishonour lay in their readiness to dance erotically for male pleasure rather than for their own pleasure. They also systematically conflated lap dancers and 'foreign' and particularly Eastern European women, thereby reproducing an ethnonationalist affective economy characterized by the overlap between the figure of the migrant and the prostitute (Chapter 1). Similarly, many lap dancers (Chapter 3), who included both migrant and Italian women, passed the whore stigma on to another category of 'other women', as they claimed their respectability against colleagues working 'dirty'– that is, women who were (also) selling sex. However, in their case, race did not appear to constitute as strong an othering device as for recreational pole dancers. I have thus suggested that the fact that Italian and migrant women were colleagues on the same work floor, rather than distant, imagined, stereotyped 'other women', ran against their crystallization of the whore stigma along ethnonationalist lines.

For the women for whom the gendered and occupational dimension of the whore stigma overlapped – that is, for cis and trans sex working women and sex workers – class was the key terrain on which they claimed their dignity and value (Chapter 4). Women selling sex negotiated their engagement in a stigmatized, hazardous and precarious occupation at the crossroads between their own and often their family members' livelihood needs and social mobility aspirations and a 'matrix of domination' (Collins 2000) consisting of capitalist exploitation, precarity, restrictive migration regimes and different forms and intensity of patriarchal violence. Frequently invested with breadwinning responsibilities towards their minor and adult dependents, migrant sex working cis and trans women appeared to find dignity and value in their cruelly optimistic (Berlant 2006) attachments to the bittersweet fruits of their labour. The Italian sex workers that I have interviewed, who arguably structurally occupied a less socially vulnerable position in virtue of their nationality/citizenship and in-country legal status, found value (also, or mainly) in their achievement of a better balance in the structurally unequal relationship between capital and labour, as they increased the economic return on their labour and the time and money that they could spend off work. Overall, therefore, women selling sex did not seem to be overly invested in the displacement of the whore stigma onto some 'other women'. I have argued that theirs was a self-contained materialist ethics, as the women's assertion of their dignity and value through or despite their work did not rest upon nor reproduce the othering of any other social group.

At this point, some may consider that the non-sex working women whose narratives I have discussed in this book lacked feminist consciousness because they did not challenge but contributed to reproducing the patriarchal division of women into 'good' or 'bad' and, therefore, their own gendered subjection. Some might thus see here a reason to suggest reversing this hierarchy of women's patriarchal-defined dis/honour by putting 'bad' women first. As a feminist researcher, however, I find this interpretation theoretically reductionist and politically unhelpful, as it too easily dismisses the structural and everyday symbolic and material violence that women are subjected to, from their different social locations. As a group of non- and sex working women posited decades ago,[3] it is instead necessary to recall that 'submission, manipulation, rejection or any combination of the three ... can be a useful self-preserving skill or life-saving strategy when used consciously on one's own behalf; each can also be self-deprecating or endangering alienations when enacted mindlessly at the mercy of others' (Pheterson 1996, 135). I thus conceive women's claims of dignity and value through the displacement of the whore stigma as a 'weapon of the weak' (J.C. Scott 1987) – that is, they were the most readily available 'tactics' (de Certeau 1984) that they could *individually* deploy to negotiate their use of sexuality outside of chastity norms without jeopardizing their human status. The third main contribution that this book has intended to make, then, goes beyond academia. By empirically tracing continuities in women's experiences of subjection to the whore stigma across the non-/sex working women binary, it aims to feed into a materialist feminist politics of liberation. As such, it situates itself in the wake of the work of scholars, activists and sex workers (these three sometimes being overlapping categories) for whom sex workers' rights are human rights and as such inseparable from an inclusive social justice agenda (among many others see Kempadoo and Doezema 1998; Agustín 2007; Kotiswaran 2011; Smith and Mac 2018).

Women, however, are not a class – let alone an internally homogeneous front (Lorde 1984; Mohanty 1988; 2003; Puar 2008). This book's fourth main contribution, then, has been to foreground how gender, race, class and nationality differently affected women's presence, position, in/visibility and value across the three sexscapes analysed – that is, the pole dance school, the night club and street sex work areas. Through their contrast, the book outlined some key elements of the matrix of domination producing their racialized and gendered segmentation (Chapter 5), the effects of which manifested in multiple ways. Recreational pole dance entrepreneurs, instructors and students were almost exclusively white Italian cis women, and I have suggested that Black women's absence from this space reflects the 'duress' (Stoler 2016) of racist and sexist constructions of sexuality marking their bodies as excessively sexual. This pleasure practice, therefore, appears to be unevenly accessible for women across race. I have discussed the prevalence of white Eastern European cis women in the lap dancing workforce and on the street at the crossroads between a political economy of migrant labour exploitation, co-constituted through restrictive EU and Italian migration laws, trans- and homophobia, and male customers' racialized desire. Indeed, transphobia profoundly shaped trans women's presence and visibility across the three sexscapes analysed in this book. They were either absent or invisible in the recreational pole dance schools and night clubs where I undertook my research, while on the street, they were simultaneously spatially secluded and the highest paid for their work, suggesting that they were ambivalently positioned as precious objects of male customers' concealed desire. Finally, I have introduced the concept of 'exotic value' to take stock of the changing value of (women's hetero)sexual desirability based on place, the racial grammar of the beholder of the (male) gaze and (women's) race manipulation skills and possibilities.

Contra the Western normative imagination that intimacy and the market are and should remain 'separate and hostile' spheres (Zelizer 2005), which lies at the core of the feminist sex wars' debate on prostitution (Chapter 4), the book showed that migrant women's livelihood and mobility strategies heavily relied on their readiness to commodify sex or care acts (Chapter 5). For most street sex working cis women, live-in care work (i.e. as *badante*) appeared to be the only realistic work alternative, while for some women working as *badante*, sex work was a flexible means through which they would buffer unemployment and/or boost their revenues and/or remittances on demand. For many street sex working women, and particularly for non-EU citizens, entry into an intimate contract, such as through employment as a *badante* or through marriage, appeared to have tactical value, as it held the promise to reside in Italy legally and thereby being able to improve their living and working conditions. Sex and care work were also synchronically articulated in migrant women's lives in ways that partly recalled and partly deviated from the 'global care chain' model (Hochschild 2000; 2004). The migration of the women in this book, in fact, similarly engendered a care deficit in their household of origin that their female kin (generally their mothers) filled in. However, they did not migrate to sell to another family the everyday care acts subtracted from their own, but to sell sex acts. Thus, the nature of the 'intimate labour' (Boris and Parreñas 2010b) performed at different levels of the chain varied, configuring what I have captured in the broader-encompassing term of 'global intimate labour chains'.

Finally, the book has also contributed to studying the politics of sexuality in modern and contemporary Italy. It has foregrounded the centrality of female prostitution in the moral and political economy of heteronormativity of the Italian nation state and the Catholic Church. It highlighted its propaedeutic role in the cultivation of men's heterosexual dispositions in times of war and peace alike and its function as a counterweight to Catholic marriage's indissoluble status (Chapter 1). Significantly, by the time I concluded my research (September 2015), Italy was the only Western European country that did not recognize any form of same-sex union *and* where, in contrast with the EU policy consensus on the adoption of the Swedish model instituting the criminalization of sex customers, major political parties called for reopening *case chiuse* (i.e. brothels) instead.

Since then, some things have changed, but others have not. Same-sex couples can now enter into a civil union but not into a marriage contract (yet) – although, currently, those who can afford it can marry abroad and demand that their marriage be recorded in the registries of their municipality of residence. However, the law does not give same-sex partners access to the so-called 'stepchild adoption', thereby denying shared parenthood over their offspring. Long after its first presentation, the Senate eventually voted down the so-called 'Zan bill' on hate crimes.[4] The Catholic Church was one of its fiercest opponents, having among other things lodged a formal diplomatic complaint based on the bill's purported infringement of the Concordat governing the diplomatic relations between Italy and the Holy See, and curtailment of religious freedom (Johnson 2021). Meanwhile, almost two hundred reform bill proposals later (Chapter 1), the Merlin Law remains unchanged, or perhaps, more precisely, untouchable. In fact, notwithstanding the seemingly widespread nostalgia for the female brothel, their reopening would be hardly morally tenable amidst the current Western consensus on the Swedish prostitution model. Hence, despite the shortcomings that most political forces, including *Comitato*, have highlighted, the Merlin Law seemingly maintains the status of the 'lesser evil' – as female prostitution itself was for the Catholic Church in Medieval Europe (Chapter 1).

Future research could take many directions. First, I do find important to explore whether and how the whore stigma plays a role in the subjectivation of trans women, and thereby pursue an even more nuanced discussion of the processes discussed in this book with regards to cis women's. Second, I consider to be both scholarly and politically compelling to pursue further ethnographic research contributing to exposing and unravelling the intersecting stigmas attached to (cis and trans) women performing erotic and/or sexual labour. The concepts of 'body work' (Wolkowitz 2006) and 'intimate labour' (Boris and Parreñas 2010a) offer ways to do so across the non-/sex working women binary, but other pathways are also possible. Speaking of the saturation of strip club research, Katherine Frank has suggested looking at 'the implications of strip club transactions beyond what happens inside the clubs' (Frank 2007, 511); for example, by including male customers' wives. Research into women buying erotic and/or sexual services from people of different genders and sexualities is still underdeveloped, at least in white-majority Western countries – there is, in fact, some scholarship on white women engaging in international sex tourism (Kempadoo 2001; see Bauer 2014 for a review). Throughout, an intersectional sensibility remains key to foster complex, nuanced and situated analyses that can contribute nurturing inclusive and effective feminist alliances and allyships within and across multiple differences.

Notes

1. The organization was recently renamed the European Sex Workers' Rights Alliance (ESWA).
2. For a recent and thorough analysis of the roots and effects of gender-based violence against women, see Committee on the Elimination of Discrimination Against Women (2017).
3. 'Alliance between Whores, Wives and Dykes: Proposal for a Work Group to Demystify and Eliminate the Division of Women into Bad, Good and Perverse.' The group first met in San Francisco in 1984. The document from which this citation is taken constitutes Appendix B of *The Prostitution Prism* (Pheterson 1996, 132–34).
4. Bill n. 2005, *Misure di prevenzione e contrasto della discriminazione e della violenza per motivi fondati sul sesso, sul genere, sull'orientamento sessuale, sull'identità di genere e sulla disabilità* (Norms to prevent and contrast discrimination and violence based on sex, gender, sexual orientation, gender identity and disability).

REFERENCES

Published Sources

Abbatecola, Emmanuela. 2019. Wanda era davvero piu' libera di Isoke? Ex-case chiuse e tratta delle migranti a confronto', in Annalisa Cegna, Natascia Mattucci and Alessio Ponzio (eds), *La prostituzione nell'Italia contemporanea. Tra storia, politiche e diritti*, Prima edizione. Spazi e Culture Del Novecento 2. Macerata: Eum, pp. 121–38.

Abu-Lughod, Lila. 1998. *Remaking Women: Feminism and Modernity in the Middle East.* Princeton, NJ: Princeton University Press.

Agustín, Laura María. 2007. *Sex at the Margins: Migration, Labour Markets and the Rescue Industry.* London: Zed.

Ahmed, Sara. 2004. 'Affective Economies', *Social Text* 22(2): 117–39. https://doi.org/10.1215/01642472-22-2_79-117.

——— . 2017. *Living a Feminist Life.* Durham, NC: Duke University Press.

Alleanza Nazionale. 1995. Pensiamo l'Italia. Il domani c'e' gia'. Valori, idee e progetti per l'Alleanza Nazionale. Tesi politiche approvate dal congresso di Fiuggi, Gennaio 1995'. Alleanza Nazionale.

Allen, Jafari Sinclaire, and Ryan Cecil Jobson. 2016. 'The Decolonizing Generation: (Race and) Theory in Anthropology since the Eighties', *Current Anthropology* 57(2): 129–48. https://doi.org/10.1086/685502.

Allison, Anne. 1994. *Nightwork: Sexuality, Pleasure, and Corporate Masculinity in a Tokyo Hostess Club.* Chicago: University of Chicago Press.

Amit, Vered. 2000. *Constructing the Field: Ethnographic Fieldwork in the Contemporary World.* London; New York: Routledge.

Amnesty International. 2016. 'Amnesty International Policy on State Obligations to Respect, Protect and Fulfil the Human Rights of Sex Workers'. POL 30/4062/2016. https://www.amnesty.org/en/documents/pol30/4062/2016/en/.

Anderson, Bridget. 2012. 'Where's the Harm in That? Immigration Enforcement, Trafficking, and the Protection of Migrants' Rights', *American Behavioral Scientist* 56(9): 1241–57. https://doi.org/10.1177/0002764212443814.

Andrijasevic, Rutvica. 2010. *Migration, Agency, and Citizenship in Sex Trafficking.* Migration, Minorities and Citizenship. Houndmills, Basingstoke; New York: Palgrave Macmillan.

Angioletti, Annamaria. 1979. 'La prostituzione in una societa alienata', in *La prostituzione* Roma: Accademia italiana di scienze biologiche e morali, pp. 1–50.

Appadurai, Arjun. 1996. *Modernity al Large: Cultural Dimensions of Globalization.* Minneapolis; London: University of Minnesota Press.

Ashforth, Blake E., and Glen E. Kreiner. 1999. '"How Can You Do It?": Dirty Work and the Challenge of Constructing a Positive Identity', *The Academy of Management Review* 24 (3): 413–34. https://doi.org/10.2307/259134.

Attwood, Feona. 2006. 'Sexed Up: Theorizing the Sexualization of Culture', *Sexualities* 9(1): 77–94. https://doi.org/10.1177/1363460706053336.

——— (ed.). 2009. *Mainstreaming Sex: The Sexualization of Western Culture*. London; New York: I.B. Tauris.

Azara, Lilioza. 2017. *L'uso politico del corpo femminile. La legge Merlin tra nostalgia, moralismo ed emancipazione*. Roma: Carocci.

———. 2022. 'The New Face of Italian Prostitution in the Aftermath of the Merlin Law: Forms, Debate and Repression.' *European Review of History: Revue Européenne d'histoire* 29 (2): 268–89. https://doi.org/10.1080/13507486.2021.2018405.

Bailey, Marlon M., and Rashad Shabazz. 2014. 'Editorial: Gender and Sexual Geographies of Blackness: Anti-Black Heterotopias (Part 1)', *Gender, Place & Culture* 21(3): 316–21. https://doi.org/10.1080/0966369X.2013.781305.

Baines, Donna, Sara Charlesworth, and Tamara Daly. 2016. 'Underpaid, Unpaid, Unseen, Unheard and Unhappy? Care Work in the Context of Constraint', *Journal of Industrial Relations* 58(4): 449–54. https://doi.org/10.1177/0022185616655981.

Balestracci, Fiammetta. 2020. *La sessualita' degli italiani. Politiche, consumi e culture dal 1945 ad oggi*. Roma: Carocci.

Barrera, Giulia. 1996. 'Dangerous Liaisons: Colonial Concubinage in Eritrea, 1890–1941', Working Paper 1. Working Papers PAS. Evanston, IL: Northwestern University.

Barry, Kathleen. 1995. *The Prostitution of Sexuality: The Global Exploitation of Women*. New York: New York University Press.

Bartky, Sandra Lee. 1990. *Femininity and Domination: Studies in the Phenomenology of Oppression*. Thinking Gender. New York: Routledge.

Barton, Bernadette. 2017. *Stripped: More Stories from Exotic Dancers*, 2nd edn. New York: New York University Press.

Barton, Bernadette, and Hannah Mabry. 2018. 'Andro-Privilege, Raunch Culture, and Stripping', *Sexualities* 21(4): 605–20. https://doi.org/10.1177/1363460717737771.

Bauer, Irmgard L. 2014. 'Romance Tourism or Female Sex Tourism?' *Travel Medicine and Infectious Disease* 12(1): 20–28. https://doi.org/10.1016/j.tmaid.2013.09.003.

Bauman, Zygmunt. 2003. *Liquid Love: On the Frailty of Human Bonds*. Cambridge; Malden, MA: Polity Press; Blackwell.

Bellassai, Sandro. 2006. *La legge del desiderio. Il progetto Merlin e l'Italia degli anni Cinquanta*, 1st edn. Saggi e monografie del dipartimento di discipline storiche dell'Universita' di Bologna. Roma: Carocci.

Berlant, Lauren. 2006. 'Cruel Optimism', *Differences* 17(3): 20–36. https://doi.org/10.1215/10407391-2006-009.

———. 2010. 'Affect & the Politics of Austerity – An Interview Exchange with Lauren Berlant', *Variant* 39/40 (Winter): 3–6.

———. 2012. *Desire/Love*. Brooklyn, NY: Punctum Books.

Berlant, Lauren, and Michael Warner. 1998. 'Sex in Public', *Critical Inquiry* 24(2): 547–66. https://www.jstor.org/stable/1344178.

Bernstein, Elizabeth. 2007. *Temporarily Yours: Intimacy, Authenticity, and the Commerce of Sex*, 1st edn. Chicago; London: University of Chicago Press.

Besnier, Niko, Susan Brownell, and Thomas F. Carter. 2018. *The Anthropology of Sport: Bodies, Borders, Biopolitics*. Oakland, CA: University of California Press.

Bhattacharya, Tithi (ed.). 2017. *Social Reproduction Theory: Remapping Class, Recentering Oppression*. London: Pluto Press.

Bianco, Giovanni. 2011. 'La Chiesa cattolica in Italia e la disciplina sulla procreazione medicalmente assistita', in Mirosław Sadowski and Piotr Szymaniec (eds), *Religia a prawo i państwo*. Wrocław: Wydział Prawa, Administracji i Ekonomii Uniwersytetu Wrocławskiego: Wydawnictwo Beta-Druk, pp. 351–83.

Bindel, Julie. 2017. *The Pimping of Prostitution: Abolishing the Sex Work Myth*. London: Palgrave Macmillan.

Bjønness, Jeanett, Lorraine Nencel, and May-Len Skilbrei (eds). 2021. *Reconfiguring Stigma in Studies of Sex for Sale*. Abingdon, Oxon; New York: Routledge.

Black Women's Blueprint. 2016. 'An Open Letter from Black Women to the Slutwalk'. *Gender & Society* 30(1): 9–13. https://doi.org/10.1177/0891243215611868.

Blanchette, Annie. 2014. 'Revisiting the "Passée": History Rewriting in the Neo-Burlesque Community', *Consumption Markets & Culture* 17(2): 158–84. https://doi.org/10.1080/10253866.2013.776307.

Bonilla-Silva, Eduardo. 2012. 'The Invisible Weight of Whiteness: The Racial Grammar of Everyday Life in America', *Michigan Sociological Review* 26: 1–15. https://doi.org/10.1080/01419870.2011.613997.

Bordo, Susan. 1993. *Unbearable Weight: Feminism, Western Culture, and the Body*. Berkeley, CA; London: University of California Press.

Boris, Eileen, and Rhacel Salazar Parreñas (eds). 2010a. *Intimate Labors: Cultures, Technologies, and the Politics of Care*. Stanford, CA: Stanford Social Sciences.

———. 2010b. 'Introduction', in Eileen Boris and Rhacel Salazar Parreñas (eds), *Intimate Labors: Cultures, Technologies, and the Politics of Care*. Stanford, CA: Stanford Social Sciences, pp. 1–13.

Borneman, John. 2017. 'Afterword: Further Questions about the Global Care Chain', *Ethics and Social Welfare* 11(3): 296–303. https://www.tandfonline.com/doi/full/10.1080/17496535.2017.1300310.

Bott, Esther. 2006. 'Pole Position: Migrant British Women Producing "Selves" through Lap Dancing Work', *Feminist Review* 83: 23–41. https://doi.org/10.1057/palgrave.fr.9400279.

Botti, Fabrizio, and Carlo D'Ippoliti. 2014. 'Don't Ask Don't Tell (That You're Poor): Sexual Orientation and Social Exclusion in Italy', *Journal of Behavioral and Experimental Economics* 49 (April): 8–25. https://doi.org/10.1016/j.socec.2014.02.002.

Bourdieu, Pierre. 1984. *Distinction: A Social Critique of the Judgement of Taste*. London: Routledge & Kegan Paul.

———. 1986. 'The Forms of Capital', in John G. Richardson (ed.), *Handbook of Theory and Research for the Sociology of Education*. New York: Greenwood Press, pp. 241–58.

———. 1989. 'Social Space and Symbolic Power', *Sociological Theory* 7(1): 14–25.

Boyle, Lex. 2005. 'Flexing the Tensions of Female Muscularity: How Female Bodybuilders Negotiate Normative Femininity in Competitive Bodybuilding', *Women's Studies Quarterly* 33(1/2): 134–49. https://www.jstor.org/stable/40005506

Bracke, Sarah. 2012. 'From "Saving Women" to "Saving Gays": Rescue Narratives and their Dis/Continuities', *European Journal of Women's Studies* 19(2): 237–52. https://doi.org/10.1177/1350506811435032.

Bracke, Sarah, and Nadia Fadil. 2012. '"Is the Headscarf Oppressive or Emancipatory?" Field Notes from the Multicultural Debate', *Religion and Gender* 2(1): 36–56. https://doi.org/10.1163/18785417-00201003.

Brennan, Denise. 2004. *What's Love Got to Do with It?: Transnational Desires and Sex Tourism in the Dominican Republic*. Latin America Otherwise. Durham, NC: Duke University Press.

———. 2010. 'Sex Tourism and Sex Workers' Aspirations', in Ronald Weitzer (ed.), *Sex for Sale: Prostitution, Pornography, and the Sex Industry*. New York: Routledge, pp. 307–23.

Brents, Barbara G., and Kathryn Hausbeck. 2010. 'Sex Work Now: What the Blurring of Boundaries around the Sex Industry Means for Sex Work, Research, and Activism', in Melissa Ditmore, Antonia Levy, and Alys Willman (eds), *Sex Work Matters: Exploring Money, Power, and Intimacy in the Sex Industry*. London; New York: Zed Books, pp. 11–22.

Brooks, Siobhan. 2010. *Unequal Desires: Race and Erotic Capital in the Stripping Industry*. Albany: State University of New York Press.

Brown, Wendy. 2005. *Edgework: Critical Essays on Knowledge and Politics*. Princeton, NJ; Oxford: Princeton University Press.

Browne, Kath, Mark Cull, and Philip Hubbard. 2010. 'The Diverse Vulnerabilities of Lesbian, Gay, Bisexual and Trans Sex Workers in the UK', in Kate Hardy, Sarah Kingston, and Teela Sanders (eds), *New Sociologies of Sex Work*. London: Routledge, pp. 209–24.

Butler, Judith. 1990. *Gender Trouble: Feminism and the Subversion of Identity*. New York; London: Routledge.

———. 1997. *The Psychic Life of Power: Theories in Subjection*. Stanford, CA: Stanford University Press.

Butler, Sandra S. 2016. 'The Undervalued Work of the Home Care Aide', *Women's Health Bulletin* 3(2): e33105. https://doi.org/10.17795/whb-33105.

Capous-Desyllas, Moshoula et al. 2020. 'Understanding the Strengths, Challenges, and Strategies of Navigating Work Life and Personal Life among Sex Workers', in Susan Dewey, Isabel Crowhurst, and Chimaraoke Izugbara (eds), *The Routledge International Handbook of Sex Industry Research*. Oxford; New York, pp. 269–82.

Carr, Joetta. 2018. 'The SlutWalk Movement: A Study in Transnational Feminist Activism', *Journal of Feminist Scholarship* 4 (4 (Spring)): 24–38.

Certeau, Michel de. 1984. *The Practice of Everyday Life*. Berkeley: University of California Press.

Cervellon, Marie-Cécile, and Stephen Brown. 2014. 'All the Fun of the Fan: Consuming Burlesque in an Era of Retromania', in June Cotte and Stacy Wood (eds), *North American Advances in Consumer Research* 42. Duluth, MN: Association for Consumer Research, pp. 271–75.

Chapkis, Wendy. 1997. *Live Sex Acts: Women Performing Erotic Labor*. London: Cassell.

Chimienti, Milena. 2010. 'Selling Sex in Order to Migrate: The End of the Migratory Dream?' *Journal of Ethnic and Migration Studies* 36(1): 27–45.

Collins, Patricia Hill. 1998. 'It's All in the Family: Intersections of Gender, Race, and Nation', *Hypatia* 13(3): 62–82.

———. 2000. *Black Feminist Thought: Knowledge, Consciousness, and the Politics of Empowerment*, rev. 10th anniversary edn. New York: Routledge.

Collins, Patricia Hill, and Sirma Bilge. 2016. *Intersectionality*. Key Concepts Series. Cambridge, UK; Malden, MA: Polity Press.

Colosi, Rachela. 2010. *Dirty Dancing? An Ethnography of Lap Dancing*. London; New York: Routledge.

Combahee River Collective. 1977. 'The Combahee River Collective Statement'. http://historyisaweapon.com/defcon1/combrivercoll.html.

Comitato per i diritti civili delle prostitute. 1983. 'Donne alla macchia decise a uscire dalla clandestinità. Le prostitute rivendicano il diritto all'esistenza.' Comitato per i diritti civili delle prostitute.

Committee on the Elimination of Discrimination Against Women. 2017. 'General Recommendation No. 35 on Gender-Based Violence against Women, Updating General Recommendation No. 19'. CEDAW/C/GC/35. Committee on the Elimination of Discrimination Against Women.

Connell, R.W., and James W. Messerschmidt. 2005. 'Hegemonic Masculinity: Rethinking the Concept', *Gender & Society* 19(6): 829–59. https://doi.org/10.1177/0891243205278639.

Constable, Nicole. 2007. *Maid to Order in Hong Kong: Stories of Migrant Workers*, 2nd edn. Ithaca: Cornell University Press.

Corbin, Alain. 1985. *Donne Di Piacere: Miseria Sessuale e Prostituzione Nel XIX Secolo*. Milano: Mondadori.

Corredor, Elizabeth S. 2019. 'Unpacking "Gender Ideology" and the Global Right's Antigender Countermovement', *Signs: Journal of Women in Culture and Society* 44(3): 613–38. https://doi.org/10.1086/701171.

Corso, Carla. 1991. *Ritratto a tinte forti*. Astrea 34. Firenze: Giunti.

Crenshaw, Kimberlé. 1989. 'Demarginalizing the Intersection of Race and Sex: A Black Feminist Critique of Antidiscrimination Doctrine, Feminist Theory and Antiracist Politics', *The University of Chicago Legal Forum* 140: 139–67.

Crowhurst, Isabel. 2019. '"We Should Tax Sex Workers to Fund Subsidies for Families": Shifting Affective Registers and Enduring (Sexual) Norms in the Italian Northern League's Approach to Prostitution', *Journal of Political Power* 12(3): 374–89. https://doi.org/10.1080/2158379X.2019.1669260.

Crowhurst, Isabel, and Adam Eldridge. 2020. '"A Cathartic Moment in a Man's Life": Homosociality and Gendered Fun on the Puttan Tour', *Men and Masculinities* 23(1): 170–93. https://doi.org/10.1177/1097184X18766578.

Cullen, Niamh. 2013. 'Morals, Modern Identities and the Catholic Woman: Fashion in Famiglia Cristiana, 1954–1968', *Journal of Modern Italian Studies* 18(1): 33–52. https://doi.org/10.1080/1354571X.2013.730272.

Curtis, Debra. 2004. 'Commodities and Sexual Subjectivities: A Look at Capitalism and its Desires', *Cultural Anthropology* 19(1): 95–121. https://doi.org/10.1525/can.2004.19.1.95.

———. 2009. *Pleasures and Perils: Girls' Sexuality in a Caribbean Consumer Culture*. New Brunswick, NJ; London: Rutgers University Press.

Dahinden, Janine. 2010. 'Cabaret Dancers: "Settle Down in Order to Stay Mobile?" Bridging Theoretical Orientations within Transnational Migration Studies', *Social Politics* 17(3): 323–48.

Davis, Angela. 1982. *Women, Race and Class*. London: The Women's Press.

Day, Sophie. 2007. *On the Game: Women and Sex Work*. London: Pluto Press.

De Castro, Arnold B., Jacqueline Agnew, and Sheila T. Fitzgerald. 2004. 'Emotional Labor: Relevant Theory for Occupational Health Practice in Post-Industrial America', *AAOHN Journal* 52(3): 109–15. https://doi.org/10.1177/216507990405200307.

Deering, Kathleen N. et al. 2014. 'A Systematic Review of the Correlates of Violence Against Sex Workers', *American Journal of Public Health* 104(5): e42–54. https://doi.org/10.2105/AJPH.2014.301909.

De Francesco, Antonino. 2012. *La palla al piede. Una storia del pregiudizio meridionale*. 1st edn. Storie. Milano: Feltrinelli.

De Genova, Nicholas. 2002. 'Migrant "Illegality" and Deportability in Everyday Life', *Annual Review of Anthropology* 31(1): 419–47. https://doi.org/10.1146/annurev.anthro.31.040402.085432.

Del Boca, Angelo. 1969. *The Ethiopian War, 1935–1941*. Chicago: University of Chicago Press.

Deller, Ruth A., and Clarissa Smith. 2013. 'Reading the BDSM Romance: Reader Responses to *Fifty Shades*', *Sexualities* 16(8): 932–50. https://doi.org/10.1177/1363460713508882.

Dewey, Susan, and Tiantian Zheng. 2013. *Ethical Research with Sex Workers: Anthropological Approaches*. SpringerBriefs in Anthropology. Anthropology and Ethics. New York: Springer.

D'Ippoliti, Carlo, and Alexander Schuster (eds). 2011. *DisOrientamenti. Discriminazione ed esclusione sociale delle persone LGBT in Italia*. Diritti, uguaglianza, integrazione 4. Roma: Armando.

Dodds, Sherril. 2013. 'Embodied Transformations in Neo-Burlesque Striptease', *Dance Research Journal* 45(3): 75–90. https://doi.org/10.1017/S0149767713000016.

Doezema, Jo. 1998. 'Forced to Choose – Beyond the Voluntary v. Forced Prostitution Dichotomy', in Kamala Kempadoo and Jo Doezema (eds), *Global Sex Workers: Rights, Resistance, and Redefinition*. New York: Routledge, pp. 34–50.

———. 2001. 'Ouch! Western Feminists' "Wounded Attachment" to the "Third World Prostitute"', *Feminist Review* 67(1): 16–38. https://doi.org/10.1080/01417780150514484.

———. 2013. 'How Was it for You? Pleasure and Performance in Sex Work', in *Women, Sexuality and the Political Power of Pleasure*. Feminisms and Development. London; New York: Zed Books, pp. 251–64.

Dominijanni, Ida. 2014. *Il trucco. Sessualità e biopolitica nella fine di Berlusconi*. Saggi. Roma: Ediesse.

Donaghue, Ngaire, and Kally Whitehead. 2011. 'Spinning the Pole: A Discursive Analysis of the Websites of Recreational Pole Dancing Studios', *Feminism & Psychology* 21(4): 443–57. https://doi.org/10.1177/0959353511424367.

Douglas, Mary. 1966. *Purity and Danger: An Analysis of the Concepts of Pollution and Taboo*. London: Routledge.

Dubisch, Jill. 1995. 'Lovers in the Field: Sex, Dominance, and the Female Anthropologist', in Don Kulick and Margaret Willson (eds), *Taboo: Sex, Identity, and Erotic Subjectivity in Anthropological Fieldwork*. London; New York: Routledge, pp. 29–50.

Duits, Linda, and Liesbet van Zoonen. 2006. 'Headscarves and Porno-Chic: Disciplining Girls' Bodies in the European Multicultural Society', *European Journal of Women's Studies* 13(2): 103–17. https://doi.org/10.1177/1350506806062750.

Dworkin, Andrea. 1993. 'Prostitution and Male Supremacy', *Michigan Journal of Gender & Law* 1: 1–12.

Dyhouse, Carol. 2013. *Girl Trouble: Panic and Progress in the History of Young Women*. London; New York: Zed Books/Palgrave Macmillan.

Egan, R. Danielle. 2006. *Dancing for Dollars and Paying for Love: The Relationships between Exotic Dancers and Their Regulars*. New York: Palgrave Macmillan.

Egan, R. Danielle, Katherine Frank, and Merri Lisa Johnson (eds). 2006a. *Flesh for Fantasy: Producing and Consuming Exotic Dance*. New York: Thunder's Mouth Press.

———. 2006b. 'Third Wave Strippers: Flesh for Feminist Fantasy', in R. Danielle Egan, Katherine Frank, and Merri Lisa Johnson (eds), *Flesh for Fantasy: Producing and Consuming Exotic Dance*. New York: Thunder's Mouth Press, pp. xi–xxxiii.

Ehrenreich, Barbara, and Arlie Russell Hochschild (eds). 2004. *Global Woman: Nannies, Maids, and Sex Workers in the New Economy*, 1. Holt paperbacks edn. New York: Metropolitan Books/Holt.

Ellis, Carolyn, Tony E. Adams, and Arthur P. Bochner. 2011. 'Autoethnography: An Overview', *Historical Social Research / Historische Sozialforschung* 36(4 (138)): 273–90. https://doi.org/10.17169/fqs-12.1.1589.

Ellis, Carolyn, and Arthur P. Bochner. 2000. 'Autoethnography, Personal Narrative, Reflexivity', in Norman K. Denzin and Yvonna S. Lincoln (eds), *Handbook of Qualitative Research*, 2nd edn. Thousand Oaks, CA: SAGE, pp. 733–68.

Elson, Diane. 1998. 'The Economic, the Political and the Domestic: Businesses, States and Households in the Organisation of Production', *New Political Economy* 3(2): 189–208. https://doi.org/10.1080/13563469808406349.

El-Tayeb, Fatima. 2011. *European Others: Queering Ethnicity in Postnational Europe*. Difference Incorporated. Minneapolis: University of Minnesota Press.

Essed, Philomena. 1991. *Understanding Everyday Racism: An Interdisciplinary Theory*. Sage Series on Race and Ethnic Relations, v. 2. Newbury Park: SAGE.
European Commission. 2011. 'Report from the Commission to the Council on the Functioning of the Transitional Arrangements on Free Movement of Workers from Bulgaria and Romania' {SEC(2011) 1343 final}. Brussels: European Commission.
Evangelista, Felipe, and Rosa Vieira. 2020. 'You Must Have People to Make Business: Relations of Proximity in Small-Scale Trade in Haiti and the DRC', *Vibrant: Virtual Brazilian Anthropology* 17. https://doi.org/10.1590/1809-43412020v17d502.
Evans, Adrienne, and Sarah Riley. 2015. *Technologies of Sexiness: Sex, Identity, and Consumer Culture*. Sexuality, Identity, and Society Series. Oxford; New York: Oxford University Press.
Faier, Lieba. 2007. 'Filipina Migrants in Rural Japan and Their Professions of Love', *American Ethnologist* 34(1): 148–62. https://doi.org/10.1525/ae.2007.34.1.148.
Faludi, Susan. 1991. *Backlash: The Undeclared War against American Women*. New York: Vintage Books.
Farley, Melissa. 2004. '"Bad for the Body, Bad for the Heart": Prostitution Harms Women Even if Legalized or Decriminalized', *Violence Against Women* 10(10): 1087–1125. https://doi.org/10.1177/1077801204268607.
Fassin, Éric. 2010. 'National Identities and Transnational Intimacies: Sexual Democracy and the Politics of Immigration in Europe', *Public Culture* 22(3): 507–29. https://doi.org/10.1215/08992363-2010-007.
Favet, Lucile (ed.). 2010. 'Indoor Sex Work: Analysis and Good Practice Manual on Indoor Sex Work Settings in Seven European Cities'. Marseille: Autres Regards.
Federici, Silvia. 1975. *Wages against Housework*. Bristol: Falling Wall Press.
———. 2018. *Witches, Witch-Hunting, and Women*. Oakland, CA: PM Press.
Fella, Stefano, and Carlo Ruzza. 2013. 'Populism and the Fall of the Centre-Right in Italy: The End of the Berlusconi Model or a New Beginning?' *Journal of Contemporary European Studies* 21(1): 38–52. https://doi.org/10.1080/14782804.2013.766475.
Ferrante, Lucia. 1987. La sessualita' corne risorsa. Donne davanti al foro arcivescovile di Bologna (sec. XVII), *Mélanges de l'Ecole Française de Rome: Moyen-Age, Temps Modernes* 99(2): 989–1016. https://doi.org/10.3406/mefr.1987.2941.
Ferreday, Debra. 2008. '"Showing the Girl": The New Burlesque', *Feminist Theory* 9(1): 47–65. https://doi.org/10.1177/1464700108086363.
Field, Jessica, Anubhav Dutt Tiwari, and Yamini Mookherjee. 2020. 'Self-Reliance as a Concept and a Spatial Practice for Urban Refugees: Reflections from Delhi, India', *Journal of Refugee Studies* 33(1): 167–88. https://doi.org/10.1093/jrs/fez050.
Fitzgerald, Erin, Sarah Elspeth, M. Ed, Darby Hickey, Cherno Biko and Harper Jean Tobin. 2015. "Meaningful Work: Transgender Experiences in the Sex Trade." Red Umbrella Project; Best Practice Policy Project; National Center for Transgender Equality.
Folbre, Nancy. 1994. *Who Pays for the Kids? Gender and the Structures of Constraint*. Economics as Social Theory. London; New York: Routledge.
Foucault, Michel. 1977. *Discipline and Punish: The Birth of the Prison*. London: Allen Lane.
———. 1984. *The History of Sexuality, Volume 2: The Use of Pleasure*. London: Penguin Books.
———. 1990. *The History of Sexuality, Volume 1: The Will to Knowledge*. Harmondsworth: Penguin Books.
Franchi, Marina, and Giulia Selmi. 2020. 'Same-Sex Parents Negotiating the Law in Italy: Between Claims of Recognition and Practices of Exclusion', in Marie Digoix (ed.), *Same-Sex Families and Legal Recognition in Europe*. European Studies of Population 24. Cham: Springer International Publishing, pp. 73–93. https://doi.org/10.1007/978-3-030-37054-1.

Frank, Katherine. 2002. *G-Strings and Sympathy: Strip Club Regulars and Male Desire*. Durham, NC: Duke University Press.
———. 2006. 'Observing the Observers: Reflections on My Regulars', in R. Danielle Egan, Katherine Frank, and Merri Lisa Johnson (eds), *Flesh for Fantasy: Producing and Consuming Exotic Dance*. New York: Thunder's Mouth Press, pp. 111–38.
———. 2007. 'Thinking Critically about Strip Club Research', *Sexualities* 10(4): 501–17. https://doi.org/10.1177/1363460707080989.
Frankenberg, Ruth. 1993. *White Women, Race Matters: The Social Construction of Whiteness*. London: Routledge.
Fraser, Nancy. 2009. 'Feminism, Capitalism and the Cunning of History', *New Left Review* 56: 97–117.
Fukuyama, Francis. 1992. *The End of History and the Last Man*. New York; Toronto: Free Press; Maxwell Macmillan.
Garbagnoli, Sara. 2016. 'Against the Heresy of Immanence: Vatican's "Gender" as a New Rhetorical Device against the Denaturalization of the Sexual Order', *Religion and Gender* 6(2): 187–204. https://doi.org/10.18352/rg.10156.
Garner, Steve. 2007. *Whiteness: An Introduction*. London; New York: Routledge.
Garofalo, Anna. 1956. *L'italiana in Italia*. Bari: Laterza.
Garofalo Geymonat, Giulia. 2014. *Vendere e comprare sesso*. Bologna: Il mulino.
Genz, Stéphanie, and Benjamin A. Brabon. 2009. *Postfeminism: Cultural Texts and Theories*. Edinburgh: Edinburgh University Press.
Gewirtz, Paul. 1995. 'On I Know It When I See It', *Yale Law Journal* 105: 1023.
Gibson, Mary. 1999. *Prostitution and the State in Italy, 1860–1915*, 2nd edn. The History of Crime and Criminal Justice Series. Columbus, OH: Ohio State University Press.
Giddens, Anthony. 1992. *The Transformation of Intimacy: Sexuality, Love, and Eroticism in Modern Societies*. Stanford, CA: Stanford University Press.
Gill, Rosalind. 2003. 'From Sexual Objectification to Sexual Subjectification: The Resexualisation of Women's Bodies in the Media', *Feminist Media Studies* 3(1): 100–106. https://doi.org/10.1080/1468077032000080158.
———. 2009. 'Beyond the "Sexualization of Culture" Thesis: An Intersectional Analysis of "Sixpacks", "Midriffs" and "Hot Lesbians" in Advertising', *Sexualities* 12(2): 137–60. https://doi.org/10.1177/1363460708100916.
Gill, Rosalind, and Ngaire Donaghue. 2013. 'As if Postfeminism Had Come True: The Turn to Agency in Cultural Studies of "Sexualisation"', in Sumi Madhok, Anne Phillips, and Kalpana Wilson (eds), *Gender, Agency, and Coercion*. Thinking Gender in Transnational Times. Houndsmills, Basingstoke: Palgrave Macmillan, pp. 240–58.
Gilman, Sander L. 1985. 'Black Bodies, White Bodies: Toward an Iconography of Female Sexuality in Late Nineteenth-Century Art, Medicine, and Literature', *Critical Inquiry* 12 (1): 204–42. https://doi.org/10.1086/448327.
Gilroy, Paul. 2010. *Postcolonial Melancholia*. New York: Columbia University Press.
Ginsborg, Paul. 2007. *L'Italia del tempo presente: Famiglia, società civile, Stato, 1980–1996*. Piccola biblioteca Einaudi Nuova serie 345. Torino: Einaudi.
Giuliani, Gaia. 2019. *Race, Nation and Gender in Modern Italy: Intersectional Representations in Visual Culture*. Mapping Global Racisms. London: Palgrave Macmillan.
Giuliani, Gaia, and Cristina Lombardi-Diop. 2013. *Bianco e nero. Storia dell'identità razziale degli italiani*, 1st edn. Le Monnier università. Quaderni Di Storia. Firenze: Le Monnier università.
Goffman, Erving. 1963. *Stigma: Notes on the Management of Spoiled Identity*. Englewood Cliffs, NJ: Prentice-Hall.
Gramsci, Antonio. 1966. *La questione meridionale*. Roma: Editori riuniti.

Grandey, Alicia, James Diefendorff, and Deborah E. Rupp. 2013. 'Bringing Emotional Labor into Focus – A Review and Integration of Three Research Lenses', in Alicia Grandey, James Diefendorff, and Deborah E. Rupp (eds), *Emotional Labor in the 21st Century: Diverse Perspectives on the Psychology of Emotion Regulation at Work*. Organization and Management 48. New York: Routledge Academic, pp. 3–27.

Grant, Melissa Gira. 2014. *Playing the Whore: The Work of Sex Work*. London: Verso Books.

Greco, Giovanni. 1987. *Lo scienziato e la prostituta. Due secoli di studi sulla prostituzione*. Nuova Biblioteca Dedalo, 65. Serie "Nuovi saggi". Bari: Dedalo.

Green, Adam Isaiah. 2008. 'The Social Organization of Desire: The Sexual Fields Approach', *Sociological Theory* 26(1): 25–50. https://doi.org/10.1111/j.1467-9558.2008.00317.x.

Gribaldo, Alessandra. 2018. 'Veline, Ordinary Women and Male Savages: Disentangling Racism and Heteronormativity in Contemporary Narratives on Sexual Freedom', *Modern Italy* 23(2): 145–58. https://doi.org/10.1017/mit.2018.5.

Gribaldo, Alessandra, and Giovanna Zapperi. 2012. *Lo schermo del potere. Femminismo e regime della visibilità*. Verona: Ombre corte.

Griffiths, Kerry. 2016. *Femininity, Feminism and Recreational Pole Dancing*. Oxford: Routledge.

Grosz, Elizabeth. 1990. *Jacques Lacan: A Feminist Introduction*. London; New York: Routledge.

Gundle, Stephen. 2007. *Bellissima: Feminine Beauty and the Idea of Italy*. New Haven, CT; London: Yale University Press.

Gusmano, Beatrice, Anna Lorenzetti and UNAR. 2014. *Lavoro, orientamento sessuale e identità di genere. Dalle esperienze internazionali alla progettazione di buone prassi in Italia*. Roma: Armando.

Gutierrez Garza, Ana P. 2019. *Care for Sale: An Ethnography of Latin American Domestic and Sex Workers in London*. Oxford: Oxford University Press.

Gysels, M., R. Pool, and K. Bwanika. 2001. 'Truck Drivers, Middlemen and Commercial Sex Workers: AIDS and the Mediation of Sex in South West Uganda', *AIDS Care* 13(3): 373–85. https://doi.org/10.1080/09540120120044026.

Hajek, Andrea. 2018. 'Je Ne Suis Pas Catherine Deneuve: Reflections on Contemporary Debates about Sexual Self-Determination in Italy', *Modern Italy* 23(2): 139–43. https://doi.org/10.1017/mit.2018.10.

Hakim, Catherine. 2011. *Erotic Capital: The Power of Attraction in the Boardroom and the Bedroom*. London: Allen Lane.

Hallgrimsdottir, Helga Kristin, Rachel Phillips, and Cecilia Benoit. 2006. 'Fallen Women and Rescued Girls: Social Stigma and Media Narratives of the Sex Industry in Victoria, B.C., from 1980 to 2005', *Canadian Review of Sociology/Revue Canadienne de Sociologie* 43 (3): 265–80. https://doi.org/10.1111/j.1755-618X.2006.tb02224.x.

Hanna, Judith Lynne. 2010. 'Dance and Sexuality: Many Moves', *The Journal of Sex Research* 47(2–3): 212–41. https://doi.org/doi: 10.1080/00224491003599744.

Haraway, Donna Jeanne. 1988. 'Situated Knowledges: The Science Question in Feminism and the Privilege of Partial Perspective', *Feminist Studies* 14(3): 575–99. https://doi.org/10.2307/3178066.

Harding, Sandra. 1993. 'Rethinking Standpoint Epistemology: "What is Strong Objectivity?"' In *Feminist Epistemologies*, edited by Linda Alcoff and Elizabeth Patter, 49–82. New York: Routledge.

Harrison, Faye V. (ed.). 1991. *Decolonizing Anthropology: Moving Further toward an Anthropology for Liberation*. Arlington, VA: Association of Black Anthropologists, American Anthropological Association.

Harrison, Lieta. 1966. *L'iniziazione*. Milano: Rizzoli.

Harvey, David. 2005. *A Brief History of Neoliberalism*. Oxford; New York: Oxford University Press.

Harvey, Laura, and Rosalind Gill. 2011. 'Spicing It Up: Sexual Entrepreneurs and The Sex Inspectors', in Rosalind Gill and Christina Scharff (eds), *New Femininities: Postfeminism, Neoliberalism and Subjectivity*. London: Palgrave Macmillan, pp. 52–67. https://doi.org/10.1057/9780230294523_4.

Herzfeld, Michael. 2015. 'Anthropology and the Inchoate Intimacies of Power', *American Ethnologist* 42(1): 18–32. https://doi.org/10.1111/amet.12113.

Hirshman, Linda R., and Jane E. Larson. 1998. *Hard Bargains: The Politics of Sex*. New York: Oxford University Press.

Hochschild, Arlie Russell. 2000. 'Global Care Chains and Emotional Surplus Value', in Anthony Giddens and Will Hutton (eds), *On the Edge: Living with Global Capitalism*. London: Jonathan Cape, pp. 130–45.

———. 2003. *The Managed Heart: Commercialization of Human Feeling*, 2nd edn. Berkeley, CA: University of California.

———. 2004. 'Love and Gold', in Barbara Ehrenreich and Arlie Russell Hochschild (eds), *Global Woman: Nannies, Maids, and Sex Workers in the New Economy*, 1. Holt paperbacks edn. New York: Metropolitan Books/Holt, pp. 15–30.

Holland, Samantha. 2010. *Pole Dancing, Empowerment and Embodiment*. Houndmills, Basingstoke; New York: Palgrave Macmillan.

Holland, Samantha, and Feona Attwood. 2009. 'Keeping Fit in Six Inch Heels: The Mainstreaming of Pole Dancing', in Feona Attwood (ed.), *Mainstreaming Sex – The Sexualization of Western Culture*. London; New York: I.B. Tauris, pp. 165–81.

Honeyball, Mary. 2014. 'Report on Sexual Exploitation and Prostitution and its Impact on Gender Equality', A7-0071/2014. Committee on Women's Rights and Gender Equality.

hooks, bell. 2001. *Ain't I a Woman: Black Women and Feminism*. Pluto Classics. London: Pluto Press.

Horswill, Abbe, and Ronald Weitzer. 2018. 'Becoming a Client: The Socialization of Novice Buyers of Sexual Services', *Deviant Behavior* 39(2): 148–58. https://doi.org/10.1080/01639625.2016.1263083.

Hubbard, Philip. 2000a. *Sex and the City: Geographies of Prostitution in the Urban West*. London: Routledge.

———. 2000b. 'Desire/Disgust: Mapping the Moral Contours of Heterosexuality', *Progress in Human Geography* 24(2): 191–217. https://doi.org/10.1191/030913200667195279.

Hubbard, Philip et al. 2008. 'Away from Prying Eyes? The Urban Geographies of "Adult Entertainment"', *Progress in Human Geography* 32(3): 363–81. https://doi.org/10.1177/0309132508089095.

Hughes, Everett C. 1958. *Men and Their Work*. Glencoe, IL: Free Press.

ICRSE. 2020. 'Undeserving Victims? A Community Report on Migrant Sex Worker Victims of Crime in Europe'. ICRSE.

Ihamäki, Elina. 2013. 'Homosociality in the Sexscapes of Sortavala, Russia', *NORMA* 8(1): 27–41.

Institute for Policy Studies. 1999. 'Women and the U.S. Military in East Asia', *Institute for Policy Studies*. https://ips-dc.org/women_and_the_us_military_in_east_asia/.

ISTAT. 2012. *Rapporto annuale 2012: la situazione del Paese*. Roma: ISTAT.

Jackson, Anthony. 1987. *Anthropology at Home*. ASA Monographs 25. London; New York: Tavistock.

Jaiteh, Mariama. 2018. 'Seeking Friends with Benefits in a Tourism-Based Sexual Economy: Interrogating the Gambian Sexscape', Ph.D. dissertation. Florida: Florida International University.

Jeffreys, Sheila. 1997. *The Idea of Prostitution*. North Melbourne, Australia: Spinifex.

Jhally, Sut, and Stuart Hall. 1996. *Race: The Floating Signifier*. Northampton, MA: Media Education Foundation. http://trove.nla.gov.au/version/28484912.

Just, Sine Nørholm, and Sara Louise Muhr. 2019. 'Holding on to Both Ends of a Pole: Empowering Feminine Sexuality and Reclaiming Feminist Emancipation', *Gender, Work & Organization* 1–18. https://doi.org/10.1111/gwao.12339.

Kempadoo, Kamala. 2001. 'Freelancers, Temporary Wives, and Beach-Boys: Researching Sex Work in the Caribbean', *Feminist Review* 67(1): 39–62. https://doi.org/10.1080/01417780150514493.

Kempadoo, Kamala, and Jo Doezema (eds). 1998. *Global Sex Workers: Rights, Resistance, and Redefinition*. New York: Routledge.

King, Russell. 1993. 'Recent Immigration to Italy: Character, Causes and Consequences', *GeoJournal* 30(3): 283–92. https://doi.org/10.1007/BF00806719.

Kitchin, Rob, and Karen Lysaght. 2003. 'Heterosexism and the Geographies of Everyday Life in Belfast, Northern Ireland', *Environment and Planning A: Economy and Space* 35(3): 489–510. https://doi.org/10.1068/a3538.

Knowles, Caroline. 2000. 'Here and There: Doing Transnational Fieldwork', in Vered Amit (ed.), *Constructing the Field: Ethnographic Fieldwork in the Contemporary World*. London; New York: Routledge, pp. 54–70.

Koken, Juline, David Bimbi, and Jeffrey Parsons. 2010. 'Male and Female Escorts: A Comparative Analysis', in Ronald Weitzer (ed.), *Sex for Sale: Prostitution, Pornography, and the Sex Industry*. New York: Routledge, pp. 205–32.

Komla-Ebri, Kossi. 2002. *Imbarazzismi. Quotidiani imbarazzi in bianco e nero*. Milano; Marna: Barzago (LC): Edizioni dell'Arco.

Kontula, Anna. 2008. 'The Sex Worker and Her Pleasure', *Current Sociology* 56(4): 605–20. https://doi.org/10.1177/0011392108090944.

Kotiswaran, Prabha. 2011. *Dangerous Sex, Invisible Labor: Sex Work and the Law in India*. Princeton, NJ: Princeton University Press.

Kristeva, Julia. 1982. *Powers of Horror: An Essay on Abjection*. New York: Columbia University Press.

Krivonos, Daria, and Anastasia Diatlova. 2020. 'What to Wear for Whiteness? "Whore" Stigma and the East/West Politics of Race, Sexuality and Gender', *Intersections: East European Journal of Society and Politics* 6(3). https://doi.org/10.17356/ieejsp.v6i3.660.

Kulick, Don. 1998. *Travesti: Sex, Gender, and Culture among Brazilian Transgendered Prostitutes*. Worlds of Desire. Chicago: University of Chicago Press.

Lamen, Darien. 2014. 'Sound Tracks of a Tropical Sexscape: Tropicalizing Northeastern Brazil, Channeling Transnational Desires', in Timothy Rommen and Daniel T. Neely (eds), *Sun, Sea, and Sound: Music and Tourism in the Circum-Caribbean*. Oxford University Press, pp. 267–88.

Law, Tuulia. 2012. 'Cashing in on Cachet?: Ethnicity and Gender in the Strip Club', *Canadian Journal of Women and the Law* 24(1): 135–53. https://doi.org/muse.jhu.edu/article/473118.

Lega Nord. 2002. 'Cronistoria della Lega Nord. Dalle origini ad oggi. Settima parte', Segretaria organizzativa federale. Retrieved May 2021 from https://www.leganord.org/phocadownload/ilmovimento/storia_ln/07_lega_nord_storia2002.pdf.

Lever, Janet, and Deanne Dolnick. 2010. 'Call Girls and Street Prostitutes: Selling Sex and Intimacy', in Ronald Weitzer (ed.), *Sex for Sale: Prostitution, Pornography, and the Sex Industry*. New York: Routledge, pp. 187–203.

Link, Bruce G., and Jo Phelan. 2014. 'Stigma Power', *Social Science & Medicine* 103 (February): 24–32. https://doi.org/10.1016/j.socscimed.2013.07.035.

Lombroso, Cesare, and Guglielmo Ferrero. 1903. *La donna delinquente, la prostituta e la donna normale*. Torino: Fratelli Bocca.

Lorde, Audre. 1984. *Sister Outsider: Essays and Speeches*. Berkeley, CA: The Crossing Press.

Lutz, Helma. 2018. 'Care Migration: The Connectivity between Care Chains, Care Circulation and Transnational Social Inequality', *Current Sociology* 66(4): 577–89. https://doi.org/10.1177/0011392118765213.

Lyons, Andrew P., and Harriet D. Lyons. 2011. 'The Reconstruction of "Primitive Sexuality" at the Fin de Siècle', in Andrew P. Lyons and Harriet D. Lyons (eds), *Sexualities in Anthropology*. Malden, MA: Wiley-Blackwell, pp. 67–81.

MacKinnon, Catharine A. 2011. 'Trafficking, Prostitution and Inequality', *Harvard Civil Rights-Civil Liberties Law Review* 46(271): 271–309. https://doi.org/10.4159/9780674977761-016.

Maginn, Paul J., and Christine Steinmetz (eds). 2014. *(Sub)Urban Sexscapes: Geographies and Regulation of the Sex Industry*. Routledge Advances in Sociology 135. London; New York: Routledge.

Magubane, Zine. 2011. 'Which Bodies Matter? Feminism, Poststructuralism, Race, and the Curious Theoretical Odyssey of the "Hottentot Venus"', in Andrew P. Lyons and Harriet D. Lyons (eds), *Sexualities in Anthropology*. Malden, MA: Wiley-Blackwell, pp. 35–49.

Mahmood, Saba. 2001. 'Feminist Theory, Embodiment, and the Docile Agent: Some Reflections on the Egyptian Islamic Revival', *Cultural Anthropology* 16(2): 202–36. https://doi.org/10.1525/can.2001.16.2.202.

Mai, Nicola. 2013. 'Embodied Cosmopolitanisms: The Subjective Mobility of Migrants Working in the Global Sex Industry', *Gender, Place & Culture* 20(1): 107–24. https://doi.org/10.1080/0966369X.2011.649350.

———. 2016. '"Too Much Suffering": Understanding the Interplay between Migration, Bounded Exploitation and Trafficking through Nigerian Sex Workers' Experiences', *Sociological Research Online* 21(4): 159–72. https://doi.org/10.5153/sro.4158.

———. 2018. *Mobile Orientations: An Intimate Autoethnography of Migration, Sex Work, and Humanitarian Borders*. Chicago: University of Chicago Press.

Mai, Nicola et al. 2021. 'Sexual Humanitarianism: Understanding Agency and Exploitation in the Global Sex Industry'. Policy Report. London: Kingston University.

Mainardi, Arianna. 2018. '"The Pictures I Really Dislike Are Those Where the Girls Are Naked!" Postfeminist Norms of Female Sexual Embodiment in Contemporary Italian Digital Culture', *Modern Italy* 23(2): 187–200. https://doi.org/10.1017/mit.2018.6.

Makhakhe, Nosipho Faith et al. 2017. 'Sexual Transactions between Long Distance Truck Drivers and Female Sex Workers in South Africa', *Global Health Action* 10(1). https://doi.org/10.1080/16549716.2017.1346164.

Malta, M. et al. 2006. 'A Qualitative Assessment of Long Distance Truck Drivers' Vulnerability to HIV/AIDS in Itajai, Southern Brazil', *AIDS Care* 18(5): 489–96. https://doi.org/10.1080/09540120500235241.

Marcasciano, Porpora, Cathy La Torre, and Monica Pasquino. 2013. Un transito lungo 30 anni, *Movimento Identità Transessuale*. http://www.mit-italia.it/wp-content/themes/mit-theme/pdf/un-transito-lungo-30-anni.pdf.

Marchetti, Sabrina. 2016. '"Domestic work is work"? Condizioni lavorative delle assistenti familiari in Italia, tra finzioni e realta' in Claudia Alemani et al. (eds), *Viaggio nel lavoro di cura. Chi sono, cosa fanno e come vivono le badanti che lavorano nelle famiglie italiane*. Roma; Bari: Ediesse, pp. 101–23.

Marcus, George E. 1995. 'Ethnography in/of the World System: The Emergence of Multi-sited Ethnography', *Annual Review of Anthropology* 24: 95–117. https://doi.org/10.1146/annurev.an.24.100195.000523.

Mazzone, Umberto, and Claudia Pancino (eds). 2008. *Sortilegi amorosi, materassi a nolo e pignattini. Processi inquisitoriali del XVII secolo fra Bologna e il Salento*. Roma: Carocci.

McCarthy, Vanessa, and Nicholas Terpstra. 2019. 'In the Neighborhood: Residence, Community, and the Sex Trade in Early Modern Bologna', in Jacqueline Murray and Nicholas Terpstra (eds), *Sex, Gender and Sexuality in Renaissance Italy*. New York: Routledge, pp. 53–74.

McCaughey, Martha, and Christina French. 2001. 'Women's Sex-Toy Parties: Technology, Orgasm, and Commodification', *Sexuality & Culture* 5(3): 77–96. https://doi.org/10.1007/s12119-001-1031-2.

McClintock, Anne. 1995. *Imperial Leather: Race, Gender, and Sexuality in the Colonial Conquest*. New York: Routledge.

McNair, Brian. 2002. *Striptease Culture: Sex, Media and the Democratization of Desire*. London: Routledge.

McRobbie, Angela. 2009. *The Aftermath of Feminism: Gender, Culture and Social Change*. Thousand Oaks, CA; London: SAGE.

Merrill, Heather. 2006. *An Alliance of Women: Immigration and the Politics of Race*. Minneapolis: University of Minnesota Press.

Meyers, Diana T. 2002. *Gender in the Mirror: Cultural Imagery and Women's Agency*. Oxford; New York: Oxford University Press.

Miller-Young, Mireille. 2010. 'Putting Hypersexuality to Work: Black Women and Illicit Eroticism in Pornography', *Sexualities* 13(2): 219–35. https://doi.org/10.1177/1363460709359229.

Mingione, Enzo, and Fabio Quassoli. 2000. 'The Participation of Immigrants in the Underground Economy in Italy', in Russell King, Gabriella Lazaridis, and Charalampos G. Tsardanidēs (eds), *Eldorado or Fortress: Migration in Southern Europe*. New York: St. Martin's Press, pp. 29–56.

Minichiello, Victor, John Scott, and Denton Callander. 2013. 'New Pleasures and Old Dangers: Reinventing Male Sex Work', *Journal of Sex Research* 50(3–4): 263–75. https://doi.org/10.1080/00224499.2012.760189.

Mintz, Sidney W., and Richard Price. 1992. *The Birth of African-American Culture: An Anthropological Perspective*. Boston, MA: Beacon Press.

Missero, Dalila. 2019. 'Playboys and the Cosmo Girls: Models of Femininity in Italian Men's and Women's Magazines and the Popularization of Feminist Knowledge', *AG About Gender – Rivista Internazionale Di Studi Di Genere* 8(16). https://doi.org/10.15167/2279-5057/AG2019.8.16.1103.

Moe, Nelson. 2002. *The View from Vesuvius: Italian Culture and the Southern Question*. Studies on the History of Society and Culture 46. Berkeley, CA: University of California Press.

Moghadam, Valentine M. 2013. *Modernizing Women: Gender and Social Change in the Middle East*, 3rd edn. Boulder, CO: Lynne Rienner.

Mohanty, Chandra Talpade. 1988. 'Under Western Eyes: Feminist Scholarship and Colonial Discourses', *Feminist Review* 30(1): 61–88. https://doi.org/10.1057/fr.1988.42.

——— . 2003. '"Under Western Eyes" Revisited: Feminist Solidarity through Anticapitalist Struggles', *Signs: Journal of Women in Culture and Society* 28(2): 499–535. https://doi.org/10.1086/521238.

Montemurro, Beth, Colleen Bloom, and Kelly Madell. 2003. 'Ladies Night Out: A Typology of Women Patrons of a Male Strip Club', *Deviant Behavior* 24(4): 333–52. https://doi.org/10.1080/713840221.

Moore, Henrietta L. 2001. 'Afterword: A "Masterclass" in Subjectivity', in Gail Currie and Celia Rothenberg (eds), *Feminist (Re)Visions of the Subject: Landscapes, Ethnoscapes, and Theoryscapes*. Lanham, MD: Lexington Books, pp. 261–65.

Morris, Penelope. 2013. '"Let's Not Talk about Italian Sex": The Reception of the Kinsey Reports in Italy', *Journal of Modern Italian Studies* 18(1): 17–32. https://doi.org/10.1080/1354571X.2013.730271.

Mosse, George Lachmann. 1996. *Sessualità e nazionalismo. Mentalità borghese e rispettabilità.* Roma; Bari: Laterza.

Moukarbel, Nayla. 2009. 'Not Allowed to Love? Sri Lankan Maids in Lebanon', *Mobilities* 4(3): 329–47. https://doi.org/10.1080/17450100903195409.

Mulvey, Laura. 1975. 'Visual Pleasure and Narrative Cinema', *Screen* 16(3): 6–18. https://doi.org/10.1007/978-1-349-19798-9_3.

Murphy, Alexandra G. 2003. 'The Dialectical Gaze: Exploring the Subject-Object Tension in the Performances of Women Who Strip', *Journal of Contemporary Ethnography* 32(3): 305–35. https://doi.org/10.1177/0891241603032003003.

Nader, Laura. 1972. 'Up the Anthropologist: Perspectives Gained from Studying Up', in Dell Hymes (ed.), *Reinventing Anthropology*. New York: Vintage Books, pp. 248–311.

Nagel, Joane. 2003. *Race, Ethnicity, and Sexuality: Intimate Intersections, Forbidden Frontiers.* New York: Oxford University Press.

Nagle, Jill (ed.). 1997. *Whores and Other Feminists.* New York: Routledge.

NSWP. 2013. 'NSWP Consensus Statement on Sex Work, Human Rights, and the Law', *Global Network of Sex Work Projects*, 16 December 2013. Retrieved May 2015 from https://www.nswp.org/resource/nswp-consensus-statement-sex-work-human-rights-and-the-law.

O'Connell Davidson, Julia. 2014. 'Let's Go Outside: Bodies, Prostitutes, Slaves and Worker Citizens', *Citizenship Studies* 18(5): 516–32. https://doi.org/10.1080/13621025.2014.923703.

O'Connell Davidson, Julia, and Bridget Anderson. 2007. 'The Market for Migrant Domestic and Sex Workers: Research Report'. R000239794. Economic and Social Research Council.

Oso, Laura. 2016. 'Transnational Social Mobility Strategies and Quality of Work among Latin-American Women Sex Workers in Spain', *Sociological Research Online* 21(4): https://journals.sagepub.com/doi/10.5153/sro.4129.

———. 2018. 'Survival within a Multi-circuited Maze: Latin American Sex Workers in Spain', in Christian Groes and Nadine Fernandez (eds), *Intimate Mobilities: Sexual Economies, Marriage and Migration in a Disparate World*. New York: Berghahn Books, pp. 101–21.

Oso-Casas, Laura. 2010. 'Money, Sex, Love and Family: Economic and Affective Strategies of Latin American Sex Workers in Spain', *Journal of Ethnic and Migration Studies* 36(1): 47–65. https://doi.org/10.1080/13691830903250899.

Owen, Louise. 2012. '"Work That Body": Precarity and Femininity in the New Economy', *The Drama Review* 56(4): 78–94. https://doi.org/muse.jhu.edu/article/491894.

Palmisano, Leonardo. 2010. *La città del sesso. Dominazioni e prostituzioni tra immagine e corpo.* Bari: Caratteri mobili.

Pankhurst, Richard. 1974. 'The History of Prostitution in Ethiopia', *Journal of Ethiopian Studies* 12(2): 159–78.

Parca, Gabriella. 1959. *Le italiane si confessano.* Firenze: Parenti.

———. 1965. *I sultani. Mentalità e comportamento del maschio italiano.* Milano: Rizzoli.

Parent Duchâtelet, Alexandre Jean Baptiste B. 1840. *On Prostitution in the City of Paris*. T. Burgess.

Parreira, Christina. 2021. 'The Lady and the Tramp: Management of Stigma in the Nevada Brothel', in Jeanett Bjønness, Lorraine Nencel, and May-Len Skilbrei (eds), *Reconfiguring Stigma in Studies of Sex for Sale*. Oxford; New York: Routledge, pp. 169–84.

Parreñas, Rhacel Salazar. 2004. 'The Care Crisis in the Philippines: Children and Transnational Families in the New Global Economy', in Barbara Ehrenreich and Arlie Russell Hochschild (eds), *Global Woman: Nannies, Maids, and Sex Workers in the New Economy*, 1. Holt paperbacks edn. New York: Metropolitan Books/Holt, pp. 39–54.

———. 2010. 'Homeward Bound: The Circular Migration of Entertainers between Japan and the Philippines', *Global Networks* 10(3): 301–23. https://doi.org/10.1111/j.1471-0374.2010.00288.x.

Pateman, Carole. 1988. *The Sexual Contract*. Cambridge: Polity Press.

———. 2002. 'Self-Ownership and Property in the Person: Democratization and a Tale of Two Concepts', *The Journal of Political Philosophy* 10(1): 20–53. https://doi.org/10.1111/1467-9760.00141.

Patriarca, Silvana. 2005. 'Indolence and Regeneration: Tropes and Tensions of Risorgimento Patriotism', *The American Historical Review* 110(2): 380–408. https://doi.org/10.1086/ahr/110.2.380.

Peano, Irene. 2012. 'Excesses and Double Standards: Migrant Prostitutes, Sovereignty and Exceptions in Contemporary Italy', *Modern Italy* 17(4): 419–432. 10.1080/13532944.2012.706994

———. 2013. 'Opaque Loves: Governance and Escape in the Intimate Sphere of Nigerian Sex Workers', *Etnografia e Ricerca Qualitativa* 3. https://doi.org/10.3240/75030.

Peirano, Mariza G.S. 1998. 'When Anthropology is at Home: The Different Contexts of a Single Discipline', *Annual Review of Anthropology* 27(1): 105–28. https://doi.org/10.1146/annurev.anthro.27.1.105.

Pheterson, Gail. 1996. *The Prostitution Prism*. Amsterdam: Amsterdam University Press.

Phillips, Anne. 2013. 'Does the Body Make a Difference?' in Sumi Madhok, Anne Phillips, and Kalpana Wilson (eds), *Gender, Agency, and Coercion*. Thinking Gender in Transnational Times. Basingstoke, Hampshire; New York: Palgrave Macmillan, pp. 143–56.

Philpott, Anne, and Krissy Ferris. 2013. 'Could Watching Porn Increase Our Expectations of (Safe) Pleasure? An Exploration of Some Promising Harm-Reduction Practices', in Susie Jolly, Andrea Cornwall, and Kate Hawkins (eds), *Women, Sexuality and the Political Power of Pleasure*. Feminisms and Development. London; New York: Zed Books, pp. 200–228.

Piketty, Thomas. 2014. *Il capitale nel XXI secolo*. Milano: Bompiani.

Pilcher, Katy. 2011. 'A "Sexy Space" for Women? Heterosexual Women's Experiences of a Male Strip Show Venue', *Leisure Studies* 30(2): 217–35. https://doi.org/10.1080/02614367.20 10.512048.

———. 2012. 'Dancing for Women: Subverting Heteronormativity in a Lesbian Erotic Dance Space?' *Sexualities* 15(5–6): 521–37. https://doi.org/10.1177/1363460712445979.

Piscitelli, Adriana. 2020. 'From Clients to "Friends" or "Lovers": Latin American Sex Workers Coping with the Economic Crisis in Spain', in Susan Dewey, Isabel Crowhurst, and Chimaraoke Izugbara (eds), *The Routledge International Handbook of Sex Industry Research*. Oxford; New York: Routledge, pp. 283–92.

Platt, Lucy et al. 2018. 'Associations between Sex Work Laws and Sex Workers' Health: A Systematic Review and Meta-Analysis of Quantitative and Qualitative Studies', *PLOS Medicine* 15(12): e1002680. https://doi.org/10.1371/journal.pmed.1002680.

Pollack, Shoshana, and Amy Rossiter. 2010. 'Neoliberalism and the Entrepreneurial Self: Implications for Feminism and Social Work', *Canadian Social Work Review/Revue Canadienne de Service Social* 27(2): 155–69. https://www.jstor.org/stable/41669933.

Pollard, John F. 2008. *Catholicism in Modern Italy: Religion, Society and Politics since 1861*. Christianity and Society in the Modern World. London; New York: Routledge.

Ponzio, Alessio. 2019. La prostituzione uomo-uomo in Italia attraverso alcuni esempi letterari degli anni Cinquanta e Sessanta, in Annalisa Cegna, Natascia Mattucci, and Alessio Ponzio (eds), *La prostituzione nell'Italia contemporanea. Tra storia, politiche e diritti*, Prima edizione. Spazi e culture del Novecento 2. Macerata: Eum, pp. 105–19.

Price-Glynn, Kim. 2010. *Strip Club: Gender, Power, and Sex Work*. Intersections. New York: New York University Press.

Probyn, Elspeth. 2010. 'Writing Shame', in Gregory J. Seigworth and Melissa Gregg (eds), *The Affect Theory Reader*. Durham, NC: Duke University Press, pp. 71–90.

Puar, Jasbir K. 2007. *Terrorist Assemblages: Homonationalism in Queer Times*. First edition. Next Wave: New Directions in Women's Studies. Durham, NC: Duke University Press.

———. 2008. 'Feminists and Queers in the Service of Empire', in Chandra Talpade Mohanty, Robin L. Riley, and Minnie Bruce Pratt (eds), *Feminism and War: Confronting US Imperialism*. London; New York: Zed Books, pp. 47–55.

Puwar, Nirmal. 2004. *Space Invaders – Race, Gender and Bodies Out of Place*. Oxford: Berg.

Radner, Hilary. 1993. 'Pretty is as Pretty Does: Free Enterprise and the Marriage Plot', in Jim Collins, Hilary Radner, and Ava Collins (eds), *Film Theory Goes to the Movies*. AFI Film Readers. New York: Routledge, pp. 79–97.

Razavi, Shahra, and Silke Staab. 2010. 'Underpaid and Overworked: A Cross-National Perspective on Care Workers', *International Labour Review* 149(4): 407–22. https://doi.org/10.1111/j.1564-913X.2010.00095.x.

Regehr, Kaitlyn. 2012. 'The Rise of Recreational Burlesque: Bumping and Grinding Towards Empowerment', *Sexuality & Culture* 16: 134–57. https://doi.org/10.1007/s12119-011-9113-2.

Riezzo, Irene et al. 2016. 'Italian Law on Medically Assisted Reproduction: Do Women's Autonomy and Health Matter?' *BMC Women's Health* 16(1): 44. https://doi.org/10.1186/s12905-016-0324-4.

Rinaldi, Cirus. 2019. '"Conformarsi deviando". Una riflessione storico-sociale sul sex work maschile', in Annalisa Cegna, Natascia Mattucci, and Alessio Ponzio (eds), *La prostituzione nell'Italia contemporanea. Tra storia, politiche e diritti*, Prima edizione. Spazi e culture del Novecento 2. Macerata: Eum, pp. 87–103.

Rivers-Moore, Megan. 2013. 'Affective Sex: Beauty, Race and Nation in the Sex Industry', *Feminist Theory* 14(13): 153–69. https://doi.org/10.1177/1464700113483242.

Roberts, Ron, Amy Jones, and Teela Sanders. 2013. 'Students and Sex Work in the UK: Providers and Purchasers', *Sex Education* 13(3): 349–63. https://doi.org/10.1080/14681811.2012.744304.

Robillard, Chantal. 2010. 'Honourable Señoras, Liminal Campesinas and the Shameful Other: Re-Defining Femininities in Bolivia', *Culture, Health & Sexuality* 12(5): 529–42. https://doi.org/10.1080/13691051003668308.

Rochat, Giorgio. 1973. *Il colonialismo italiano*. Torino: Loescher.

Ross, Becki L. 2010. 'Sex and (Evacuation from) the City: The Moral and Legal Regulation of Sex Workers in Vancouver's West End, 1975–1985', *Sexualities* 13(2): 197–218. https://doi.org/10.1177/1363460709359232.

Rossiaud, Jacques. 2013. *Amori venali. La prostituzione nell'Europa medievale*, trans. Paola Donadoni. Roma; Bari: GLF editori Laterza.

Rubin, Gayle. 1975. 'The Traffic in Women: Notes on the "Political Economy" of Sex', in Rayna Reiter (ed.), *Toward an Anthropology of Women*. New York: Monthly Review Press, pp. 157–210.

———. 1984. 'Thinking Sex: Notes for a Radical Theory of the Politics of Sexuality', in Carole Vance (ed.), *Pleasure and Danger: Exploring Female Sexuality*. Boston, MA: Routledge, pp. 267–319.

———. 2010. 'Blood under the Bridge: Reflections on "Thinking Sex"', *GLQ: A Journal of Lesbian and Gay Studies* 17(1): 15–48.

Rylko-Bauer, Barbara. 2014. *A Polish Doctor in the Nazi Camps: My Mother's Memories of Imprisonment, Immigration, and a Life Remade*. Norman, OK: University of Oklahoma Press.

Sagar, Tracey et al. 2015. 'The Student Sex Work Project – Research Summary'. Centre for Criminal Justice and Criminology, Swansea University.

Said, Edward W. 1979. *Orientalism*. 1st edn. New York: Vintage Books.

Sanders, Teela. 2005. *Sex Work: A Risky Business*. Cullompton, Devon; Portland, OR: Willan.

Sanders, Teela, and Kate Hardy. 2014. 'Students Selling Sex: Marketisation, Higher Education and Consumption', *British Journal of Sociology of Education* 36(5): 1–19. https://doi.org/10.1080/01425692.2013.854596.

Saraceno, Chiara. 2004. 'The Italian Family from the 1960s to the Present', *Modern Italy* 9(1): 47–57. https://doi.org/doi:10.1080/13532940410001677494.

Sassen, Saskia. 1991. *The Global City: New York, London, Tokyo*. Princeton, NJ: Princeton University Press.

Sbacchi, Alberto. 2005. 'Poison Gas and Atrocities in the Italo-Ethiopian War (1935–1936)', in Ruth Ben-Ghiat and Mia Fuller (eds), *Italian Colonialism*. Italian and Italian American Studies. New York: Palgrave Macmillan, pp. 47–56.

Scambler, Graham. 2007. 'Sex Work Stigma: Opportunist Migrants in London', *Sociology* 41(6): 1079–96. https://doi.org/10.1177/0038038507082316.

Schettini, Laura. 2019. *Turpi traffici. Prostituzione e migrazioni globali 1890–1940*. Roma: Biblink.

Scott, James C. 1987. *Weapons of the Weak: Everyday Forms of Peasant Resistance*. New Haven, CT: Yale University Press.

Scott, Joan W. 2009. 'Sexularism'. EUI RSCAS DL 1. Gender and Europe, Ursula Hirschmann Annual Lectures. Florence: European University Institute.

Scott, John, Christian Grov, and Victor Minichiello (eds). 2021. *The Routledge Handbook of Male Sex Work, Culture, & Society*. Routledge International Handbooks. New York: Routledge.

Serughetti, Giorgia. 2013. *Uomini che pagano le donne. Dalla strada al web, i clienti nel mercato del sesso contemporaneo*. Roma: Ediesse.

———. 2019. 'Innocenza e pericolo. Discorsi sulla "prostituta" dalla legge Merlin alle proposte di riformà, in Annalisa Cegna, Natascia Mattucci, and Alessio Ponzio (eds), *La prostituzione nell'Italia contemporanea. Tra storia, politiche e diritti*, Prima edizione. Spazi e Culture Del Novecento 2. Macerata: Eum, pp. 53–71.

Seymour, Mark. 2016. *Debating Divorce in Italy: Marriage and the Making of Modern Italians 1860–1974*. Palgrave Macmillan.

Shanley, Mary Lyndon. 1990. 'A Case against Pregnancy Contracts: Embodied Selves, Liberal Theory and the Law', *Politics and the Life Sciences* 8(2): 216–20.

———. 1993. '"Surrogate Mothering" and Women's Freedom: A Critique of Contracts for Human Reproduction', *Signs: Journal of Women in Culture and Society* 18(3): 618–39. https://doi.org/10.1086/494822.

Shaver, Frances M. 2005. 'Sex Work Research: Methodological and Ethical Challenges', *Journal of Interpersonal Violence* 20(3): 296–319. https://doi.org/10.1177/0886260504274340.

Siebler, Kay. 2014. 'What's so Feminist about Garters and Bustiers? Neo-Burlesque as Postfeminist Sexual Liberation', *Journal of Gender Studies* 24(5): 1–13. https://doi.org/10.1080/09589236.2013.861345.

Singh, Yadu Nath, and Anand Narayan Malaviya. 1994. 'Long Distance Truck Drivers in India: HIV Infection and Their Possible Role in Disseminating HIV into Rural Areas', *International Journal of STD & AIDS* 5(2): 137–38. https://doi.org/10.1177/095646249400500212.

Skeggs, Beverley. 1997. *Formations of Class and Gender: Becoming Respectable*. Theory, Culture & Society. London; Thousand Oaks, CA: SAGE.

Skinner, Jonathan. 2007. 'The Salsa Class: A Complexity of Globalization, Cosmopolitans and Emotions', *Identities: Global Studies in Culture and Power* 14(4): 485–506. https://doi.org/10.1080/10702890701578480.

———. 2016. 'Tango Heart and Soul: Solace, Suspension and the Imagination in the Dance Tourist', in Mark Harris and Nigel Rapport (eds), *Reflections on Imagination: Human Capacity and Ethnographic Method*. Anthropological Studies of Creativity and Perception. London: Routledge, pp. 61–76.

Slyomovics, Susan. 2015. *How to Accept German Reparations*. Philadelphia, PA: University of Pennsylvania Press.

Smith, Molly, and Juno Mac. 2018. *Revolting Prostitutes: The Fight for Sex Workers' Rights*. London; New York: Verso.

Sorcinelli, Paolo. 1993. *Eros. Storie e fantasie degli italiani dall'Ottocento a oggi*. Roma; Bari: Laterza.

Spronk, Rachel. 2012. *Ambiguous Pleasures: Sexuality and Middle Class Self-Perceptions in Nairobi*. New York, NY: Berghahn Books.

Standing, Guy. 2011. *The Precariat: The New Dangerous Class*. London; New York: Bloomsbury.

Stefani, Giulietta. 2007. *Colonia per maschi. Italiani in Africa Orientale: una storia di genere*, 1st edn. Documenta 5. Verona: Ombre corte.

Stoler, Ann Laura. 1995. *Race and the Education of Desire: Foucault's History of Sexuality and the Colonial Order of Things*. Durham, NC: Duke University Press.

———. 1997. 'Making Empire Respectable: The Politics of Race and Sexual Morality in Twentieth-Century Colonial Cultures', in Anne McClintock et al. (eds), *Dangerous Liaisons: Gender, Nation, and Postcolonial Perspectives*. Cultural Politics, v. 11. Minneapolis: University of Minnesota Press, pp. 344–73.

———. 2016. *Duress: Imperial Durabilities in Our Times*. Durham, NC: Duke University Press.

Suzuyo, Takazato, and Kutsuzawa Kiyomi. 1999. 'The Base and the Military: Structural Violence against Women', *Review of Japanese Culture and Society* 11/12: 66–78.

Sweeney, Brian N. 2017. 'Slut Shaming', in Kevin L. Nadal (ed.), *The SAGE Encyclopedia of Psychology and Gender*. Thousand Oaks, CA: SAGE, pp. 1579–80.

Tabet, Paola. 2004. *La grande beffa. Sessualità delle donne e scambio sessuo-economico*. Soveria Mannelli (Catanzaro): Rubbettino.

Tambor, Molly. 2006. 'Prostitutes and Politicians: The Women's Rights Movement in the Legge Merlin Debates', in Penelope Morris (ed.), *Women in Italy, 1945–1960: An Interdisciplinary Study*, 1st edn. Italian and Italian American Studies. New York: Palgrave Macmillan, pp. 131–45.

TAMPEP. 2015. 'TAMPEP on the Situation of National and Migrant Sex Workers in Europe Today'. https://tampep.eu/wp-content/uploads/2017/11/TAMPEP-paper-2015_08.pdf.

———. 2021. 'Solidarity with Sex Workers That Demand the Right to Work'. *TAMPEP*. https://tampep.eu/solidarity-with-sex-workers-that-demand-the-right-to-work/.

Tarchi, Marco. 2003. 'The Political Culture of the Alleanza Nazionale: An Analysis of the Party's Programmatic Documents (1995–2002)', *Journal of Modern Italian Studies* 8(2): 135–81. https://doi.org/10.1080/13545710320000078248.

Tatafiore, Roberta. 2012. *Sesso al lavoro. La prostituzione al tempo della crisi*, Bia Sarasini (ed.). Milano: Il saggiatore.

Tavuzzi, Michael M. 2007. *Renaissance Inquisitors: Dominican Inquisitors and Inquisitorial Districts in Northern Italy, 1474–1527*. Leiden; Boston, MA: Brill.

Teti, Vito. 1993. *La razza maledetta. Origini del pregiudizio antimeridionale*. Indagini. Roma: Manifestolibri.
Trachman, Mathieu. 2009. 'La Banalité de l'échange: Entretien Avec Paola Tabet', *Genre, Sexualité & Société* 2. https://doi.org/10.4000/gss.1227.
Treccani. 2003. 'Puttana in "Sinonimi e Contrari"', *Treccani*. https://www.treccani.it/vocabolario/puttana_(Sinonimi-e-Contrari).
——. n.d. 'Dònna in Vocabolario on line', *Treccani*. Accessed 26 January 2022. https://www.treccani.it/vocabolario/donna.
Tsang, Eileen Yuk-Ha. 2019. *China's Commercial Sexscapes: Rethinking Intimacy, Masculinity, and Criminal Justice*. Toronto: University of Toronto Press.
Turner, Victor W. 1979. 'Betwixt and Between: The Liminal Period in Rites de Passage', in William Armand Lessa and Evon Z. Vogt (eds), *Reader in Comparative Religion: An Anthropological Approach*, 4th edn. New York: Harper & Row, pp. 234–43.
Turno, Michela. 2003. *Il malo esempio. Donne scostumate e prostituzione nella Firenze dell'Ottocento*. Generazioni. Firenze: Giunti: Comune di Firenze.
Tyler, Imogen. 2021. *Stigma: The Machinery of Inequality*. London: Zed Books.
Tyler, Imogen, and Tom Slater. 2018. 'Rethinking the Sociology of Stigma', *The Sociological Review* 66(4): 721–43. https://doi.org/10.1177/0038026118777425.
UK Network of Sex Work Projects. 2008. 'Keeping Safe – Safety Advice for Sex Workers in the UK'. UK Network of Sex Work Projects.
Vance, Carole (ed.). 1984a. *Pleasure and Danger: Exploring Female Sexuality*. Boston, MA: Routledge.
——. 1984b. 'Pleasure and Danger: Toward a Politics of Sexuality', in Carole Vance (ed.), *Pleasure and Danger: Exploring Female Sexuality*. Boston, MA: Routledge, pp. 1–27.
Vertovec, Steven. 2007. 'Super-Diversity and its Implications', *Ethnic and Racial Studies* 30(6): 1024–54. https://doi.org/10.1080/01419870701599465.
Vianello, Francesca Alice. 2016. 'La salute delle assistenti familiari', in Claudia Alemani et al. (eds), *Viaggio nel lavoro di cura. Chi sono, cosa fanno e come vivono le badanti che lavorano nelle famiglie italiane*. Roma: Ediesse, pp. 125–49.
Vietti, Francesco. 2010. *Il paese delle badanti*. Melusine 91. Roma: Meltemi.
Walkowitz, Judith R. 1980. *Prostitution and Victorian Society: Women, Class, and the State*. Cambridge; New York: Cambridge University Press.
Walley, Christine J. 2015. 'Transmedia as Experimental Ethnography: The Exit Zero Project, Deindustrialization, and the Politics of Nostalgia', *American Ethnologist* 42(4): 624–39. https://doi.org/10.1111/amet.12160.
Walters, Suzanna Danuta. 2016. 'Pleasure and Danger: Sexual Freedom and Feminism in the Twenty-First Century', *Signs: Journal of Women in Culture and Society* 42(1).
Wanrooij, Bruno P.F. 1990. *Storia del pudore. La questione sessuale in Italia, 1860–1940*. 1st edn. Saggi. Venezia: Marsilio.
Waterston, Alisse. 2014. *My Father's Wars: Migration, Memory, and the Violence of a Century*. Innovative Ethnographies. New York: Routledge.
Waterston, Alisse, and Barbara Rylko-Bauer. 2006. 'Out of the Shadows of History and Memory: Personal Family Narratives in Ethnographies of Rediscovery', *American Ethnologist* 33(3): 397–412. https://doi.org/10.1525/ae.2006.33.3.397.
Weitzer, Ronald John (ed.). 2010. *Sex for Sale: Prostitution, Pornography, and the Sex Industry*. 2nd edn. New York: Routledge.
Werbner, Pnina. 2007. 'Veiled Interventions in Pure Space: Honour, Shame and Embodied Struggles among Muslims in Britain and France', *Theory Culture Society* 24(2): 161–86. https://doi.org/10.1177/0263276407075004.

Whitehead, Kally, and Tim Kurz. 2009. '"Empowerment" and the Pole: A Discursive Investigation of the Reinvention of Pole Dancing as a Recreational Activity', *Feminism & Psychology* 19(2): 224–44. https://doi.org/10.1177/0959353509102218.

Willson, Margaret. 1995. 'Afterword. Perspective and Difference: Sexualization, the Field, and the Ethnographer', in Don Kulick and Margaret Willson (eds), *Taboo: Sex, Identity, and Erotic Subjectivity in Anthropological Fieldwork*. London; New York: Routledge, pp. 251–75.

Willson, Perry. 2011. *Italiane: Biografia del Novecento*. Roma; Bari: Laterza.

Wilson, Ara. 2012. 'Intimacy: A Useful Category of Transnational Analysis', in *The Global and the Intimate: Feminism in Our Time*. Berlin, Boston, MA: Columbia University Press, pp. 31–56. https://doi.org/10.7312/prat15448-002.

Wolkowitz, Carol. 2006. *Bodies at Work*. London: SAGE.

World Bank. 2003. 'Truck Drivers and Casual Sex: An Inquiry into the Potential Spread of HIV/AIDS in the Baltic Region'. World Bank Working Paper no. 37. Washington, DC: World Bank.

World Health Organization et al. 2013. 'Implementing Comprehensive HIV/STI Programmes with Sex Workers: Practical Approaches from Collaborative Interventions'. Geneva: World Health Organisation.

Wynn, L.L. 2007. *Pyramids & Nightclubs: A Travel Ethnography of Arab and Western Imaginations of Egypt, from King Tut and a Colony of Atlantis to Rumors of Sex Orgies, Urban Legends about a Marauding Prince, and Blonde Belly Dancers*. Austin: University of Texas Press.

Wynter, Sylvia. 2003. 'Unsettling the Coloniality of Being/Power/Truth/Freedom: Towards the Human, After Man, Its Overrepresentation – An Argument', *CR: The New Centennial Review* 3(3): 257–337. https://doi.org/10.1353/ncr.2004.0015.

Yeates, Nicola. 2004. 'Global Care Chains', *International Feminist Journal of Politics* 6(3): 369–91. https://doi.org/10.1080/1461674042000235573.

Yeğenoğlu, Meyda. 1998. *Colonial Fantasies: Towards a Feminist Reading of Orientalism*. Cambridge: Cambridge University Press.

Young, Hershini Bhana. 2017. *Illegible Will: Coercive Spectacles of Labor in South Africa and the Diaspora*. Durham, NC: Duke University Press.

Young, Iris Marion. 2005. 'Throwing Like a Girl: A Phenomenology of Feminine Body Comportment, Motility, and Spatiality', in Iris Marion Young (ed.), *On Female Body Experience: 'Throwing like a Girl' and Other Essays*. Studies in Feminist Philosophy. New York: Oxford University Press, pp. 27–45.

Yuval-Davis, Nira. 1997. *Gender and Nation*. London; Thousand Oaks, CA; New Delhi: SAGE.

Zambelli, Elena. 2018. 'Between a Curse and a Resource: The Meanings of Women's Racialised Sexuality in Contemporary Italy', *Modern Italy* 23(2): 159–72. https://doi.org/10.1017/mit.2017.64.

———. 2019. 'Intimate Others and Risky Tenants: Disentangling the Economy of Affect Shaping Women's Migratory Projects in Italy', *Journal of Political Power* 12(3): 425–42. https://doi.org/10.1080/2158379X.2019.1669265.

Zambelli, Elena, Arianna Mainardi, and Andrea Hajek. 2018. 'Sexuality and Power in Contemporary Italy: Subjectivities between Gender Norms, Agency and Social Transformation', *Modern Italy* 23(2): 129–38. https://doi.org/10.1017/mit.2018.11.

Zelizer, Viviana A.R. 2005. *The Purchase of Intimacy*. Princeton, NJ: Princeton University Press.

Zimmerman, Mary K., Jacquelyn S. Litt, and Christine E. Bose. 2006. *Global Dimensions of Gender and Carework*. Stanford University Press.

Zincone, Giovanna. 1998. 'Illegality, Enlightenment and Ambiguity: A Hot Italian Recipe', *South European Society and Politics* 3(3): 45–82. https://doi.org/10.1080/13608740308539547.

Zucca, Gianfranco. 2016. 'Viaggio nel lavoro di cura. Una ricerca azione sulle trasformazioni del lavoro domestico', in Claudia Alemani et al. (eds), *Viaggio nel lavoro di cura. Chi sono, cosa fanno e come vivono le badanti che lavorano nelle famiglie italiane*. Roma: Ediesse, pp. 35–78.

Blogs and News

AP news wire. 2021. 'Italy's Grillo Derided for Defending Son in Sex Assault Case', *The Independent*, 20 April. https://www.independent.co.uk/news/world/europe/italys-grillo-derided-for-defending-son-in-sex-assault-case-giuseppe-conte-beppe-grillo-milan-italy-sardinia-b1834736.html.

BBC News. 2012. 'Berlusconi Sex Trial: Parties "Were Burlesque Games"', *BBC News*, 20 April, sec. Europe. https://www.bbc.com/news/world-europe-17783784.

———. 2013. 'Spain Unemployment Rate Hit a Record: Youth Rate at 55%', *BBC News*, 24 January. https://www.bbc.co.uk/news/business-21180371.

Corriere della Sera. 2007. '"Mandiamo i bamboccioni fuori di casa"', *Corriere Della Sera*, 4 October. https://www.corriere.it/politica/07_ottobre_04/padoa_bamboccioni.shtml.

D'Amico, Valentina. 2014. 'Tanti buoni motivi per iniziare un corso di pole dance', *Pole Dance Italy* (blog). http://www.poledanceitaly.com/2014/09/motivi-iniziare-corso-pole-dance/.

———. n.d. 'Scuole di Pole Dance in Italia', *Pole Dance Italy* (blog). Accessed 28 January 2022. https://www.poledanceitaly.com/scuole-pole-dance-italia/.

Decriminalize Sex Work. 2021. 'Heroes of the Month: Scientists for Sex Worker Rights', *Decriminalize Sex Work* (blog), 3 March. https://decriminalizesex.work/march21-hero/.

De Gregorio, Concita. 2011. 'Le altre donne', *L'Unità*, 18 January. https://giovannitaurasi.wordpress.com/2011/01/19/le-altre-donne-di-concita-de-gregorio/.

Desiderio, Alfonso. 2008. 'Le basi militari in Italia', *Affarinternazionali* (blog), 2 July. https://www.affarinternazionali.it/archivio-affarinternazionali/2008/07/le-basi-militari-in-italia/.

Di Rosa, Valeria. 2020. '2.000 è il numero di donne che …' *Trasportare Oggi in Europa* (blog), 20 April. https://trasportale.it/2000-donne-lavorano-come-camionisti-in-italia/.

Eretica. 2013. 'Violenza, la donna (non) e' oggetto di stato', *Il Fatto Quotidiano*, 16 December. https://www.ilfattoquotidiano.it/2013/12/16/violenza-la-donna-non-e-oggetto-di-stato/814972/.

FuoriPorta. n.d. 'Mostra virtuale dedicata alle case di tolleranza'. Accessed 26 January 2022. https://www.fuoriporta.org/itinerari/mostra-virtuale-dedicata-alle-case-di-tolleranza/.

Gibson, M. 2020. 'Impact of Female Commercial Truck Drivers on the Trucking Industry', *Beroe*, 3 May. https://www.beroeinc.com/article/impact-of-female-commercial-truck-drivers-on-the-trucking-industry-/.

Holmes, Godfrey. 2019. 'Cavalese Cable-Car Disaster: It's 20 Years since a US Aircraft Killed 20 People in the Dolomites and Still No One Accepts Responsibility', *The Independent*, 3 February. https://www.independent.co.uk/news/long_reads/cavalese-cable-car-disaster-us-aircraft-deaths-trentino-20-1998-italy-dolomites-lake-garda-responsibility-air-force-a8184771.html.

Human Rights Watch. 2019. 'Why Sex Work Should Be Decriminalized', *Human Rights Watch* (blog), 7 August. https://www.hrw.org/news/2019/08/07/why-sex-work-should-be-decriminalized.

ICRSE. 2013. 'International Day of Protest against the Violent Abuse and Murder of Sex Workers – in Memorial of Jasmine and Dora'. International Committee on the Rights of Sex Workers in Europe. 14 July 2013. http://www.sexworkeurope.org/de/news/general-news/international-day-protest-against-violent-abuse-and-murder-sex-workers-memorial.

International Pole Sports Federation. 2017. 'Pole Sports Recognition Announcement', *International Pole Sports Federation*, 2 October. http://www.polesports.org/news/04-10-17-gaisf-status/.

Johnson, Miles. 2021. 'Vatican Lobbies against Italy's Anti-Homophobia Law', *Financial Times*, 22 June. https://www.ft.com/content/49c488e3-f08f-4d53-ab2e-dfec9c71a3a1.

Jones, Gavin. 2013. 'Official Statistics Hide True Scale of Italian Joblessness', *Reuters*, 11 April, sec. Business News. https://www.reuters.com/article/uk-italy-unemployment-idUKBRE93A0EG20130411.

Kelly, Annie. 2016. 'Trafficked to Turin: The Nigerian Women Forced to Work as Prostitutes in Italy', *The Guardian*, 7 August, sec. Global development. https://www.theguardian.com/global-development/2016/aug/07/nigeria-trafficking-women-prostitutes-italy.

La Stampa. 2010. 'Brunetta contro i "bamboccioni"', *lastampa.it*, 17 January. https://www.lastampa.it/politica/2010/01/17/news/brunetta-contro-i-bamboccioni-1.37028877.

McKenna, Jo. 2012. '"Bunga Bunga Nuns" Did Strip Show at Party for Berlusconi', *Independent.Ie*, 17 April. https://www.independent.ie/world-news/europe/bunga-bunga-nuns-did-strip-show-at-party-for-berlusconi-26843930.html.

Redazione. 2012. 'I conti in tasca alle ragazze: arrivano a 500 euro al giorno', *Corriere di Bologna*, 11 January. http://corrieredibologna.corriere.it/bologna/notizie/cronaca/2012/11-gennaio-2012/i-conti-tasca-ragazze-arrivano-500-euro-giorno-1902817168634.shtml.

———. 2014a. 'Padova, studentesse e massaie "rubano il lavoro" alle lucciole', *PadovaOggi*, 26 March. https://www.padovaoggi.it/cronaca/prostituzione-padova-crisi-tornano-italiane-studentesse.html.

———. 2014b. 'Rimini, da casalinghe a prostitute contro la crisi: "Ricche e felici con 10mila euro al mese"', *Today*, 23 September. https://www.today.it/citta/casalinghe-prostitute-rimini.html.

Redazione XXD. 2011. 'Una sollevazione popolare', *XXD rivista di varia donnitá*, 5 March. http://www.xxdonne.net/2012/06/una-sollevazione-popolare/.

Repubblica. 2008. 'Berlusconi: "Contro la precarieta'? Sposare mio figlio o un milionario"', *Repubblica*, 13 March. https://www.repubblica.it/2008/03/sezioni/politica/verso-elezioni-10/berlusconi-precari/berlusconi-precari.html.

Romano, Monica J. 2019. 'Le transizioni non finiscono mai', *Purpletude*, 26 February. https://purpletude.com/diversity/le-transizioni-non-finiscono-mai/.

SNOQ. 2011. 'Appello alla mobilitazione delle donne italiane domenica 13 febbraio 2011', *Se Non Ora Quando?* (blog), 30 January. https://senonoraquando13febbraio2011.wordpress.com/2011/01/30/ciao-mondo/.

Speed, Barbara. 2014. 'Pole Fitness: The Respectable Face of Pole Dancing?' *The Guardian*, 29 April, sec. Life and style. http://www.theguardian.com/lifeandstyle/2014/apr/29/pole-fitness-dancing-pole-fitness-olympics.

Testa, Davide. 2020. 'Le basi militari statunitensi sul territorio italiano: attualità delle questioni costituzionali dopo l'uccisione del generale Soleimani', *Ius in itinere* (blog), 7 February. https://www.iusinitinere.it/le-basi-militari-statunitensi-sul-territorio-italiano-attualita-delle-questioni-costituzionali-dopo-luccisione-del-generale-soleimani-25447.

Tondo, Lorenzo. 2020. 'Sex Traffickers Left Thousands of Women to Starve During Italy Lockdown', *The Guardian*, 10 July, sec. Global development. https://www.theguardian.com/global-development/2020/jul/10/sex-traffickers-left-thousands-of-women-to-starve-during-italy-lockdown-coronavirus.

Transgender Europe. 2022. 'TMM Absolute Numbers (2008–Sept 2021)', *Transrespect versus Transphobia Worldwide* (blog). https://transrespect.org/en/map/trans-murder-monitoring/.

Young, Sarah. 2018. 'These Are the Seven Most Common Sexual Fantasies', *The Independent*, 11 July, sec. Lifestyle. https://www.independent.co.uk/life-style/common-sexual-fantasies-threesomes-bdsm-public-american-a8438566.html.

Videos and Movies

Bergman, Andrew. 1996. *Striptease*. Warner Bros Pictures.

Coppola, Sofia. 2003. *The White Stripes – I Just Don't Know What To Do With Myself*. Retrieved January 2022 from https://www.youtube.com/watch?v=zS5fkPFUskQ.

Judd, Zoraya. 2012. *Zoraya Judd LA Pole Show 2012 With Snake*. Retrieved January 2022 from https://www.youtube.com/watch?v=18rEEqQUZNQ.

Laiguana, Jaume de. 2011. *Shakira – Rabiosa (English Version) Ft. Pitbull*. Retrieved January 2022 from https://www.youtube.com/watch?v=a5irTX82olg.

Marshall, Gary. 1990. *Pretty Woman*. Buena Vista Pictures Distribution.

Scafaria, Lorene. 2019. *Hustlers*. STX Films.

Index

A
abject, 30, 45, 46n8, 108
abortion, 37, 45, 47n17, 48n26, 49n34, 120
acrobatic stripper. *See* stripper/s: acrobatic
adultery, 32–33
affective economy, ethnonationalist, 29, 40–41, 68, 135, 149
agency, 2, 4, 102, 108, 115
alienation, 12, 74n2, 96
Appadurai, Arjun, 9–10
austerity, sexual-economic, 21, 42–43

B
badante, 111, 138–140, 142, 144n15, 152. *See also* contract: *badante*
Bartky, Sandra, 74n2
beauty, 18, 23n2, 43, 90
beauty pageant, 35
beauty, standards of, 7, 132
belly, view from the, 105–6
belly dance. *See* dance: 'Oriental'
Berlant, Lauren, 112
Berlusconi, Silvio, 18, 38, 40, 42–44
binary
    authenticity/commodity, 80, 83–84, 119
    backward/modern, 10, 35, 65, 92, 132–34
    body/mind, 92
    choice/coercion, 109
    clean/dirty, 89–90, 150
    clean/unclean, 149
    consumer/worker, 8
    elegance/vulgarity, 63–65
    erotic/pornographic, 63
    good/bad women, viii, 1, 4, 13, 19, 21, 23n7, 28, 30, 33, 43, 54, 76, 82, 107–8, 122, 147–48, 150, 154n3
    inside/outside, 83–84, 97–98, 106
    intimacy/market, 107, 109–10, 120, 123, 152
    leisure/work, 8–9, 13
    non-/sex working women, 8–9, 149, 151, 153
    normal/deviant, 6, 23n10, 91, 96, 100n6
    oppression/liberation, 8, 55, 80, 83, 108, 120
    pleasure/danger, 13, 52, 55, 57, 60, 72–73, 125n5
    sante/puttane, 4, 20, 44
    sexual objectification/empowerment, 24n12
    victims/whores, 113
    virgin/whore, 23n7
body work, 85, 92, 153
boundary
    affective, 124
    blurring of the, 8–9, 85, 88
    crossing, 7
    in erotic work, 99
    'healthy', 116, 123
    between lap dancing and sex work, 92
    between legitimate and illegitimate sex, 33
    between mainstream culture and the sex industry, 2

between mainstream leisure and erotic and sex markets, 9
pliable, 114
porous, 85
proper, 83
racialized, 128
in sex work, 22, 93, 119, 123
temporal, 124
Brennan, Denise, 9–10
Brooks, Siobhan, 7, 132
brothel/s, female, 28–31, 35, 37, 42, 45, 46n10, 47n15, 85, 88, 118, 122, 152
  closure of, 12, 32, 36–39, 44, 82, 115
  colonial, 31–32, 41, 47n13, 131
  fascist era, 40, 49n38
  illegal, 115
  imperial, 28, 41
  military context, 29–30
  as mythological objects, 37
  (neo)brothel, 41, 45
  nostalgia for the, 28, 40–41, 45, 153
  Museo delle Case di Tolleranza, 41, 49n38
  price list, 28, 41, 49n36
  quindicina, 82
  See also: case chiuse
bruciata, 58, 62–63
bruises, vii, 62–63, 66
burlesque, 2, 8, 14, 24n12, 54, 72
Butler, Judith, 3–4

C
capital
  cultural, 143n5
  erotic, 2, 23n2, 132
  and labour, 22, 122, 124, 150
  racialized erotic, 7, 132
  return on, 122
  symbolic, 122
capitalism
  and consumerism, 58, 121, 123
  industrial, 107
  and patriarchy, 74n2
  and pleasure, 58, 122
  and second wave Western feminism's goals, 2
  and time, 119
  See also exploitation: capitalist

care crisis, 137
care deficit, 137, 139, 152
care work, 107, 110, 125n6, 137–39, 142, 143n9, 144n15, 152. *See also* global care chain
care worker, live-in. *See badante*
case chiuse (sing. casa chiusa), 21, 28
  reopening of, 28, 40–41, 44, 49, 152–53
chastity norms, female, 4–6, 36, 54, 57, 108, 147, 151
choice, 102
  as class marker, 109
  constrained, 94, 99, 103
  empowerment through, 65
  'free choice', 2, 109, 124
  no choice, 117, 140
  smart, 90
  See also binary: choice/coercion
Church, Catholic, 21, 29, 32–33, 36, 45, 50n47, 58, 152
  and female prostitution, 32–34, 36, 45, 153
  'ideology of gender', 45, 50n48
  marriage and divorce, 33–34, 36–37, 45, 84, 152–53
civil unions, 45, 50n49, 152
class, 6–7, 11, 14, 16–18, 20–21, 24n15, 25n21, 30–31, 53, 61, 63–66, 69–70, 72–73, 106, 108–9, 125n4, 133, 141, 148–151
clean 'work', 72, 88. *See also* binary: clean/dirty
coercion, 55, 109. *See* also binary: choice/coercion
colonialism
  European, 7, 10, 22n1, 30
  Italy's, 29, 31–32, 40–41, 131
  and sexuality, 6–7, 22, 127–28
  See also brothel/s, female: colonial; brothel/s, female: imperial
Comitato per i Diritti Civili delle Prostitute (Comitato), 17, 38–39, 115, 120, 145, 153
commodification
  commodified encounters, 82
  commodified 'image', 92
  commodified kiss, 117–18
  paradoxes, 81

Index • 181

and pleasure, 80, 119
shelter from, 107
of time, 119
of women's sexuality, 9, 11, 58, 99
See also binary: authenticity/commodity
commodity
   spell, 80
   status, 82, 84
   women, commodities and modernity, 35, 78
   See also binary: authenticity/commodity; capitalism: and pleasure
consciousness
   'authentic', 4
   false, 54, 61
   feminist, 151
consumerism, 2, 35, 58, 122
   bondage of, 122
consumption, 9–10, 110, 121–22
   cycle of work and, 111
   eroticized, 84
   gendered experience of, 107
   lifestyle, 122
   and pleasure, 99, 119
   of sex, 125, 126n13
   sexualized, 8
continuum, 137
   of degrees of subjection, 106
   pole/lap dance, 64
   of sexscapes, 8–9, 17, 148
   of social relations, 125n4
contract
   badante, 138, 140
   employment, 49, 82, 89–90, 99, 130, 140
   fiancé, 124n2
   intimate, 142, 152
   marriage, 34, 50n49, 106, 109, 120, 140, 152
   social, 108–9
   sexual, 108–9
Corso, Carla, 17, 38–39, 115–16, 120, 122
Covre, Pia, 17, 39, 120–24, 145, 147
cruel optimism: *See* optimism, cruel
customer/s, female, 59, 75, 79
   dignification and gentrification potential of, 79
   male escorting rule, 86
   of recreational pole dance, viii, 1
customer/s, male, 1, 9, 14–15, 21, 23n3, 24n18, 56, 77–78, 81–82, 84, 88, 90, 95, 97, 99, 117, 121, 131, 133–34, 153
   criminalization of (*see* prostitution laws and policies: Swedish model)
   fragility, 83
   stigma on, 77, 93
   sympathy for, 93
   See also desire: concealed; desire: racialized; 'extras'

D
dance
   exotic, 7, 64, 84–85, 128, 132
   lap, vi–viii, 8, 14–15, 53, 59, 61–64, 70–71, 75–101, 127–29, 132, 141, 151
   recreational pole, vi, viii, 1–2, 9–10, 13–15, 17, 21, 24n16, 51–74, 76, 86–88, 127–28, 141, 148–49, 151
   'Oriental', 14, 63, 71–72
   See also modern: dances
dancers
   exotic, 2, 8, 15, 80, 82, 85
   lap, viii, 3, 9, 14–17, 21–22, 55, 59, 63, 66, 68–72, 75–101, 105, 129–30, 138–40, 148–49
   recreational pole, 9–10, 14, 21–22, 45, 51–74, 78–79, 92, 99, 105, 149–50
danger, 3–4
   images of invasion and, 68
   objects of shame and, 28
   polluting, 89
   See also binary: pleasure/danger
desexualisation, 21, 60, 99
desire
   concealed, 152
   and contempt, 4, 44, 64
   mutual, 108, 116
   nexus between image, female body and, 37
   object of male, 2, 60, 74n2, 74n5
   racialized, 24n15, 41, 79, 127, 129, 131–32, 141, 151
   sex, gender and, 73
   sexual, 6, 23n2, 74n2

See also sexiness: women's desire for
dignity
  mobilisation in the name of women's, 43
  and value, 9, 62, 99, 105, 112, 122, 124, 148–51
dirt, 88–89. *See also* binary: clean/dirty
dirty work, 89
disciplina (sport), 60, 73
discipline
  social and legal discipline of sexuality, 21, 29, 34, 37, 44
  of women, 105
  See also subjection: disciplinary device of
discourse, 24n14, 48, 50n48, 56, 60
  ethnonationalist, 21
  neoliberal, 90
  of sexuality, 4, 68
  in subjectivation processes, 3–5, 60
dispositions
  heterosexual, 30, 33, 152
  'natural', 107
distinction, 7, 9, 62–65, 69, 90
divorce, 47n18, 48n21, 49n34, 82, 120. *See also* Church, Catholic: marriage and divorce

E
embodiment, 65, 73, 74n2, 92, 112, 133
emotional labour. *See* labour: emotional
empowerment, 2, 56, 64, 66, 78, 148. *See also* binary: sexual objectification/empowerment
erotic capital. *See* capital: erotic
erotic entertainment
  diversification, 79
  experience, 96
  female-to-male, vi, 11, 14, 15, 53, 75, 98–99
  gentrification, 79
  industry, 2, 100n6
  market, 15, 94, 98
  market segmentation, 128–31
  services, 133–34
  venue, 58, 82, 100n2
  work in, 69, 96, 132
  See also dancers: exotic; dancers: lap
erotic labour. *See* labour: erotic
escort, 18, 25, 114, 134

forums, 116
ethics, materialist, 112–13, 122, 124, 150
ethnonationalism, political economy of, 68. *See also* affective economy: ethnonationalist
evil
  'lesser evil', 32, 153
  'necessary evil', 33
exchange
  gifts in, 33
  of labour, 109
  of men, 33
  for money, gifts and/or positions, 54
  of money for sex, 24n14, 32, 36, 42, 65
  sexual-economic, 125n4
  value, 7, 121, 135
exotic dancing. *See* dance: exotic
exotic value, 7, 17, 127, 132–35, 141, 152
exploitation
  anguish, love and, 110
  capitalist, 115, 124, 150
  and deportation, 129
  migrant labour, 22, 127, 129, 138, 141, 151
  sexual, 104
  sexual violence and, 102
  work, 121
'extras', 9, 69, 85, 87–88, 90, 92, 99

F
Foucault, Michel, 3–5, 23n6
Frank, Katherine, 79, 153
freedom, 119
  exchange for the, 33
  from, 38
  market and sexual, 92
  of movement, 131, 143n4
  religious, 153
  sexual, 10, 20, 133
  un/freedom, 57
  See also binary: oppression/liberation

G
gaze
  anthropological, 148
  beholder/s of the, 7, 59, 141, 152
  male, 60, 74n5, 117
  panoptical, 90

of the state and media, 106
white European, 128, 132
gifts, 33, 54, 108, 120
Gilroy, Paul, 40
glamour, 64–65, 73
global care chain, 137, 139, 144n16, 152
global intimate labour chain, 139–40, 142, 152
globalization
   cultural dimension of, 10
   of recreational pole dance, 10, 55, 73
   of the sex market, 29

H
healing
   effect, 59
   metaphors of, 21
   natural, 60
   potential, 59, 99
heteronormativity, 3, 23n2, 60, 73, 82, 147
   political and moral economy of, 45, 108, 152
homophobia, 17, 45, 100n2, 141, 145, 151
homosexuality, 32, 49
   female, 33–34
   male, 29, 33, 47n17
honour
   clause, 48
   'honour crimes', 38
   and shame, 63
   women's patriarchal-defined dis/honour, 4, 22, 37, 73, 121, 150
human rights, 116, 151

I
imagination, 10, 79, 110, 117, 128. *See also* binary: intimacy/market
inequality/ies, 2, 5, 10, 108, 122–23, 137
International Committee on the Rights of Sex Workers in Europe (ICRSE), 145, 154n1
intersectionality, 6, 23n5
intimacy, 108, 111
   as affects, 107, 117
   architecture of, 82
   and money, 106
   as space, 107–08, 117
   undesired, 93

vehicle of, 118
work and, 96, 107, 116–17, 142
See also binary: intimacy/market; intimate Other; labour: intimate
intimate Other, 20, 25n21

L
labour
   emotional, 9, 15, 78, 80, 82, 100n3
   erotic, 5, 7–9, 15, 18, 80, 134, 149, 153
   intimate, 127, 137–40, 142, 152–53
   sexual, 5, 7, 108, 149, 153
   See also capital: and labour; global intimate labour chain; market: labour
lap dancers. *See* dancers: lap
leisure
   activities, 14, 71
   commercial, 35
   and fitness activity, 2
   and pleasure, 1, 3
   practice, 19, 53
   site/s, 11, 81, 107
   time, 3, 148
   See also binary: leisure/work; boundaries: mainstream leisure and erotic and sex markets; pleasure
love, 22, 80, 95–96, 105, 111–12, 118, 120
   of family, church and nation, 49n34
   in, 83, 87, 95–96
   'love proof', 37
   and money, 107
   power of, 93, 96
   weddings, 49

M
Madonna/whore. *See* binary: good/bad women
Marcasciano, Porpora, 17, 24n19
market, 18, 107, 118
   capitalist, 109
   gendered and racialized labour market, 104, 138, 141
   labour, 11, 50n44, 97, 100n8, 131, 136–37
   pleasures of the, 122
   rationality of the, 90
   recreational pole dance, 13, 53, 66–67, 72, 128

See also binary: intimacy/market; erotic
 entertainment: market; freedom:
 market and sexual; marriage: market;
 sex market
marriage, 34, 74n8, 94, 105–6, 140–41
 by capture, 6
 no 'genuine', 104
 informal, 49
 market, 6, 30
 and prostitution, 31, 33, 37, 82, 108–9,
  120, 125n4
 and reproduction, 29, 36, 38, 44, 121
 sex outside of, 4, 33, 37, 58
 for social mobility, 120
 virginity at, 34
 See also Church, Catholic: marriage and
  divorce; contract: marriage
matrix of domination, 3, 11, 22, 23n5, 127,
 150–51
McClintock, Anne, 46n8, 132
meretrice isolata. *See under* prostitute, female
meretrix publica. *See under* prostitute, female
Merlin Law. *See under* prostitution laws and
 policies
Merlin, Lina, 36
migration, 10, 130, 137, 139, 143n10, 148,
 152
 anxieties, 40
 authorities, 140
 circular, 111, 123, 140
 containing, 40–41
 halting, 40
 internal, 35
 irregular, 49n33
 laws, 22, 41, 94, 111, 127, 129, 135, 151
 regimes, 150
 status, 18, 103, 130–31, 133–34, 142
 third-party mediation, 130
modern, 92
 consumers, 58
 dances, 35
 industrial imperialism, 30
 Italians, 92
 Italy, 29–30, 33, 44, 47, 133, 152
 nation state, 48n23
 patriarchy, 108
 pre-, 132
 sexual entrepreneur, 90

subjectivities, 10
vanguards, 92
white Western woman, 78
woman, 56, 78, 92
See also binary: backward/modern
modernity, 10, 21, 35, 64, 148
 sexual-economic, 35
 sexuality and, 57, 73
 stage of, 6, 57
 trope, 65
 Western, 57–58, 78, 92, 133
 See also binary: backward/modern
modernization, 21, 34–35, 44
morality, 6, 31, 38, 47n17, 70, 141
Movimento Identità Trans (MIT), 17, 24n19
Mulvey, Laura, 74n5
Museo delle Case di Tolleranza. *See under*
 brothel/s, female

N
nation, 23, 30, 40, 42, 49n34, 106, 135
 abjects of the, 30
 -making, 29
 (re)building the, 35
 state, 21, 29, 33, 48n23, 120, 152
neoliberal
 attack, 71
 discourse, 90
 policies, 10, 145
 reforms, 43
night club/s, vi, 9, 14–15, 21–22, 24n17,
  54, 64, 66, 68–69, 71, 73, 75–101,
  103, 127–132, 134, 140–41, 142n3,
  143n5, 148, 151

O
objectification, sexual, 2, 74n2. *See
 also* binary: sexual objectification/
 empowerment
oppression
 internalized, 24, 54, 61, 74n2
 intersecting structures of, 9, 17, 121, 124
 sexual, 59
 See also binary: oppression/liberation
optimism, cruel, 112, 150
original sin, 32, 64
'Oriental' dance. *See* dance: 'Oriental'
other, 131, 149

female, 6, 9, 16, 21–22, 53, 61, 69, 73, 128
the 'other women', 42–43, 54, 63, 87, 124, 149–50
See also intimate Other; self: and the other
othering, 113–14, 150
  device, 150
  processes, 8–9, 20, 72, 80, 99, 149
  subjectivation and, 8

P

Pateman, Carole, 108–09
performativity, gender, 60
Pheterson, Gail, 4–5
pleasure, 1, 3, 20, 74n2, 74n5, 76, 78, 108
  male customers', 1, 9, 11, 14, 55–56, 76, 80, 82–84, 103, 149
  promise of, 123
  recreational pole dancers', vii, 1, 3, 21, 57–61, 65
  of sexuality, 72
  sexual, 78, 85, 118
  See also binary: pleasure/danger; capitalism: and pleasure; commodification: and pleasure; market: pleasures of the; sexscapes: *sexscapes of pleasure*
pleisure, 3, 8–9, 11, 13–14, 24n16, 51–74, 79, 128, 148–49
  racialization of, 127–28
pornography, 2, 49, 79, 98, 108. *See also* binary: erotic/pornographic
postcolonial melancholia, 40, 45
power, 4, 45
  beauty for, 43
  consumer buying, 65–66, 68
  erotic, 7, 54, 133, 141
  hierarchies of, 6–8
  imbalance, 16
  imperial, 40
  relations of, 2, 8, 12, 80, 105, 109, 125, 149
  sexuality and, 5
  of sexuality, 55, 73, 78, 89
  See also binary: sexual objectification/empowerment; empowerment; love: power of; stigma: power

precarity, 43, 91, 97, 124, 150
Pretty Woman (movie), 100, 117, 126n12
Pretty Woman fantasy, 96
prostitute, female, 4, 7, 21, 23n9, 24n14, 31, 90, 108, 111, 146
  meretrice isolata, 30
  meretrix publica, 32
  overlap with the figure of the migrant, 40–41, 44, 68, 149
prostitution, female, 28, 108, 136
  in the history of 'modern' Italy, 21, 21n48, 29–32, 34–36, 43–45, 146, 152
  See also brothels, female; Church, Catholic: and female prostitution; marriage: and prostitution; prostitution laws and policies; sex work
prostitution laws and policies
  Convention for the Suppression of the Traffic in Persons and the Exploitation of the Prostitution of Others, 36
  Merlin Law, 32, 34, 36–37, 40–42, 44, 85, 100n5, 146, 153
  Regolamento Cavour, 29–30, 32, 46n7
  Swedish model, 28, 46n5, 152–53
prostitution, male, 24n19, 34, 108. *See also* sex work, male
puttana, 18–19, 89, 105. *See also* binary: *santa/puttana*; whore
puttan tour, 19

R

race, 6–7, 11, 22n1, 23n5, 31, 40, 43, 47n17, 48n25, 127–28, 131–36, 141–42, 148, 150–51
  manipulation skills and possibilities, 7, 134–35, 141, 152
racial grammar, 7, 128, 141
recreational pole dance. *See* dance: recreational pole
recreational pole dance schools, viii, 1, 3, 9, 13–14, 51–74, 86–87, 141, 128, 151
recreational pole dancers. *See* dancers: recreational pole
remittances, 105, 111, 135, 142, 152
rescue, 96, 106
respectability, 1, 45, 55, 61, 64–66, 73, 99, 112, 147

female respectability line, 43, 45, 70
  ideology of, 6, 31, 122
  journey to, 21, 70–72
  marker, 138
  narratives, 14
  as a national/ist property, 45, 67
  'respectable' sexuality, 108, 123
  tactics, 3, 9, 53, 60–61, 63, 65, 69, 72–73, 80, 89, 99, 149–50
Rossiaud, Jacques, 33

S
sacrifice/s, 22, 60, 62, 80, 112–13, 120
santa/puttana. *See under* binary
self, 4
  -determination, 120
  -dignification, 98, 99
  -entrepreneurship, 22
  entrepreneurial, 91
  fragmentation and loss of the, 74n2
  forfeiture of the, 117
  individual, 114
  -making, 10
  and the other, 46
  outward-oriented, 59
  -presentation, 23n2, 70, 73
  -preserving, 151
  relational, 61, 114
  -reliance, 70, 95, 98
  -respect, 112
  risk-taking and flexible, 90
  -sufficiency, 71
  technologies of the, 3, 5
sex customers, criminalisation. *See* prostitution laws and policies: Swedish model
sex market, 5, 8, 11–12, 16, 29, 39–40, 97, 114, 119, 127, 134–41
  segmentation of the, 135–42
sex wars, 8, 22, 80, 83, 93, 102, 108–9, 116, 120, 125n5, 149, 152
sex work, 4, 8–11, 16–18, 21–22, 24n13, 24n19, 32, 71, 85, 88, 92, 98, 102–26, 128, 134–142, 143n9–12, 144n20, 147, 149–52
  indoors, 16, 39, 85, 115–20, 134–35, 140, 143n9
  LGBTQI+, 34
  male, 24n19
  street, 16, 102–106, 110–115, 135–42, 144n20, 151
  trans women in, 10, 16–17, 29, 39, 41, 45, 102, 105, 110, 115, 123, 136–37, 140–42, 150, 153
  See also boundary: in sex work
sex workers, 5, 8, 43, 50n46, 89, 91, 96, 99, 102, 107, 109–10, 114–124, 125n7, 125n10, 126n11, 145–48, 150–51
sex workers' organisations. *See Comitato per i Diritti Civili delle Prostitute (Comitato)*; International Committee on the Rights of Sex Workers in Europe (ICRSE)
sex working women, 3, 5, 8, 16, 19–20, 22, 39–40, 62, 85–86, 99, 102–114, 123–24, 135–142, 148, 150–52. *See also* binary: non-/sex working women
sex trafficking, 113–114, 136, 143n10
sexiness
  performance of, 9, 56–57, 61, 73
  technologies of, 60
  women's desire for, 53, 55
sexism, 4–5, 37, 108
  and ageism, 78
  and racism, 6–7, 22, 40–41, 127–29, 131, 134, 141–42, 151
sexscape, 9–11, 15, 24n15, 80, 99, 124
  sexscapes of pleasure, 11
  Western, 53, 58, 72, 78–79, 147
sexual double standard, 6–7, 33
sexual entrepreneur, 90
sexuality, 1, 3–4, 6–9, 11–14, 18–19, 125n4, 143n7, 148, 151
  construction of Black women's, 128, 141, 151
  male split, 23n5
  moral and political economy of, 4, 21, 27–50, 152
  and women's status, 1, 4, 7–9, 11, 13, 21–22, 28, 44, 53, 56, 80, 91, 99, 107, 124, 128, 147, 151
  See colonialism: and sexuality; discipline: social and legal discipline of sexuality; discourse: of sexuality; modernity: sexuality and; power: sexuality and; whore: sexuality of the; whore stigma

sexualization of culture, 1, 8
Skeggs, Beverley, 65, 148
slut, 23n10, 128
slut-shaming, 5, 23n10
Slut Walks, 128, 142n1
sodomy, 32–33, 47n17
status, 79, 110, 120
   human, 5, 151
   of sport, 56, 60
   See also commodity: status; migration: status; sexuality: and women's status
stigma, 20, 63, 96, 110
   gendered, 4–5, 77, 80, 93, 96, 100n6
   intersecting, 153
   management strategies, 118
   power, 149
   sex work, 38, 44, 118, 149
   See also whore stigma
stigmata, 63
stigmatization, 3–6, 9, 13–14, 16, 21, 24n14, 25n20, 42, 65–66, 68, 89, 91, 94–95, 99, 108, 112, 121, 123, 124, 150
strip club/s, vi, 1, 13–14, 53–54, 56, 61, 64, 69, 134, 153
   association, 21
   background, 57
   genealogy, 13, 60
   imaginary, 57
stripper/s, 2–3, 13, 23n3, 60, 64, 72, 80, 131, 148
   acrobatic, 15, 88, 129–30, 132
   glamorization of the, 10, 14, 53, 55, 78
   heels, 57
   male-to-female, 100n6
subject, 4, 23n7, 46n8, 109, 112
   dignified subject position, 96, 99, 122, 124
   'prostitute', 24n14, 34
   'whore', 19
   'woman', 3–5, 19, 34, 59
subjection, 4, 38, 121, 129, 150–51
   disciplinary device of, 5, 9, 149
   gendered, 73, 150
   paradox of, 3–4
   to the whore stigma, 3, 18, 20, 90, 99, 106, 122
subjectivation, 3, 8, 20, 22, 147–49, 153

'Swedish' model. *See under* prostitution laws and policies

T

Tabet, Paola, 125n4
tactics, 23n4, 151. *See also* respectability: tactics
taste, 79
technologies of the self. *See under* self
technologies of sexiness. *See under* sexiness
traffic
   of commodities and people, 75
   'traffic' in men, 33
   See also sex trafficking
transphobia, 17, 45, 140–42, 145, 151

V

victim blaming, 106
violence, 20, 25n21, 38, 144, 154n4
   discursive and material, 150
   domestic, 43
   gender-based, 21, 50n45, 140, 147, 154n2
   institutional, 38
   male, 38, 106, 115, 124
   military, 49
   patriarchal, viii, 150
   physical, 4, 126n10
   police, 38
   racist and colonial, 40–41
   sexual, 4, 38–39, 48n29, 48n32, 102, 116, 126n10
   against sex working women, 19, 39, 48n32
   structural, 40
   symbolic, 72
   against women, 19, 39, 43, 46, 120, 145
virgin, ixn2, 30, 37, 58, 121, 149. *See also* binary: virgin/whore; marriage: virginity at
vulgarity, 65, 74n7. *See also* binary: elegance/vulgarity

W

weapon of the weak, 151
whiteness, 17, 40, 131
   economic value of, 136
   Italians', 67, 133

political economy of, 128
whore, 4, 23n7, 24n10, 47n12, 146–47, 149
  as intimate Other, 20
  metonym of the, 9, 60–61
  sexuality of the, 55, 64
  as symbol of political subversion, 109
  and woman, 18–20
  See also binary: good/bad women; binary: Madonna/whore; binary: victims/whores; whore stigma

whore stigma, 3–6, 8–9, 11, 18, 20–22, 23n10, 53–55, 58–60, 62, 69, 72–73, 79–80, 89–90, 95, 99, 105–107, 112–113, 121, 124, 147–51, 153. *See also* subjection: to the whore stigma
Wolkowitz, Carol, 85, 92

Z

Zelizer, Viviana, 106–7

www.ingramcontent.com/pod-product-compliance
Lightning Source LLC
Chambersburg PA
CBHW051546020426
42333CB00016B/2122